*by Jay Stringer*

Unwanted: How Sexual Brokenness
Reveals Our Way to Healing

Desire: The Longings Inside Us and the
New Science of How We Love, Heal, and Grow

*Desire*

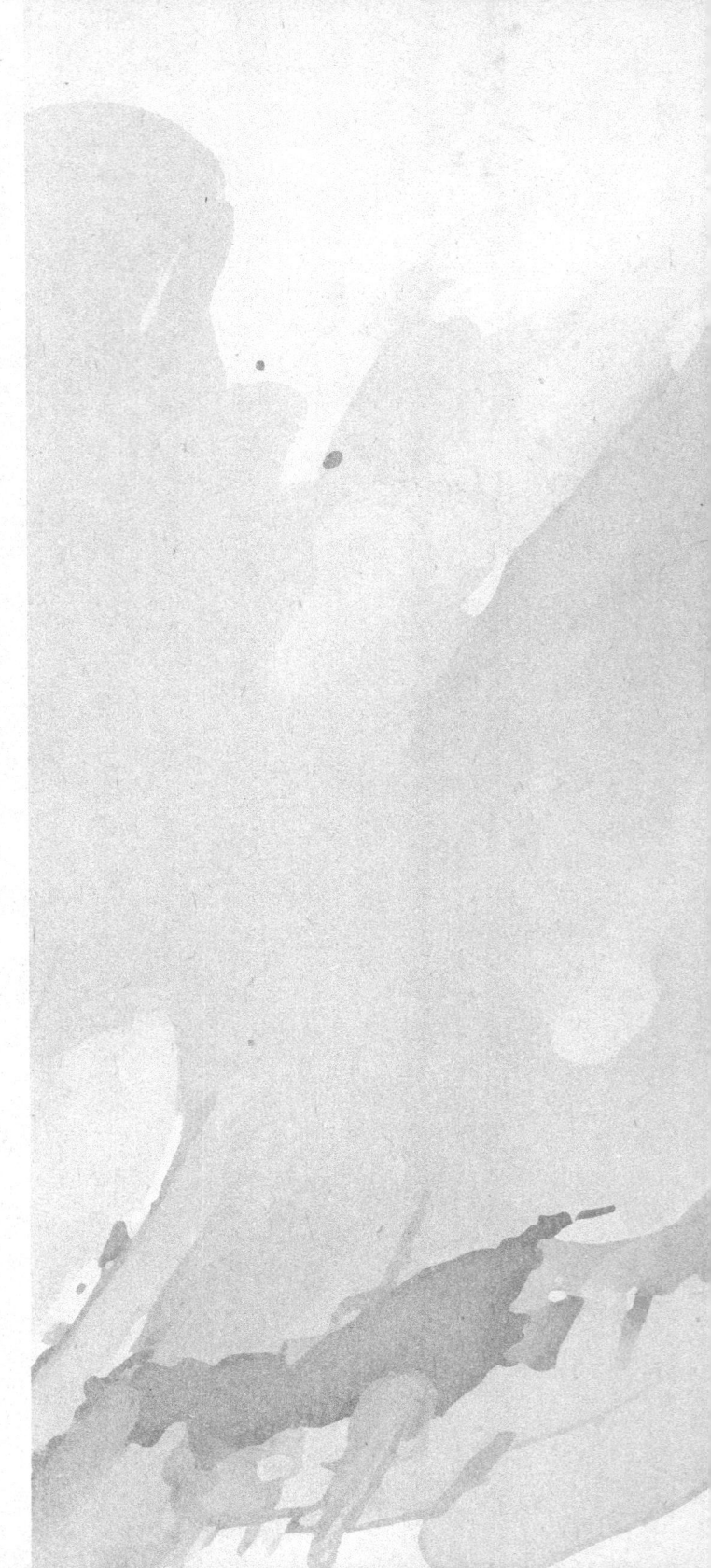

CONVERGENT

*New York*

# *Desire*

THE LONGINGS

INSIDE US

AND THE

NEW SCIENCE

OF HOW

WE LOVE, HEAL,

AND **GROW**

Jay Stringer

CONVERGENT
An imprint of Random House
A division of Penguin Random House LLC
1745 Broadway, New York, NY 10019
convergentbooks.com
penguinrandomhouse.com

Hardcover ISBN 9780593728277
Ebook ISBN 9780593728284

Printed in the United States of America on acid-free paper

1st Printing

FIRST EDITION

BOOK TEAM: PRODUCTION EDITOR: *Mark Birkey* • MANAGING EDITOR: *Allie Fox* •
PRODUCTION MANAGER: *Jenn Backe* • COPY EDITOR: *Phil Newman* •
PROOFREADERS: *JoLeigh Buchanan, Michael Fedison, Rachael Clements, Jennifer Hilty* •
INDEXER: *Gina Guilinger*

*Title page image from AdobeStock/Hurca!*

*Book design by Barbara M. Bachman*

The authorized representative in the EU for product safety and compliance
is Penguin Random House Ireland, Morrison Chambers, 32 Nassau Street,
Dublin D02 YH68, Ireland. https://eu-contact.penguin.ie

To the readers who will look up at the stars
and plumb the depths,
that their hearts may become fully alive.

And to Amos and Iona—whose desires provoke me,
again and again, to be young again.

# Contents

# Author's Note

Throughout this book, I'll share stories of people I've met as a psychotherapist and researcher. To protect their identities, each character is a composite drawn from multiple individuals, carefully chosen to highlight key inflection points in their journeys related to desire. As you read their stories, I encourage you to look for moments when you may have felt something similar. Let their narratives inspire you to excavate your own.

*Introduction*

# The Civil War of Desire

YOU ARE ENGAGED IN A CIVIL WAR WITH DESIRE. DESIRE IS THE birthplace of your greatest joys, but it's also responsible for your deepest heartaches. It fuels your search for romance, personal growth, and meaningful work. It drives you to seek what truly makes you happy, to cultivate greater intimacy and purpose, even as it exposes you to some of life's harshest experiences.

For all of us, the desire for love can open the door to betrayal. Desire for success can reveal our darkest greed and envy, and reckless desires can inflict immense pain on ourselves and those we love. Desire has the power to turn us into the best or worst version of ourselves.

In response, most of us adopt strategies—whether we're aware of them or not—in hopes of finding relief. Some of us suppress what we really want as a way of avoiding the disappointment of unfulfilled desires, or even the disillusionment that follows their fulfillment. Others of us sabotage our desires, turning them into burdensome demands on others for validation or approval, or making choices that undermine our well-being and keep us from facing the real work of growth. Regardless of how we navigate these complexities, one thing remains clear: Most of us could use some help in our relationship to desire.

Desire problems can't be blamed on personal shortcomings alone. We're living through an unprecedented moment in history. In the past, there was greater clarity surrounding gender roles and societal expectations—who would earn the income, who would care for the baby, and what (and who) defined "the good life." Now, we have access to choices that previous generations would have never conceived of, brought on by an increasingly digitized world, rapid geopolitical and social upheavals, a wealth of new knowledge about health and well-being, and evolving moral frameworks. Our struggle is no longer the tyranny of having too few choices, but the overwhelm of too many.

To further complicate matters, we're flooded with competing messages about how to handle desire. Many of us grew up in families or religious communities where desire was synonymous with something bad, selfish, or—God forbid—sexual. Then, as adults, we encountered a chorus of experts and social media influencers urging us to pursue our "one wild and precious life" while offering little practical guidance on how to do so. We're left wondering:

Why do I feel like something is "off" inside me, even though I think I had a decent childhood?

How can I feel so lonely and still want so much more from people at the same time?

Why does sex either feel underwhelming . . . or make me feel out of control?

Why is getting healthy—or staying motivated—so much harder than it should be?

This leaves us grappling with bigger questions about sex and relationships, the tension between personal fulfillment and family expectations, how success should be defined, and how we can cultivate authentic connections amid the noise. Bereft of wise guides, we scrape together input from friends, magazines, social media, and other less-than-ideal sources. Consequently, our relationship status with desire is . . . complicated.

## *Your Brain on Desire*

The number of times a day our brain wants something is staggering. On average, adults make around thirty-five thousand (mostly subconscious) decisions daily, including what we will eat, what we will wear, who we will talk to, what we will say, and how we'll express ourselves.[1] We see a donut and we want food. We witness someone making a difference in the world and start questioning our own worth. We long for the latest Apple product. We see children playing and remember painful moments from our childhood, wondering why we didn't have similar experiences. We see a couple who genuinely seems to be in love, and suddenly our romantic relationship or singleness feels agonizing. Throughout the day, we are constantly collecting, interpreting, and acting on complex signals.

But what if the apparatus that helps us feel, interpret, and choose our desires is faulty, or at least misunderstood? As a licensed therapist and mental health researcher on the topic of desire, I've learned that most people are unaware of the formative stories, dynamics, and underlying motivations that shape these everyday longings. If the machinery directing so much of our decision-making is underdeveloped—if it's driving us toward pain instead of flourishing—shouldn't that haunt us? What's more, shouldn't we desire to repair it? Rather than suppressing or indulging desires, maybe it's time to develop curiosity about them.

Through my research and clinical work, I've had a front row seat to the civil wars of desire in over seven thousand men and women. I've counseled people who were navigating childhood trauma, extramarital affairs, sexual-desire discrepancies (in which one partner wants sex more or less than the other), the harmful effects of shameful religious systems like purity culture, depression, and professional confusion and burnout. I've concluded that it's not a question of *if* we will experience a major desire-related problem, but *when*.

## *There's More to Desire Than Sex*

When we hear "desire," our minds often jump straight to sex. But in doing so, we miss the bigger picture. Sex is one of desire's most powerful expressions, but desire is boundless, infusing every aspect of our lives. It is the energizing force that awakens our curiosity, the fire that fuels our ambition, the longing that propels us toward something more.

Even when we do talk specifically about sexual desire, the conversation remains far too narrow. We're seduced into thinking that a missing piece of sex education, a new tip to spice things up, or the latest clickbait article promising "mind-blowing" sex will finally unlock our erotic potential. But these quick fixes distract us from what truly matters—the personal and relational development that leads to true intimacy. Ironically, this lack of growth is precisely what keeps us from the passion and meaning we crave in sex. To unlock the full potential of desire (including better sex), we need to embrace it as a holistic force that extends far beyond the bedroom.

## *Desire Problems Are Not Random*

As a therapist, my role is to create a safe yet challenging context where clients can explore the full spectrum of their relationship with desire—whether it's their deepest, wildest longings or past experiences that they've been too ashamed to acknowledge. I'm writing this book to offer you a similar experience.

At some point in our lives, we will face a significant challenge in our relationship to desire. We might long to fix something broken or missing inside of us, but have no idea how to do it. We might hope for something more in a relationship or career but feel powerless to make it happen. Desire problems could also manifest as anxiety or depression, when we begin to question whether our life holds any real meaning. In these moments, it's important to recognize that our desire problems are normal, but they are never random. The recurring conflicts we face have an uncanny way of revealing truths about ourselves and our stories that we've been unable or unwilling to confront.

When I researched my first book, *Unwanted,* I sought to delve into the meaning of common unwanted sexual behaviors like infidelity and out-of-control porn use. I received thousands of emails from people who were beginning to get curious about their story and sexual behaviors for the first time. They told me that they never received any education on sexual health, and many shared tragic stories of sexual abuse. Others wondered aloud why certain porn searches were so alluring to them. It got to the point where some of my friends began calling me "the fantasy whisperer" because so many people were asking me to interpret their sexual desires. It was a beautiful season of life, because I saw how eager people were to resist the two great paradigms of our time: *pathologizing* desires or *dismissing* them as inconsequential. Curiosity about our desires creates a middle path, and it's a path we need now more than ever.

*Unwanted* was able to answer some sexual-desire questions, but many it could not. As I continued my clinical work and paid closer attention to the problems facing my clients and society at large, I realized that the topic of desire was so much larger and more beautiful than I had previously understood. My clients and readers needed more than just guidance on outgrowing an unhealthy behavior. They needed a road map for how to be human—a means to better understand the human search for connection, purpose, and love. It's a big aspiration, but so are the desires within us.

The word "desire" itself hints at this meaning. It originates from the Latin word *desidus,* meaning "the lack of the star." It evokes a sense of being lost, a lack of orientation, and yet a longing to find a way home. It's likely you're reading this book because you've lost a star. You found a romantic partner and they turned out to be a piece of work. The career you once desired now leads to burnout. The family you love looks far more troubled than you ever imagined. The personal goals you invested significant resources and hope in have come back void.

Research shows that our desires are constantly changing. During adolescence, we desire independence from our parents and family culture.[2] In our twenties and thirties, we tend to be more motivated by professional goals, money, and the approval of others, whereas in the second half of life, we might find ourselves wanting more time with friends or grandchildren, good palliative care for terminal illness, and to pass along an enduring legacy.[3]

We are most likely to lose our North Star when our lives feel upended. But it happens, even when we're experiencing beauty and growth. A fabulous meal, a friend who genuinely cares, or a moment of personal success can leave us wondering why we've settled for so little throughout our life. Misery and beauty both alter our inner world—and in the process push us to abandon old desires in search of new ones.

In this way, desire is always a conversation between significant loss and great expectation. The search can be both heart-wrenching and exhilarating. Either way, your life is about to get interesting.

### *Our Desires Are Shaped by Forces We May Not Even Be Aware Of*

Consider a couple that wishes their home had a lush, green lawn. At first glance, their desire seems innocuous. But in the U.S. we owe our fixation on tidy, manicured yards to wealthy French and English aristocrats in the seventeenth and eighteenth centuries.[4] At the time, maintaining a lawn required a tremendous amount of labor and resources, making it a status symbol for the affluent. If our preferences for something as seemingly benign as lawns can be shaped by historical context, how much truer is this for our more consequential desires, such as our vocations, romantic partners, and vision of the "good life"?

Our desires are often shaped by what others want us to want—whether it's a beauty product, a tech gadget, a wellness trend, or a food craving. We rarely consider the multibillion-dollar industries behind them, all designed to stir our desires and open our wallets. Sexual desires are no exception. Pornography, in particular, has played a significant role in reshaping sexual norms. One striking example is the rise of sexual choking over the last fifteen years. A 2011 study found that 13 percent of women reported being choked by a partner.[5] In 2019, another study found 38 percent of women had experienced unwanted acts like slapping, choking, gagging, or spitting during otherwise consensual sex.[6] By 2024, a survey found that 61 percent of women had been choked during sex.[7] This rapid shift raises important questions about consent, safety, and who—and what—is shaping our desires.

The stakes are high: If we don't interrogate the origins of our desires, we surrender their authorship to others—whether to trauma, corporations, or cultural scripts. We might believe we're choosing freely, but our desires are consistently shaped by unseen forces. The question isn't just "What do I want?" but "Why do I want it?" Until we ask, we'll keep prioritizing the desires we've been sold over the ones that might set us free.

### Desire Is a Mirror

In *Harry Potter,* the Mirror of Erised ("desire" spelled backwards) reflects a person's most ardent longings, often rooted in their deepest wound. When Harry looks into the mirror, he sees the image of his parents, who died after he was born. In the same way, our desires—healthy and not—hold a mirror up to our personal stories, reflecting our wounds, unfulfilled longings, and deepest passions.

I once worked with a client who wanted to sculpt his body into an Adonis-like beauty and be the most fashionable man in any room he entered. The taproot of this desire lay in grade school, where his classmates mocked him for his chubby belly and discount shoes. Childhood humiliation set up his quest for mastery in adulthood. As he began recognizing that his desires were messengers pointing to unaddressed trauma, he shifted his focus from conquering those stories of childhood embarrassment to healing them. His need for physical perfection transformed into a longing for deeper connection with his friends.

What did you desire as a kid? Maybe it was to be like Mike (remember the Michael Jordan commercials?), to play the electric guitar, to grow up on the prairie in another lifetime, or to travel to the moon. How did your family engage these desires? Did they cultivate them, ignore them, delight in them, or prioritize someone else's desires over yours?

As we age, our raw childhood desires tend to wane. We learn that becoming Michael Jordan, Bono, Laura Ingalls Wilder, Sally Ride, or Lance Armstrong probably isn't in the cards, and we set out to find a workable ratio between stability and passion. We know we must pay the bills, but we also want to preserve the divine spark of spontaneity within. Many of us get in the habit of choosing stability over honoring our desire for passion. Each time we do this, we set up problems that our future self will have to deal with.

We'll explore this in greater detail in Part One, but if you feel some combination of numb, stuck, lonely, depressed, or unfulfilled, know that these symptoms are calling you back to a robust relationship to desire. Within your childhood longings are clues to what your soul most deeply wants. It's your adult duty to study them and ask how they might be beckoning you to make a necessary change.

## Who Is This Book For?

This book is written for humans. You might identify as straight or gay or bi or male or female or non-binary. You might be married (happily or miserably), in a lifelong partnership, single (happily or unhappily), widowed, or altogether disillusioned with the categories of singleness, dating, open relationships, or marriage. Although we all come to this conversation from different vantage points and will arrive at different conclusions, I hope the journey ahead will be similar for each of us: a commitment to engaging the stories, problems, and beauty of our lives with hospitality, integrity, and delight. Our life is speaking to us through our desires, but I wonder how well we are listening.

So, how is your relationship to desire? How do you feel like it's going? Maybe your desires feel out of control, because you can't seem to turn them off. Or maybe it's the opposite: You're wondering if anyone has invented a defibrillator for passion, because feeling emotionally flat or uninspired has become normal for you. There's a good chance you're somewhere in the middle: You have a deep appreciation for desire but find yourself occasionally surprised at how desperate or entitled you can become with someone you love. Maybe you didn't even know you had a relationship with desire in the first place.

Regardless of where you find yourself on that continuum, desire is central to all that is beautiful and heartbreaking in your life—and therefore worthy of your full engagement. If you want to transform your relationship to desire, learn what informs it.

Ultimately, that's what we're after: a holistic approach to desire. In Chapter One, I'll introduce you to five core longings uncovered through my research with thousands of couples and fifteen years of clinical practice. Together, they'll help you make sense of your challenges, move through them with kindness, and achieve breakthroughs that felt out of reach until now. These five desires aren't just ideas; they are the foundation of human flourishing and a map to reclaiming your life. I hope that they lead you to love your story and gain deeper clarity about the meaning and hope embedded within your longings. May this journey into the heart of desire help you find the love and wonder you've been longing for.

## A Resource to Go Deeper

If you're looking for an additional resource to help with this journey, I've created a hands-on companion to this book, the *Desire Workbook*. It's designed to help you dive deeper into the book's insights and apply them directly to your life. Through guided reflection, journaling prompts, and thought-provoking exercises, the workbook allows you to explore your five core longings on a personal level. The workbook is more than just a set of exercises—it's a tool for transformation, helping you unpack your story, break through barriers, and realign your desires with your true self. My recommendation would be to not just read this book, but use the workbook to excavate your story and actively author its future.

*Desire*

## CHAPTER I

# The Five Core Desires

AS A RESEARCHER AND PSYCHOTHERAPIST, I AM ENDLESSLY curious about desire. While we naturally dread facing issues connected to our love lives, self-worth, or careers, these struggles have so much to reveal to us. The dilemma is that we tend to pathologize our difficulties, thinking, *I'm so messed up. What's wrong with me?* Other times, we downplay their significance with a dismissive "It's not that big of a deal." Both responses hinder our growth. What we need is a third way, one that encourages us to engage our problems with uncommon kindness and curiosity.

This search for deeper understanding inspired me to create the Holistic Desire Survey, working with researchers to gather insights from over four thousand men and women worldwide. Participants answered deeply vulnerable questions about their childhood, trauma, romantic relationships (if partnered), mental health, sexual desires, and their lives' deepest longings.

The Holistic Desire Survey revealed that our desires and the problems we encounter related to them are far from random. While some individuals and couples are flourishing and enjoying deep satisfaction in their desires and relationships, others are struggling immensely, stuck in unwanted patterns. We have much to learn from both groups. Their courageous responses illuminate the precise reasons many of us remain stuck in negative cycles. They also reveal that while common solutions—like improving communication, medication, or prioritizing sex—can be helpful, they often oversimplify and overlook the far more complex patterns at play. We might believe we've identified the root cause, only to discover later that, like water damage, the issue has spread into areas of our lives we hadn't considered. Armed with insights from the survey, however, we'll learn to address problems holistically—viewing them as interconnected systems rather than isolated issues. This approach will help us stop wasting our lives fighting ourselves and our partners, and instead, start focusing on what really matters to each of us.

One of my greatest takeaways from the research is the value of embracing a "learn-it-all" mindset. The moment we feel certain we know what is going on inside of us or in a relationship, we risk closing ourselves off to new insights. Our goal, then, is not to draw hard-and-fast conclusions, or succumb to self-loathing or resignation, but to approach life's challenges with patience and curiosity.

## *The Danger of Partial Truths*

As I reflected on the Holistic Desire Survey, I began noticing a pattern I had not appreciated in my clinical work. Many individuals and couples turned to me as a last resort, often after trying various therapeutic approaches. Many of them had tried some combination of talk therapy, somatic therapy, couples counseling (if in a relationship), EMDR, Internal Family Systems, or life coaching. Some had ventured into plant-based medicine, while others had sought wisdom from popular books like *The Body Keeps the Score* (to explore trauma) or *Come As You Are* (to learn more about human sexuality). Despite all their efforts, they hadn't achieved the outcomes they desired.

I realized that this wasn't because their previous therapies or the books they'd read weren't valuable—though it's true that not all therapists are created equally. Instead, the issue stemmed from a failure to integrate these diverse perspectives into a cohesive, holistic understanding.

Whether it's trauma, relationships, or personal growth, our focus on a single paradigm can lead us to overlook or even devalue other important perspectives. American psychologist Abraham Maslow famously remarked, "If the only tool you have is a hammer, you tend to see every problem as a nail." Many clients experience something similar with their preferred tool. It initially works well . . . until it doesn't. When the paradigm fails to deliver results, they prematurely conclude that something is broken in them, in the relationship, or in the therapy field. Few realize the real issue lies in a lack of integration.

As we discussed in the Introduction, desire is at the center of all that is good, true, and beautiful in our world. Yet for too long, we've been walking through life's complex terrain without a map. If we do not develop a holistic relationship to desire, we risk spending our entire lives as underdeveloped humans, missing meaning, and living with half-hearted passions.

## Our Five Core Longings: Developing Holistic Desire

Through my research and clinical practice, I've identified five essential desires that predict the quality of our individual and relational well-being. I'll introduce you to these now, and I'll spend the rest of the book demonstrating how they can help you understand the roots of your challenges and what it might take for you to build a better life. By cultivating each desire, you can unlock the breakthroughs you've been longing for in your personal journey and relationships.

The five core longings are:

A desire for wholeness: our longing to heal the wounds of childhood and make sense of our past

A desire for growth: our longing to live with authenticity and strength through life's deepest challenges

A desire for intimacy: our longing to know and be known

A desire for pleasure: our longing for touch, vitality, and sexual connection

A desire for meaning: our longing for clarity, purpose, and a life that matters

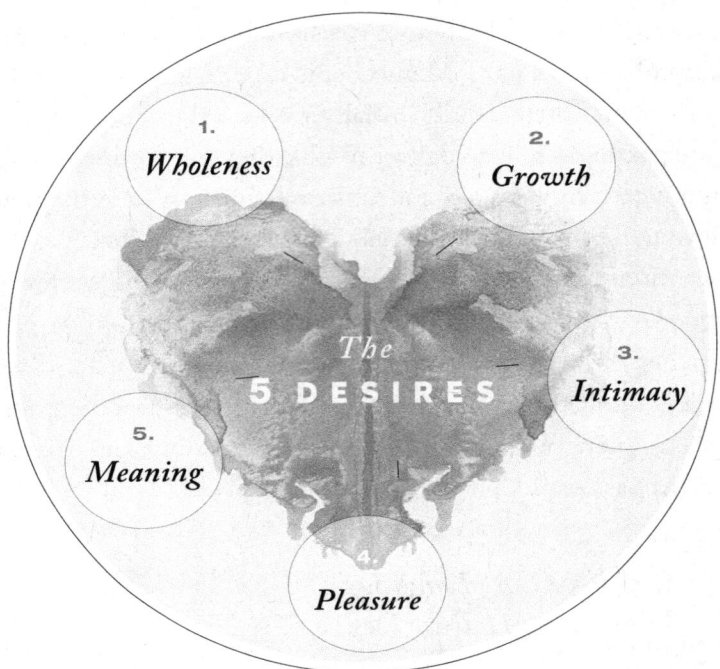

The book is divided into five parts, each dedicated to one of the core desires. While we'll explore each desire independently, it's important to recognize that they are more interconnected than we might realize. For example, as we begin to heal our childhood stories, it can shift the way we approach desires for growth, intimacy, and purpose. Or, when our marriage reveals that we are emotionally and sexually underdeveloped, it may prompt us to examine our early family dynamics and the lack of education around healthy sexuality. Each desire is deeply intertwined with the others.

Our goal throughout this book is to cultivate curiosity for how these desires are at work in our day-to-day lives. For example, my client's desire to sculpt his body into perfection had far more to do with escaping his story than embracing it with kindness. What we're all longing for is an integrated life. Developing a holistic relationship to desire is the key to creating it.

As you progress, you may find that one or two of the desires come naturally to you, while others are quite underdeveloped. This is a normal part of the journey. The chapters will empower you to build on your strengths and gently lean into the areas that require growth. While there's plenty to learn about the science of desire and the practical tools for its cultivation, this journey is less about acquiring information and more about cultivating curiosity about your own story and pondering where you might want it to go.

Now let's explore each desire in a bit more detail before we dive into them specifically in the next five parts of the book.

### ONE. A DESIRE FOR WHOLENESS:
### EXCAVATING YOUR CHILDHOOD STORY

As we explored earlier, your childhood is the foundation of your relationship to desire. We often believe we're in the driver's seat of our adult decisions, but have you ever wondered why you steer toward some desires and away from others? Part One will guide you to excavate the formative experiences of your childhood, revealing the stories that have shaped you into the person you are today, and providing clues into the origins of your deepest longings.

The two key questions for seeking wholeness are:

EXCAVATE YOUR STORY: How has my family shaped my relationship to desire?

TRAUMA AND DESIRE: How does childhood trauma shape my desires?

### TWO. A DESIRE FOR GROWTH:
### THE CRUCIBLE OF SELF-DEVELOPMENT

Desire problems serve as a *crucible* for personal growth, yet many of us have not been taught how to value the badlands of our soul. Instead of stepping into this crucible, we avoid it by filling our days with distractions and pursuits that give us the illusion of progress—like optimizing our health or building financial security. While some of these desires may seem beneficial, they often lead us away from the deeper work required for true transformation.

Part Two will explore the inner work necessary to become our strongest, most authentic self. But be warned: While we all want a better life, it will likely cost us the one we have.

The two key questions in this part are:

DEVELOPING A GROWTH MINDSET: Do I have hospitality for
  life's struggles?

NEEDING YOU TO NEED ME: How am I burdening others with
  my need for validation?

## THREE. A DESIRE FOR INTIMACY: RESPONDING TO THE CLARION CALL TO LOVE AND BE LOVED

Part Three is written primarily for couples—those who are currently in, have been in, or hope to be in romantic relationships. Intimacy struggles are often seen as indicators of what is wrong in a relationship. In reality, they may be signs that the relationship is working exactly as it should. Relationship challenges have an uncanny way of exposing unsettling truths about us, and for that reason, they act as a clarion call—a strong and clear signal for couples to take action. If we avoid the call, the issues will persist; but if we heed it, we can begin to satisfy our deep need to love and be loved.

The two key questions of this section are:

CONFRONTING SABOTAGE: How am I sabotaging intimacy in
  my relationship?

CULTIVATING LOVE: How can I learn to love and be loved?

## FOUR. A DESIRE FOR PLEASURE:
## DEVELOPING A HEALTHY RELATIONSHIP
## TO OUR SEXUALITY

It's no secret that most of us received inadequate sex education in adolescence and early adulthood. But the shortcomings of our education are just the tip of the iceberg when it comes to how unprepared we are to navigate the incredible power of sex. Sex has the potential to reveal our deepest vulnerabilities, provoke us to make life-changing decisions, and heal us in ways we can't even begin to imagine. The complexity is that most of us have learned to use sex for the exact opposite reasons. We don't like our emotional and physical vulnerabilities revealed during sex; we resist the growth it can provoke; and so we either use it like an opiate to numb pain or avoid it altogether to protect ourselves from additional harm. Part Four will teach you how to experience sex that is revelatory, provocative, and ultimately healing.

The two key questions of the sexual knowledge chapters are:

SEX REVEALS WHAT I DESIRE AND FEAR: Will I allow sex to be a source of revelation?

ALLOWING SEX TO PROVOKE AND HEAL: How can I outgrow unhealthy sexual patterns and cultivate healthier ones?

## FIVE. A DESIRE FOR MEANING:
## FINDING YOUR CALLING

The final part of the book invites you to cultivate a life of meaning and purpose. Without a clear vision of where we want to go and the personal agency to get there, life can feel unfulfilling. In developing a holistic relationship with desire, we learn to outgrow our constant need for external validation through people and achievements. Instead, we learn to pursue desires that are not only authentic but also serve the common good. If you stay with me until the end, you'll discover how to chart a course toward a meaningful life, navigate inevitable setbacks, and become a transitional character—someone who influences lasting change in their family and community.

The two key questions here are:

WAKING UP: What are the core traits I can develop to live a meaningful life?

CULTIVATING DESIRE: What are the key pillars of a meaningful life?

I SUSPECT ONE OR two of these five realms of desire will resonate most deeply with you, but I strongly encourage you to read all of them in order. Each part is integral to the others. If you don't know your story, you can't grow in authenticity. Without authenticity, you can't experience intimacy. If intimacy is lacking in your romantic relationship, sexual pleasure will diminish. And if you're unsure who you are, meaninglessness will pervade your life.

Wholeness, Growth, Intimacy, Pleasure, and Purpose are not à la carte menu items that we get to choose from. Think of them as a five-course meal, where each desire informs, builds on, and energizes the others. Because of this interconnectedness, some concepts will resurface throughout the book, allowing us to revisit and deepen our understanding of each desire.

As part of the research for this book, I developed a self-assessment to help you identify which desires are flourishing, which ones may be underdeveloped, and how you can chart a course for growth. You can access this self-assessment by visiting https://www.holisticdesire.com. It will score your responses and highlight areas of your desires that might need more attention. This assessment is optional and confidential.

## Entering, and Choosing, a Critical Period

In treatment, many of my clients come to a surprising realization: They might not truly *want* to get well. It's not that they enjoy their suffering; quite the opposite. They've come to treatment because they recognize that their former way of life has become untenable, a source of existential and relational dread. But soon into their journey, they discover that healing involves pain, learning requires unlearning, and growth entails anxiety. None of us is prepared for these challenges at the beginning. Thus, we find ourselves straddling two worlds—dead in one, powerless to be born in the other.[1]

Civil wars of desire can rage on for decades, if not a lifetime, if we don't choose to enter what's called a "critical period" of transformation. Neuroscientist Gul Dolen at Johns Hopkins University notes that critical periods are finite windows of time, ranging from days to years, when the brain is impressionable and open to new learning.[2] While these periods occur most reliably (and unconsciously) during childhood—the time when songbirds learn to sing and humans learn to walk—we also have the potential to enter them in adulthood through intentionality or crisis. Falling in love, dedicating ourselves to prayer or spiritual practice, or immersing ourselves in a new culture can each be intentional ways to enter a critical period. Life will also ask us to travel through dismal places. But heartache and crisis alone are not enough to create a critical period. We must choose it.

The life you desire will require you to let go of the life you've built. This book will guide you, but it will only be effective if something in your heart allows, even desires, a more curious and honest relationship with desire. Along the way, you should expect resistance. There will be fatigue, family drama, and crises of many kinds that will tempt you to turn back to the familiar. The truth is, there is never an ideal time for a critical period, because of the inevitable disruption it will usher in. But when you choose the path of growth, you're embarking on a journey that has the power to define your life.

The most effective way to enter a critical period is to be honest with yourself and at least one other trusted person about the confusion and difficulties you're facing. In a trauma-filled world, we become so accustomed to avoiding pain or chasing superficial pursuits that we don't even recognize all the ways our relationship with desire has been compromised. Change doesn't happen in abstraction; it requires us to carefully read the text of our story and share it with someone who cares.

From here, we will begin an excavation into the first of our five desires: a desire for wholeness. While I believe all five longings are foundational to a flourishing life, this first one may hold the deepest significance. Our childhood stories shape the quality, direction, and decisions of our adult lives in the most dramatic of ways, yet many of us have never taken the time to study them with the attention and care they deserve. It's time to learn your story and truly listen to your life.

# PART ONE

# A Desire for
# *Wholeness*

—

**SATISFYING**

**OUR NEED**

**FOR**

**HEALING**

## CHAPTER 2

# Let the Excavation Begin

*The greatest burden a child must bear
is the unlived life of its parents.*

—CARL JUNG

WHEN LAUREN WAS A CHILD, HER MOTHER GOVERNED HER desire. When she wanted ice cream, her mother refused: too much sugar. When she asked for concert tickets, her mom declined: The drive into the city would take forever. When she expressed interest in attending a liberal arts college, her mother countered, "I'll only pay for your first two years at a local community college." Although it would take Lauren years to recognize, her mother had obstructed her relationship to desire, and that went on to shape the trajectory of her life.

Parents are meant to steward their children's needs for authenticity, play, and belonging, but sadly, many are squanderers and swindlers. In Lauren's case, she wanted more out of life, but her mother conditioned her to reduce her expectations and taught her that wanting more was unhealthy, unreasonable, and even dangerous. Although it was never spoken, the message Lauren internalized was: "Your desires are too much. Keep them small and the family and our relationship will run smoother."

Lauren ended up marrying a practical man who sometimes mirrored her mother's rigidity. He became intense and sometimes intimidating when his expectations weren't met. Recently she had gone out to dinner with a friend; when her husband saw the credit card charge, he cornered her, asking why she needed to spend so much on an entrée, and did she really need to order a second glass of wine? Lauren and her kids, like many who live under a controlling authority figure, habitually suppressed their desires to reduce the potential for hostility. But one day, when her husband yelled at her son over a trivial matter, something in Lauren broke. She knew from experience how a child's brightness could slowly dim in the shadow of an oppressive parent. She sought out a licensed therapist.

In our first few sessions, Lauren shared openly about her marriage. It was one thing to feel a mild depression and a complete lack of sexual desire for her husband, but another to watch her children be ruled by a severe man. Although she was focused on her immediate circumstances and her desire for change, I invited her to see that the over-governance of her husband and her anger at her son's mistreatment were not only present-day dilemmas, but a set of clues to understanding her story. They were windows into what she'd experienced as a child but never had the language to name. As tedious as it may seem, especially when you're facing a crisis, current problems need to be studied before they can be solved.

## *Parents Pass Along Their Desire Baggage*

Imagine a child growing up in a religious home where clothing, music, and movie choices are all strictly censored for modesty. His parents say nothing about the topic of sex and opt him out of sex education at school for fear that the knowledge will corrupt him. As puberty approaches, he can't shake the fear that his burgeoning sexual desires are sinful. Torn between a desire to learn about sex and the reproach of his parents, he retreats into the world of porn, where he can pursue his curiosities in secret. If these childhood templates aren't interrupted, they will continue into adulthood, with the boy growing to see himself as broken.

Or consider the opposite scenario: a child whose every desire is immediately gratified. Instead of preparing their child for the road, as the old saying goes, these parents prepare the road for the child. The child's wishes for toys are always granted. They receive excessive praise for achievements rather than for effort, and they are overprotected in social situations where they might encounter difficulties. Their parents conflate satisfying a child's every desire with love and condition their child to expect the world to orbit around them.

In this scenario, the child is not only unprepared to navigate challenges but also accustomed to experiencing quick relief from an outside source. When adversity arises, particularly in adolescence or young adulthood, the child may have a low tolerance for difficulty. This conditioning can make them more likely to turn to substances or harmful coping mechanisms that promise a familiar, temporary relief. As an adult, this individual might be frustrated at themselves when they make unhealthy choices, but they have not appreciated all the ways they were conditioned to seek out temporary relief rather than learn how to move through challenges in a healthy, meaningful way. It's all too easy to fight our problems instead of addressing the patterns embedded within them.

We all are born with raw, untamed desires: the impulses to play, express ourselves, and connect with others. These desires are inherently good, but, just as our first crayon drawings probably weren't masterpieces, our childhood wants and needs rarely emerge in refined ways. The role of the parent is to allow these desires to be expressed, but also to gently and consistently guide the child in developing them.

Children who are consumed by raw desires are not entitled brats who have inherited a genetic predisposition to selfishness, but rather boys and girls whose family and culture have failed to provide the proper foundation for cultivating the wild, undulating power of desire. Without solid ground beneath them, the result is that they grow up personally and relationally underdeveloped, with desires to match.

Bestselling author and theologian Ronald Rolheiser offers insight into a response: It's not about satisfying their every whim or criticizing them for being selfish; it's about teaching them to connect those longings to a greater sense of communal life. For example, if a child has a raw desire for food, he suggests helping them connect it to "the much deeper joy of dining, of sharing food, life, and love within family and community."[1] A raw desire for a sugary pastry makes complete sense, but a good parent might invite the child to discipline this desire through forming a Saturday morning tradition of going to the local bakery as a family, or buying all the ingredients to make treats from scratch and then share a few with neighbors and friends. The unrefined energy of a child isn't harmful or selfish—it's waiting to be initiated.

As a culture, however, we are much more comfortable telling a child to suppress their raw and unrefined desires than we are teaching them how to cultivate them. Instead of seeing a child throw a fit and thinking, *I love that she knows what she wants!* we tend to think, *Her parents better address that, or she's going to be an entitled brat.* We deploy shame because it's easier to critique than it is to honor. Wanting always has been, and always will be, disruptive to those of us who desire control.

## *A Lesson I Learned from My Son*

I experienced this firsthand with my son during the Covid-19 pandemic. Like many parents, we were navigating seismic changes in both work and family life, and my son's behavior began to shift as well. At seven, he was increasingly rude to his sister, ignored my requests around the house, and began challenging any decision I made. I tried to make him understand how much of a royal pain he was being, without using those exact words. When that didn't work, I reacted with anger and attempted to enforce compliance through control.

One day my wife asked me to leave for the afternoon to figure out what was happening within me. That afternoon, I realized that my son was beginning to assert his independence, and I was framing his challenges as obstacles to be controlled, not as a sign of the growing, independent self that was emerging in him.

The next day, he saw a billboard in Seattle saying that fifty-three gallons of water go into making one store-bought egg. He threw three eggs against our backyard fence and told me I was looking at 159 gallons of water wasted. I was wildly irritated . . . if immensely impressed by his pandemic mathematics. But in that moment, I recognized that my son wasn't just being difficult; he was changing. The playful, innocent boy I had known now wanted to assert himself. He didn't need me to double down on my "obey me" mentality. He needed delight and direction so much more than he needed his spirit squelched.

After a few days of consistent kindness toward my son, making sure my attempts to connect weren't driven by guilt, I invited him to join me on the back deck. I made him his favorite drink and said, "I've made your desire for disruption something bad, but it's not. You're challenging me more because there's more you want to express and experience—and those are very good things." Then, an idea came to me: *Ask him what he might want to destroy next.*

He thought for a second before a mischievous smile filled his face. "I'd like to destroy your trophies," he said. Our family was preparing to move from Seattle to New York City, and my parents had dropped off a childhood bin full of trophies: sports awards and a second-place award from the state science fair. My son picked up the science fair trophy and placed it on the backyard grass. Then he grabbed my high school baseball bat and swung it with gusto, smashing it into hundreds of pieces. He turned around with sheer delight and said, "Your trophy is cheap plastic!"

What a metaphor. Children are trophy destroyers. They expose the things parents care about too much and set them free through faithful disobedience. The question for all of us is: In our formative years, did we have people around us who were mature enough to see the glory in our unrefined expressions? If our family system or the elders in our lives lacked patience and delight for our earliest longings, it's likely that our relationship to desire will need a biopsy.

## Provisional Self vs. True Self

As a result of our upbringings, each of us has developed a provisional personality—a patterned way of maneuvering through the world to make our life work. This provisional self is not our true self. It's a set of strategies and habits, formed in response to unhealthy family dynamics and adverse childhood experiences. Too often, our identities are formed at the cost of developing a soul.

For instance, I've worked with many members of the armed forces whose true selves were emotionally tender, but their childhood required hardness to survive. I've also worked with therapists who, deep down, wished they could live free from the demands of caring for others on a day-to-day basis. But their childhoods conditioned them to prioritize holding the family together by providing emotional support at the expense of their own desires. Both kinds of people felt that they had to cut off core parts of themselves and form provisional identities to survive their family dynamics. The journey to wholeness cannot take place until we acknowledge these provisional selves and invite them to honorably die.

Jungian psychoanalyst and author James Hollis notes that somewhere around midlife, these provisional personalities begin to decompensate and break down.[2] This is why it's essential to engage your story whenever you're facing significant personal or relational upheaval. What looks like your world falling apart may in fact be the implosion of your provisional self. The patterns and personas that helped us survive must be honored, but they also must pass away for something truer to emerge.

We look to the past not to blame our parents or excuse our actions, but because the narrative contains clues to unlocking destructive patterns and implementing lasting change. The person we are today is directly related to the quality of care our parents provided, the adverse childhood experiences we underwent, and the ways we learned how to navigate life as a result. Therefore, the journey to developing our true self will require we excavate landscapes that many of us hold as sacred, if not off-limits: family.

While most of us intuitively understand that our upbringings shape our adult lives, we often adopt a posture of dismissiveness, or even amnesia, when it comes to our parents. Most of my clients acknowledge that their childhoods weren't perfect; still, they would rather believe their desire problems stem from personal flaws or fixed traits in their personality than consider how their parents or family system might have set them on their current path. As a result, they feel a deep sense of self-contempt for their inadequacies or become engrossed in the latest health trends to improve what they don't like about their life.

The way out of these cycles is to honestly confront our family system, specifically our parents, and who we had to become in response to the dynamics of our childhood home.

## Your Parents Weren't Doing the Best They Could

You might be thinking: *This is a lot to put on my parents. They were doing the best they could.* The idea that parents are doing the best they can is common, even among therapists. We cling to this belief because it helps us avoid the pain in our own stories. It's easier to say things like "My dad did better than his dad" or "That happened so long ago, I need to take responsibility for myself" than to face the hurt and manipulation we experienced as children. Every client I've worked with has found it easier to identify their own flaws than to show kindness for their younger self, who felt powerless or heartbroken.

As a therapist and a father, I no longer believe that anyone's parents are doing their very best. Parenting requires consistent effort, patience, emotional resilience, and a willingness to support children through all kinds of challenges. There are times when all of this feels exhausting, and we all fall short. Even when I do give my best, I often feel grief and anger because I know I am giving my kids something better than I received. Parenting is an incredible honor, even as it reveals the depths of our selfishness.

Dr. David Schnarch, founder of Crucible Approach Therapy, points to a German saying: *Stressen Engel, Haus Teufel,* meaning "Street Angel, House Devil."[3] It describes parents who behave much better outside the home than in it. Children see this contrast and instinctively know that their parents aren't truly giving them the best they can. They know full well that if they were to engage a colleague, friend, or superior the way they treat their children, it would cost them those relationships or their career.

When my daughter was six, she addressed this dynamic with me directly. "When Mom is home," she said, "you're not as rigid with me when we do math homework. But when she is gone, you can get meaner." As parents, my spouse and I have strived to give our children language to express their experiences, but it's always a bit jarring when they reflect our behaviors so accurately. My daughter had mapped my mind, highlighting the stark contrast between how I act when my spouse is around and when she is not. She knew that I knew that what I was doing was wrong.

The idea that parents are doing their best is a comforting illusion, but it prevents us from acknowledging the harm done to us. It keeps us from confronting the ways we fail to offer our best to our partners or children today. When parents don't accurately see the harm they received, they won't see the harm they intentionally do to their own children.

Let's return to Lauren's story to see how she started to map her own desire problems after years of denying their source.

### *What If You Engaged Your Story?*

After several sessions with Lauren, the matrix of her relational struggles began to make sense. Unbeknownst to her, she had married a man who, like her mother, also governed her desires. She would hurl her hopes and dreams into the sky like clay pigeons, only for them to be shot down by the twelve-gauge shotgun of practicality. Even before marrying him, she remembered being ruled by a strong inner critic who would critique her for not having the courage to pursue what she wanted.

Lauren knew her mom's mother had died when she was fourteen, but she had never considered how that trauma might have shaped her mother's parenting. After the death, Lauren's mom was forced to become the primary mother figure to her three younger siblings. This role led her to foreclose her adolescent dreams of becoming a singer and going to college. Unwittingly or not, Lauren's mother adopted a belief that duty and sacrifice must be chosen over cultivating personal desire.

Lauren's story shows us that desire problems build over generations, quietly shaping our lives. Only by stepping back to examine our family's legacy of desire can we find the courage to defy these cycles. By breaking free from inherited patterns, we empower not only ourselves but also future generations to embrace a richer and more fulfilling sense of desire.

What legacy of desire did your family leave for you? This is the foundational question to ask yourself—and it's also where we'll start in Part One. Everything else we explore in the book will be built on this foundation.

Origin stories contain clues into the struggle for our true or authentic self. But like any great story, the protagonist is caught between staying loyal to the world she knows—a safe and predictable existence—or risking it all for a wild and unpredictable adventure. If we don't engage the dynamics set in motion during our childhood, our lives will lack meaning. We will find ourselves scrolling through our social media feeds and watching movies or TV shows where we can consume the lives of others rather than cultivating our own. In the end, we become like actors on a stage: reciting lines written by someone else, playing a role in a plot devised by a powerful producer, and developing a well-crafted persona that carries us further from our authentic self.

The further we drift from our true selves, the more our relationship to desire becomes compromised. A pull toward destructive behaviors, maddening relational dynamics, or external symbols of identity—such as prestige and wealth—is a telltale sign that we are disconnected from who we truly are and what we most deeply desire. At first glance, these behaviors may seem like mere failures of integrity or limitations of character. But if we stop our analysis there, we miss an important truth: Our addictions, conflicts, and mental health challenges are, in a sense, some of the most honest dimensions of our lives.

The recurring problems we face are symptoms, revealing both what has happened to us and the way we learned to organize our lives in response. To be sure, we need to grow beyond these destructive patterns, but we also need to see that the suffering they produce is a signal that an old part of us, something no longer serving us, is aching to die so that something new and vital can emerge.

Desire is the way back to the authentic life force within us. We can't let our underdeveloped desires or destructive choices convince us that we've never experienced true aliveness or an innocence in our longings. Perhaps, like Lauren, you can't remember a time when you felt free to pursue deep desires. Or maybe you've resigned yourself to the belief that your desires can't be trusted. No matter where you are in your journey, the chapters ahead will help you see the struggles in your life as clues to your childhood story and the seeds of your greatest potential.

## CHAPTER 3

# How Was My Relationship to Desire Formed?

*If you fly away from yourself,*
*your prison will run with you.*

—GUSTAVE THIBONE,
FRIEND OF SIMONE WEIL

WHEN CHARLES ENTERED THERAPY AT TWENTY-SEVEN, HE believed his problems stemmed from impulse control—specifically, binge drinking and out-of-control porn use. His first therapist had taken an addiction-focused approach, working to manage his behaviors through accountability, attending recovery meetings, and utilizing internet monitoring. It felt empowering at first, because it gave him something concrete to tackle. But over time, the constant focus on what was wrong with him and the message that he was powerless to change began to feel suffocating.

A few months later, Charles switched therapists, hoping for a different perspective. His new therapist took a less pathologizing approach, suggesting he explore "ethical porn" and take a one-month break from alcohol to manage his habits. It felt like a welcome change at first, but it didn't help Charles understand what was driving him toward these behaviors or why he always seemed to struggle in romantic relationships. Whenever he started to get serious with someone, Charles would fear losing his independence and retreat into his porn use. His emotional withdrawal and compulsions left him frustrated with himself, and his partners would inevitably break up with him.

Around that time, Charles confided in a friend about his longing to experience a stable, healthy relationship. The friend encouraged him to look deeper than just fixing behaviors and explore the "why" behind his patterns. This led Charles to me, and we began unearthing the deeper story influencing his struggles.

A few sessions into treatment, Charles shared a memory that started to make sense of his life. He told me that he couldn't stop thinking about his high school girlfriend that week. He'd seen an Instagram story of her on a road trip with her current boyfriend, and it brought up a family dynamic from high school that he'd forgotten, involving his parents' strict control over his social life.

At sixteen, Charles was texting his girlfriend one day when his mom noticed him smiling. She demanded to know if he was dating someone. Avoiding eye contact, he replied, "Yeah." His mom threw a kitchen towel on the counter and launched into a litany of critiques: the "C" on a recent report card, his reluctance to continue playing piano, and his growing self-centeredness, evidenced (to her) by his waning interest in family activities. She told him that dating was a distraction and that grades, not women, would allow him to reach his full potential. His dad backed her up. From then on, Charles would turn in his phone to his mom after dinner. He could start dating again after he was accepted into a "good" college.

After the breakup, Charles felt trapped at home and alienated at school. He retreated to his room, where porn became a constant companion. But after a few months, he felt disgusted over some of the content he was watching. This self-loathing led him to start drinking from his parents' always-stocked liquor cabinet. Charles wisely remarked, "It sucked. The things I used to help me get through the breakup were also the behaviors that made me feel like crap about myself."

His mother's overbearing nature created a bind: She demanded his loyalty to family and academics, but in doing so, she sabotaged Charles's ability to pursue anything outside of her control. His natural desire to explore other interests and relationships was framed as a mild form of rebellion, setting him up to be isolated in a home full of traps—unlimited internet access and a full bar. When his parents eventually caught him drinking, they used it as additional proof of his immaturity.

A decade later, Charles explained, his primary coping strategies remained the same, but now he saw them as irrefutable evidence that something was clearly wrong with him. I invited him to consider a new perspective: His behaviors were telling a story about something that had gone wrong around him. His parents had blocked his desires and handed him over to a gauntlet of traps that no adolescent would have been able to avoid. The entire story felt like a setup.

The crucial point is this: The damage we carry from our families often doesn't show up in memories alone, but in the repetitive problems of our adult life. Charles's personal and relational struggles weren't just the result of poor impulse control and immaturity. They revealed the moments when his deeper desires were blockaded by his family system. Instead of trying to fix our patterns, we need to study them. By doing so, we can cultivate an imagination for what our younger selves might have needed in order to move through those binds, with the support and guidance of our healthier, adult selves.

This chapter will guide you in excavating your story and uncovering the hidden forces that shape your relationship to desire. We'll consider how your family system has influenced your habits, impulses, and emotional needs. We'll explore what a healthy family system looks like, identify your attachment style (and the wounding that comes from insecure attachment), and examine four experiences we need to receive in order to feel secure in life. Once you gain awareness of where you're starting from, you'll be able to understand the meaning behind your current problems and begin to author the future direction of your story. Making sense of your past is the most effective way to transform your relationship to desire.

## *Understanding Your Attachment*

There is a growing, and now well-established, body of evidence that suggests the quality of our attachments to caregivers plays a significant role in the quality of our adult lives. From childhood through adolescence, we pass through many difficult developmental states, where we need to rely on our caregivers to offer us soothing, emotional regulation, and nourishment. When we receive consistent care, we tend to thrive, but when our caregivers are absent or become a source of dysregulation, significant problems ensue.

For example, if we lacked affection or attention from our parents, we might find our adult desires revolve around seeking reassurance and validation from our partners or professional colleagues. On the other hand, if we experienced an emotionally suffocating parent, we might find ourselves gravitating toward experiences of freedom and autonomy as adults, but struggling to allow ourselves to be deeply known.

The implication of establishing a secure attachment cannot be overstated. A sobering reality is that if you had received better care in your formative years, it's likely that much of the anxiety, depression, and relational strife you face today could have been reduced.[1] Children who grow up with insecure attachments learn that their big feelings, such as anger or distress, will not lead to connection, but to separation. As Dr. Bessel van der Kolk, author of *The Body Keeps the Score,* says, children from these types of family systems are in effect being "conditioned to give up when they face challenges later in life."[2]

You might be wondering if this puts too much pressure on parents. The good news is, a secure emotional bond doesn't take perfection from the parent.[3] Research shows that when a parent turns toward their child's needs and bids for attention around 50 percent of the time, they can still foster a secure attachment.[4]

## *The Four S's*

Dr. Dan Siegel, clinical professor of psychiatry at the UCLA School of Medicine, developed a simple and clear framework for understanding secure attachment: the 4 S's: Seen, Safe, Soothed, and Secure.

- *Seen* means having a parent who is attuned to both our physical and emotional needs. They are in sync with us, whether we feel sad, happy, or anything in between.

- *Safe* refers to being in a home environment that is emotionally, physically, and sexually safe.
- *Soothed* involves the recognition that children will inevitably experience intense emotions and need a parent who is kind and strong enough to help them process and regulate those feelings.
- *Secure* is the result of consistently being seen, safe, and soothed, along with the education and life experiences necessary to feel confident in life.

We will spend the rest of the chapter exploring these categories and the consequences we experience when they are not provided to us. Many of our desires, and the challenges we face surrounding them, are rooted in the attachment experiences we did or did not receive during our childhood. This framework helps us understand the fundamental conditions that support emotional well-being and shape our ability to form secure, healthy relationships later in life.

### Secure Children Seek Belonging and Authenticity

When children experience secure attachment, they are able to pursue two fundamental, but often conflicting, human experiences: belonging and authenticity. Many of us feel that belonging to a community or a family requires us to compromise some aspect of our authenticity. Others try to be authentic, but struggle to find a place where they truly fit. A healthy family system, however, provides a child nearly two decades of training in how to experience deep connection with others (belonging) while also cultivating and expressing their unique individuality (authenticity).

When families value the 4 S's, parents and children feel supported in their relationships with one another while also being encouraged to explore their authentic desires. In such an environment, family members are free to take personal risks, knowing that failure is not only accepted but a natural part of growth and discovery. And after they return from their adventures, they can anticipate connection and support.

The Holistic Desire Survey found that children whose desires were supported by their parents were 3.18 times more likely to score highly in terms of adult desire.[5] Do you see the implication? When children had supportive relationships, they were free to pursue authentic desires. Our childhood family system forms the blueprint for how we approach our future and the type of life we will eventually create.

Here's how that influence plays out across the four attachment types:

## SECURE ATTACHMENT

A securely attached child believes that relationships will be a place where they are deeply known and cared for. As adults, they seek meaningful connection and are able to communicate their desires openly. Their relationship to desire is healthy—they can express their needs, are less susceptible to unhealthy cravings, and have the flexibility to adjust and be patient with themselves and others.

## AVOIDANT ATTACHMENT

An avoidant attachment often stems from a family system that tends to dismiss emotions and desires. Adults with avoidant attachment may struggle to connect with their internal world. They find it difficult to know or express what they truly want and may keep their desires hidden. This leads to an underdeveloped relationship with their desires, often opting for less meaningful pursuits to avoid vulnerability or acknowledgment of their deeper longings. These individuals often find themselves pushing away intimacy, leading to frustration or withdrawal from romantic partners or friends.

## ANXIOUS (OR AMBIVALENT) ATTACHMENT

An anxious, or ambivalent, attachment typically arises from a family system where a child's needs were met inconsistently, or with conditions. Adults with this attachment style feel anxious and preoccupied with managing their image or securing love. They may feel intense hope when a relationship seems promising, but experience profound despair when it begins to unravel. Their relationship to desire gets compromised, too, as they tend to use it to seek external validation and soothing through people or material things, rather than having a healthy sense of what they need and how to find security.

## DISORGANIZED ATTACHMENT

A disorganized attachment develops in chaotic family systems, where a child may have experienced various forms of abuse (emotional, physical, sexual, neglect, etc.). Adults with disorganized attachment struggle to form healthy relationships and are more easily drawn into destructive behaviors. They may desire connection and soothing, but often find themselves reenacting the dysfunctional dynamics of their youth, endlessly stuck in cycles of self-sabotage and unhealthy relational patterns.

### *Evaluate Your Attachment to Understand Your Desires*

When Charles and I explored the topic of attachment, he recognized that his parents dismissed his desires and conditioned him to prioritize their own wants and needs, essentially orbiting his life around their control. While he also exhibited traits of anxious attachment, his core experience was that his longings were devalued or outright ignored—a hallmark of avoidant attachment. Over time, he learned to attach to unhealthy behaviors, including reliance on porn and alcohol, to find soothing and manage the big emotions of anger and sorrow that he felt.

Our ability to name what we want, how we express those desires, and the belief that our longings will come to fruition are all shaped by our attachment style. However, most of us tend to view the challenges of our adult life as isolated problems with our personalities, circumstances, or relationships. In reality, these challenges are echoes of our past, inviting us to learn our attachment story.

We examine the past not to find excuses for our desire-related problems, but because narrative holds the key to understanding our behavior, as well as any change we might be wanting to make in our relationship to desire. By excavating our past, we can better recognize where our desires were supported or neglected, and how that impacts our core longings.

To begin evaluating the type of attachment you had with your parent(s), consider your current relationships, whether romantic, familial, or social, and reflect on these questions:

- Do you become preoccupied with managing your image around others, needing to be seen favorably?
- Do you genuinely expect relationships to be a place where you're deeply seen and known?
- When you encounter a problem, do you dismiss the issue as unimportant or become emotionally withdrawn?
- When life becomes chaotic and people around you fail to honor or protect you, do you think, *Just another day in my messed-up life?*

The questions that resonate with you will serve as some of your first clues to understanding your attachment patterns.

To guide you further, let's take a deeper look at the 4 S's of attachment—Seen, Safe, Soothed, and Secure. Our early experiences with these core needs are foundational. They influence our patterns of relating to others, our self-worth, and the ambitions and relationships we pursue later in life. They're not just clues to understanding our past; they actively shape our desires in the present. As you deepen your understanding of these dynamics, you'll be better equipped to resolve challenges and gain clarity on the passions you truly want to pursue.

## SEEN: A HOME MARKED BY MATURE ATTUNEMENT

Attunement is the experience of being truly seen—when someone understands what makes us tick, what pisses us off, and what brings delight. It's the ability to read our emotional landscape, recognizing when we're happy, upset, confused, or full of wonder. In childhood, mature attunement might look like a parent noticing the sad look on our face after we get off the school bus. With genuine concern, they ask how we're feeling and make space for our big emotions. It's a parent who longs to care for our needs—whether it's a hug when we're upset or celebrating our joy when we are excited about something. Attunement communicates to a child: *I see you, and I delight in you. Your emotions and desires matter, and I am here to honor them.* It's this kind of care that encourages children to be confident in their ability to feel both belonging and authenticity.

Dr. Victoria Leong is a neuroscientist researching the link between social interaction and learning in parents and young children. She found that when infants engaged in joint play with their parents, they played longer with objects and showed fewer moments of inattentiveness compared to when they played alone.[6] Another study showed that when a parent offered a direct gaze—looking directly at their baby—the child vocalized more frequently, which in turn increased synchronization from the adult.[7]

The benefit of being seen by a mature caregiver is that it increases our capacity to synchronize with ourselves and others. While some worry that overly encouraging a child's desires might spoil them, the evidence suggests the opposite: Children whose desires are nurtured develop secure attachments, which lay a foundation for their well-being. They love to play, learn, and connect with the world inside and around them, and the experience of positive attunement continues to pay dividends throughout their adult life.

Do you want to know what truly drives unhealthy or entitled behavior in adolescents and adults? It stems from individuals with high anxiety who have never learned how to self-soothe and who lack the experience of supportive relationships. Cultivating a child's desires isn't indulgence; it's an investment in their future emotional health and resilience.

In my research, I looked at individuals who reported the highest childhood desires scores. These individuals:

- ✔ Were encouraged to desire
- ✔ Felt loved, even when they did not get what they wanted
- ✔ Did not feel guilty or ashamed of their desires
- ✔ Felt their desires were seen and supported by their family members

As expected, these individuals were more likely to report positive relationships with their parents. Conversely, individuals who weren't encouraged to desire as children had negative relationships with their parents and would go on to struggle with multiple desire-related issues as adults, including low confidence, recurring intimacy challenges, and a lack of purpose. Mature attunement brings delight and future flourishing, but when it's absent or when we're asked to attune to our parents more than they attune to us, it can set us on a path toward lifelong challenges.

## The Cost of Being Manipulatively Seen

In counseling and therapeutic circles, attunement is often seen as an entirely positive trait. But attunement is much like breathing; if you're alive, you're attuning. The question is: To what?

Many of my clients mistakenly conclude that their parents lacked attunement, overlooking more problematic and even more sinister motivations. It's not always that a parent was devoid of attunement; it's that they were attuned to something else. A parent might neglect their child's well-being because they're highly attuned to their own career, their next alcoholic drink, or a more successful sibling.

In many families, parents claim they are doing things "for the kids," but upon closer examination, manipulation, rather than generosity, is at play. A friend once shared that his father would take him and his siblings out for hamburgers and ice cream. Instead of ordering something for himself, he would go around licking each child's ice cream and eating several fries, citing a "dad tax." When the children pushed back, the father flipped it back on them: *Don't you see I'm doing something special for you?* What began as a family outing became a scenario that instilled powerlessness and humiliation in my friend and his siblings.

## *The Cost of Being Unseen: Disengagement*

Whereas mature attunement brings delight, a lack of it leads to life-long grief. Our childhood may not feel overly traumatic; it might just feel blank or monochromatic. Psychiatrist Dr. Curt Thompson puts it well: "We can grow up in homes where the food finds the table, the money finds the college funds, and the family finds the church each Sunday; but somehow our hearts remain undiscovered by the two people we most need to know us—our parents." A lack of attunement leaves us scanning distant horizons, hopeful, eager, even desperate for someone capable of delighting in us.

When a parent consistently fails to attune to a child, it creates a disengaged family system. Disengagement occurs when a parent chooses to withdraw physically or emotionally from their child's life. This can include a parent who spends excessive hours at work; avoids developmentally appropriate conversations about topics like sex, nutrition, or self-care; and consistently deprioritizes a child's needs. Many of my clients have believed that neglect is a lesser evil than physical abuse, but in fact, neglect is the most common form of childhood abuse. And because our brains process physical and emotional pain in similar areas, it can be just as harmful to our functioning.[8]

Growing up in a disengaged home leaves you feeling unprepared for life. You might struggle with intimacy and problem-solving and rely too heavily on external validation. Essential life skills—such as budgeting, time management, or cooking—may feel daunting or out of reach. Moreover, my research shows that individuals raised by disengaged parents are more likely to experience physical and sexual trauma outside the family.

Disengaged children grow up into adults with desire problems. Some turn to behaviors like compulsive sex, hookups, or emotionally fused relationships in the hopes of receiving what they missed growing up: being seen and enjoyed. While these behaviors might work temporarily, they lack real intimacy and therefore lead to feelings of shame and isolation. At this critical moment, adults tend to battle against their destructive desires instead of recognizing the deeper truth: These behaviors are simply a way to return to a familiar state of disengagement and judgment that they experienced growing up. Ultimately, compulsive behaviors and emotionally fused relationships are not chosen for their pleasure or connection; they reinforce the expectations that were formed in childhood.

## SAFE: A HOME MARKED BY STABILITY

Children need to feel—and be—safe before they can thrive and move into the world with confidence. Safety is not just the absence of harm. It also involves parents offering healthy vigilance to protect their children from outside threats, like bullies or harmful content, while also providing consistent attunement to prevent emotional neglect. When children grow up consistently feeling safe at home, they develop an intrinsic belief that relationships should offer refuge. As they move into adulthood, this belief shapes what they expect from their desires, emotional needs, and relationships.

A key aspect of creating safety involves maintaining healthy boundaries. When parents set limits, whether it's saying no to riding a bike without a helmet, limiting screen time, or enforcing curfews, they are teaching children that desires need to be disciplined if they are to develop in a healthy way. Over time, children internalize that their parents' role is to protect them, even at times from themselves, so they can continue to thrive. When boundaries are practiced with kindness, they teach children an important life lesson: You cannot always get what you want, but your needs and feelings will be seen and respected.

## How Healthy Discipline and Rigidity Differ

One question that often arises when discussing boundaries in a family system is: What's the difference between healthy discipline and rigidity? For example, couldn't Charles's parents have been looking out for his long-term success when they wanted him to prioritize academics over a high school fling? Sure. But when a parent (or culture) is too firm, overly protective, and excessively focused on compliance, the child learns that their feelings and longings are secondary to rules or achievement. This approach to parenting is a hallmark of a rigid family system.

In rigid family systems, emotional expression, mistakes, and vulnerability are met with harsh consequences, creating an environment that suppresses emotional growth and incubates powerlessness and shame. When a child's raw desires are constantly met with disapproval, their home lacks the emotional safety needed to learn from mistakes. Behaviors often labeled "rebellious" or "immature" are the child's attempts to assert their will and navigate their feelings in an environment where a tyrant rules without accountability. In these cases, the child is trying to figure out who they are while also pushing back against the constraints of a controlling system.

The root of the word "discipline" is *disciple*, which means "to teach." This is the litmus test of healthy discipline: teaching children to understand their emotions, impulses, and the connection between their behavior and its consequences. However, in rigid systems, discipline can become punitive or emotionally unsafe. Here, children are not taught to befriend and manage emotions, but to fear them, both in themselves and in others. In these environments, children may be yelled at or physically punished to make them "calm down." But this doesn't soothe them; it shuts down their nervous system, sending them into survival mode or a freeze state. The child hasn't calmed down; they've shut down—and there is a world of difference between the two.

## *Abdication Isn't Safe Either*

While rigid families suppress emotions, abdication of parental responsibility can create another type of unsafe environment where children are left to navigate life with little guidance. Dr. Jonathan Haidt, author of *The Anxious Generation,* observes that many parents today, especially those of iGen children (born between 1996 and 2012), have been overprotective of their kids' physical safety while being under-protective of their activities online. Too many children are given unrestricted access to the internet, social media, video games, pornography—experiences that can pave the way for compulsive behaviors, addiction, and mental health challenges like anxiety and depression.

A parent's abdication is never neutral. Failing to provide adequate boundaries and connection opens the door for harm to find their child—whether through abusive relationships or problematic behaviors. Without consistent and compassionate parental presence, negative influences will fill the void.

## *How an Unsafe Childhood Impacts Desire*

An unsafe childhood, whether stemming from emotional neglect, rigidity, or the abdication of parental oversight, has lasting effects on how we relate to desire. The absence of safety in a child's environment impacts their desires in three key ways:

1. **A HARSH INNER CRITIC:** There's an adage in psychology that the way we are spoken to as children becomes our inner voice. This is especially true of children raised in unsafe homes. When a parent is dismissive or humiliating, that pain doesn't just vanish. It becomes internalized as a critical inner voice that stunts a child's ability to experience joy, play, and vulnerability. As adults, we may suppress our true desires for fear that

they'll be critiqued or dismissed. Alternatively, we may only pursue desires that align with perfectionism, as a way of feeling acceptable and avoiding the risk of judgment. If we don't address the harm we experienced as children, this self-contempt will often grow into contempt for others over time.

2. **SELF-DESTRUCTIVE BEHAVIORS:** Studies on Adverse Childhood Experiences (ACEs) show that abuse, neglect, and family dysfunction increase the likelihood of early initiation into self-destructive behaviors, such as illicit drug use, by two to four times.[9] Lacking protection, children pursue these behaviors as a temporary refuge from pain. These patterns help individuals avoid emotional discomfort, but they also re-create the unsafe conditions they've grown accustomed to. The cycle of self-sabotage can perpetuate feelings of inadequacy, leading to resigning to the belief that they will never have a healthy, fulfilling life.

3. **UNDERDEVELOPED SEXUAL AND RELATIONAL DESIRES:** An unsafe home environment also affects our sexual and relational desires. In research for my book *Unwanted*, I found that rigid families have a particularly strong effect on people's sexual issues and fantasies. For example, men who were powered over by their fathers were more likely to pursue fantasies and sex acts that gave them a feeling of power over others. Similarly, women raised in homes with strict mothers were two and a half times more likely to fantasize about being used or treated harshly. Sexual preferences are not random; they can be negatively shaped by unhealthy relational dynamics and survival strategies we develop in response to those influences. By understating the origins of our desires, we can make conscious choices to reshape them into more embodied and fulfilling expressions.[10]

Rather than feeling ashamed or dismissive of these patterns, we need to ask questions like: Are these desires leading me toward the person I want to become? Are they fulfilling my deep need for inti-

are set up to sacrifice their own well-being to manage parental emotions and expectations, often in exchange for the "privilege" of being the favored child. Make no mistake, however: The "privileges" of enmeshment are a form of psychological grooming. Enmeshment interferes with a child's ability to develop their own desires because their goodness is being consumed to satisfy the parent's emotional hunger.

One common manifestation of enmeshment occurs when emotional intimacy between partners breaks down and a child is relied on to fill the void. For instance, a father might lavish attention on his daughter, calling her his "princess," while neglecting his spouse, the "queen" whom he vowed to love and support. Similarly, a mother might turn to her child for comfort and validation when her spouse is emotionally unavailable. In some cases, both parents may even compete for a child's affection, each looking to them to fill different emotional needs.

This dynamic is especially challenging in a single-parent household or when a spouse faces significant health challenges. However, even in these circumstances, a healthy parent does not enmesh. Instead, they might say, "I am having a really hard time right now, but I am so thankful to have a therapist and supportive friends." Parents can be honest about their struggles while maintaining boundaries that allow the child to be a child, not a surrogate spouse.

### ENMESHMENT AND GENDER

Emotional enmeshment affects both boys and girls, but my research shows that women are 42 percent more likely than men to report high levels of enmeshment. This pattern aligns with the traditional gender roles around caregiving and emotional labor. I also learned that there are two factors that significantly reduce the likelihood of experiencing enmeshment:

1. **SUPPORT FOR PURSUING ONE'S OWN DESIRES**: Children who are encouraged to explore their own desires were 21 percent less likely to experience enmeshment.

2. SEX EDUCATION: Children who received a solid sex education by the time they reached adulthood were 18 percent less likely to experience enmeshment. Teaching children about their bodies, boundaries, and quality relationships helps them form healthy, independent identities.

### ENMESHMENT HINDERS HEALTHY DESIRE

Enmeshment complicates a child's relationship with their own desires. On one hand, they feel responsible for meeting their parent's needs and expectations, but on the other, they have an innate longing to separate and forge their own path. Caught in this tension, some children suppress their own needs, constantly deferring to the desires of others. Others engage in a two-step dance of showing outward loyalty while secretly striving to break free. In both cases, the patterns established in childhood evolve into ingrained personality structures. One person constantly defers to others' needs, while the other appears outwardly supportive but secretly lives with a sense of entitlement, an imitation form of independence.

## *Healing the Past by Choosing to Soothe Ourselves as Adults*

Whether our parents were disengaged, sadistic, or emotionally enmeshed, healing comes when we, as adults, commit to bringing comfort in the ways we were denied it—even when doing so feels risky or unfamiliar.

For years, the client whose father forced him to throw away his blanket saw himself as an overly sensitive kid. But as he began to understand the lack of emotional comfort he received, he grieved for the boy who never had the kindness of a parent's soothing presence. In the months that followed, he decided to share this painful memory with his partner, and for his birthday, he was given a beautiful Pendleton blanket. Each Saturday morning, he now reads a book, wrapped in that symbol of beauty and comfort. The blanket is not a replacement for the one his father made him discard, but a symbol of the comfort he is now free to seek for himself. Wholeness comes when we find healthy ways to experience the soothing we desired and deserved.

Finally, let's look at the last "S": Secure.

### SECURE: A HOME
### MARKED BY CONFIDENCE

When children are seen, safe, and soothed on a consistent basis, they feel secure in who they are and in their connection with others. This feeling of security enables a child to show vulnerability, make mistakes, and have confidence in voicing their desires without fear of punishment or rejection.

This sense of security does not come from growing up in a perfect family, but from one that takes care to repair ruptures.[11] Parental ruptures include moments of irritation, saying something harsh, prioritizing rules over relationship, or disengaging from a child's needs. Healthy parents are mindful of these moments and seek to repair the harm done. Instead of blaming their child, they first take responsibility for their reactions. Before an apology is ever uttered, they've done the necessary work to understand what motivated them to do harm. Whether they intended to cause pain or not, healthy parents take responsibility for the impact of their choices.

An apology is only half of repair. The other half is changed behavior. Parents must reflect on their actions, work through their reactivity with a therapist or trusted adult, and be mindful of how their energy affects the family. Phrases like "that was not my intent" avoid accountability and display a lack of care for the other. As a society, if we want children to grow up into adults who can engage conflict with integrity, they first need to see it modeled at home.

Children, too, will rupture. We see this when they treat family members with disrespect or fail to follow through on promises. However, a child's rupture is quite different from that of an adult due to the inherent power differential and the fact that a child's brain doesn't fully develop until their mid- to late twenties. A secure parent understands that children need to rupture, and it's in these moments when they most need an adult who can navigate it with both kindness and strength. After all, how else will children learn, if not in the safety of their home? Most of the time, children don't need to learn how to obey or listen better. Instead, they need to be truly discipled—taught the skills necessary to navigate relationships with wisdom, kindness, and playfulness.

## The Cost of Feeling Insecure

Children from dysfunctional family systems are often kept from learning the information they need to feel confident in life—including education about their bodies and sexuality. Many of my clients grew up in religious families that avoided these topics entirely or offered only abstinence-based education, leaving them in the dark while they navigated puberty. Imagine a child who suddenly gets their period or experiences ejaculation for the first time, unaware of what is happening. Silence is a recipe for profound body insecurity.

Sheila Gregoire, Rebecca Lindenbach, and Joanna Sawatsky, authors of *The Great Sex Rescue*, surveyed over twenty thousand Christian women and discovered troubling findings that highlight the harms of this abdication. In their research, 41.4 percent did not learn about female orgasm until adulthood. Many also reported feeling extremely embarrassed about their periods throughout their teenage years. As adults, these women were 55 percent more likely to have poor marital satisfaction, 74 percent more likely to have below-average sexual satisfaction, and five times less likely to have solid self-esteem.[12] By avoiding these critical conversations, parents set up a pattern of chronic insecurity and confusion about what children should and shouldn't know.

## The Roots of Disordered Desires

Throughout history, many philosophers and theologians have discussed the notion of disordered desires—those longings that start as good but become twisted inside of us. Some have called these "idols" or "God substitutes" because of their power over us. For example, a desire for prestige starts as a natural longing to be seen and honored, but it can devolve into an endless search for validation and recognition. Similarly, greed takes a good desire for material security or comfort and turns it into an obsessive quest for wealth at any cost. A desire for power, when rooted in a secure or creative place, can be healthy, but it becomes disordered when it shifts into a need to control or manipulate others. Even a beautiful desire for pleasure, when taken to extremes, can lead to a hedonic treadmill, causing harm to others in the process.

The gift of secure attachment is that it rightly orders our desires. We long to be seen, safe, soothed, and secure, but how do we handle these desires when they are unmet? The good news is that even if we didn't experience secure attachment growing up, we can still change. Through growing self-awareness, healthy relationships, and intentional emotional work to understand our story, we can rewire how we approach our desires.

## The 4 S's and Charles's Growth in Desire

Let's return to Charles's story to see these concepts in action. As therapy progressed, Charles and I focused on the internal conflict that his family of origin created around desire. Like all adolescents, Charles naturally developed a growing desire to separate from his family and establish his own identity (authenticity). Whenever he attempted to assert this desire, however, his parents set up a rigid and enmeshed system designed to keep him close (manipulative belonging).

Charles's parents did "see" him, but in a manipulative way. They used academics as a tool for amputating his desires. And while they wielded excessive control in some areas, they failed to keep him safe in other areas, like the internet and alcohol use. As a result of his powerlessness and unlimited access to unhealthy behaviors, Charles sought soothing in unhealthy ways.

In therapy, Charles began to recognize how he had projected these dynamics with his family on to the women he dated. He saw each girlfriend as someone who would inevitably trap him in a cycle of emotional enmeshment and control. Initially, he thought his struggles with pornography, relationships, and career were insurmountable and unrelated. Over time, he came to understand that these behaviors were messengers, alerting him to an attachment story that he needed to face.

Charles began healing his relationship with desire the moment he stopped seeing himself as the disappointing adolescent his parents had painted him to be. By reinterpreting his story, he started viewing himself with more compassion. He no longer saw himself as merely impulsive or immoral, but as someone who had never been given the emotional support or relational tools to grow. The more he felt secure within his own identity (authenticity), the more he was able to outgrow unhealthy behaviors and pursue more mature, fulfilling relationships (belonging). Over time, he began to set goals that aligned with his true desires, instead of defining success on his parents' terms.

### Conclusion

As you've moved through the chapter, what insights have you gained? What attachment style did you form with your parents or caregivers, and how has that influenced your adult life? Are there wounds there that need to be healed?

Reflecting on the 4 S's, which aspects did you receive, or fail to receive, in childhood? Are there gaps that now shape the challenges you face today? Understanding what happened in the past is crucial, because if our diagnosis of our problems is wrong, the treatment plan will be ineffective.

My hope is that these insights have stirred a desire within you to heal. When we recognize how our family system shaped us, it helps us understand the desires our lives orbit around. In the process, we begin to assess whether those desires are leading us toward wholeness or if they are attempts to repeat or reverse dysfunctional patterns. In doing so, we take our first significant steps in developing a more holistic and authentic life of desire.

But there is another equally important dimension of childhood that can distort our relationship to desire: trauma. While we often associate trauma with life-threatening events, trauma is not just what happened to us. It's about what happens inside our minds and bodies when no one is there to witness our pain. Trauma is to desire what cancer is to the body. If we don't address it, it will slowly erode our capacity for healthy longing, leading to numbness, destruction, and disconnection.

## CHAPTER 4

# How Does Trauma Shape My Desires?

*Trauma is a fact of life. It does not,*
*however, have to be a life sentence.*

—DR. PETER LEVINE

### Sam

Sam spent his childhood in the shadow of his older sister's tennis career. She was one of the best players in the state, but it wasn't all-natural talent. His parents spent thousands of dollars they barely had to support her desires—moving three times so she could be closer to a coach or a better school tennis program. She competed in a tournament nearly every weekend, and Sam had to attend them all. He was bored out of his mind, but learned to pass the time drawing comics.

In middle school, his grades started slipping, which finally got his parents' attention. They criticized him consistently: "Why can't you be more like your sister, a good student and athlete?" He couldn't figure out why they cared. It seemed like they were only concerned with his sister and their next high-profile social connection. Now, at thirty-four, Sam is a stay-at-home dad, supporting his wife's thriving law career. He's a good dad, spends time drawing with his kids, but is also depressed. He drinks more than he'd like to admit and uses cash to buy his bourbon so it doesn't show up on his credit card statement. He feels invisible and is unsure of what he truly wants.

### Brittany

Brittany was fourteen years old when her parents' divorce shattered her stability. She eventually got involved in a local church that had a well-respected youth director. The summer between her freshman and sophomore years, she spent considerable time with him on various summer trips. He began grooming her and eventually abused her. Brittany felt deeply conflicted. She craved his attention and loved his touch, but she was also hearing messages from other leaders that she was supposed to make sure that her body was not a "stumbling block" to men.

When the youth pastor stopped talking to her, she felt a deep sense of rejection and rage at herself for wanting his connection. Now, as a thirty-seven-year-old woman, she struggles to integrate sexual desire into her life. When she experiences it, she either feels dirty or overcome by intense, out-of-control longings. She's had seasons of having a lot of sex, but to reduce the inner madness, she has been avoiding it for the last year.

### Gregory

At age twelve, the poet Gregory Orr was responsible for a hunting accident that claimed his younger brother's life. The anguish overwhelmed him, and his parents were so devastated by the loss that they couldn't even speak to him about it. His faith community was no refuge either, offering hollow reassurances that the tragedy was all part of God's plan. It wasn't until a librarian introduced Gregory to poetry that he began to find a way to understand his emotions and what was happening inside of him.

### Mabel

At age eight, Mabel went to a friend's birthday sleepover. She struggled with occasional bedwetting, and her mom packed a diaper just in case. As she pulled her pajamas from her overnight bag, the diaper fell out in front of her friends. The shock and laughter were immediate and loud. Mabel became the target of jokes throughout elementary school. Later, in middle school, she battled severe acne. Though her mom took her to various treatments, she never asked Mabel how she was feeling and never acknowledged the emotional toll it took.

Now fifty, Mabel has built a successful interior design career and survived breast cancer. But she constantly feels like her body is betraying her. She doesn't hate it; she's just exhausted by its constant demands for attention.

### Childhood Trauma Shapes
### Our Problems and Our Desires

Each of these four stories involves a formative experience of trauma that profoundly shaped the trajectory of a person's life. Many of us know—at least in theory—that trauma from long ago can create problems that consume us today. The question is: Do we understand how?

Trauma, derived from the Greek word for "wound," encompasses both physical injuries and the emotional scars we carry inside. While the word might evoke scenes of life-threatening events, leading us to dismiss or minimize our own experiences as inconsequential, the reality is that trauma exists on a continuum. Psychologists often distinguish between "big T" traumas—such as war, abuse, or natural disasters—and "small t" traumas, which may include experiences like bullying, divorce, or chronic stress.

Many people believe trauma is most evident through invasive or heartbreaking memories. In reality, its effects are more subtle. Trauma reveals itself in the longings we chase, our emotional reactions to the world, and the negative, recurring beliefs about who we are. The telltale sign that we have been through a trauma is in our fight, flee, freeze, and fawn responses. How do you react when faced with the threat of exposure, powerlessness, or pain? Do you flee the exposure of shame, or fight to regain control over the situation before vulnerability overwhelms you? Do you freeze in moments of pain, or fawn before others to mitigate the potential for harm? Often, what may look like our personality, or our personal flaws, is more likely the ongoing imprint of trauma.

Mental health is the journey of integration—of acknowledging and incorporating all the parts of our history into a coherent sense of self. Trauma teaches us that healing is not about forgetting, but about embracing our wounds and allowing them to inform how we will choose to live in the future. While seeking to overcome or forget the pain in our story is understandable, it will never lead us to a meaningful life.

The unhealthy dynamics and reactive patterns of our adult life are speaking to us about the adverse childhood experiences we've endured. Rather than putting pressure on us to just "grow up," we can see how they reveal where something got stuck when we were growing up. To find wholeness, our desire to experience kindness for our bodies must exceed our impulse to avoid, numb, or control them.

## *Trauma Impacts Our Bodies, Behaviors, Beliefs, and Bonds*

In this chapter, we will explore how trauma impacts our *bodies*, the *behaviors* we engage in, the *belief* systems we develop, and the *bonds* we form with others. Let's explore how each of these dimensions uniquely affected Brittany's life.

When Brittany first came to see me, her life appeared stable, but she confided that her heart felt dull and her eyes had lost the spark they'd had when she was a girl. She had been engaging in hookups with older men, drawn to their power and the hope of finding connection. But each time, the men would pull away, saying they couldn't leave their families or start a life with her. Exhausted by the rejection, she attempted to shut down her desire for romance and focus solely on her career.

Brittany saw her relational and sexual problems as evidence that she was screwed up and incapable of having a healthy relationship. I introduced her to the concept that behavioral patterns are messengers, pointing to the ways she was repeating dynamics formed during her trauma—longing for deep connection, but being used by older men. As she processed this, tears filled her eyes. "I'm so messed up. What kind of girl would want that type of connection?"

Brittany knew the youth pastor had groomed and abused her, but what she felt the most anger toward were the desires she'd had as a teenager. Her body longed to be seen, safe, soothed, and secure, and her pastor positioned himself precisely where these needs were most vulnerable. After the trauma, she felt like she could no longer trust her body, and her adult sexual behaviors became reenactments of this adverse experience. The more she pursued these desires, the more they reinforced harsh beliefs about who she was. Her attempts at bonding followed a similar, painful script: seeking older men who would use her, while simultaneously isolating from those who might offer real care and tenderness. Trauma had infiltrated nearly every aspect of Brittany's life, even if she hadn't connected the dots between her past and her present.

This raises a question I want you to consider as you reflect on your own life: What stories of harm have you concluded are irrelevant to your current self? As we explore the ways trauma impacts our bodies, behaviors, beliefs, and bonds, I encourage you to approach your own experiences with curiosity. Be open to the possibility that your unaddressed trauma might be shaping your desires in ways you haven't yet recognized.

## BODIES

Trauma doesn't just reside in our minds; it's embedded within the body. Candace Pert, the pioneering neuroscientist, coined the term *bodymind* to describe this intrinsic connection between body and mind.[1] We often mistakenly believe that trauma is solely a mental issue—limited to harmful thoughts or memories. But it's far more complex than that. Trauma takes place in the body and alters its physiological state, affecting everything from our nervous system to our immune response.

Here are a few examples of how trauma negatively impacts our physical health:

1. Women with severe post-traumatic stress disorder (PTSD) were found to have twice the risk of ovarian cancer as women with no known trauma exposure.[2]
2. Men sexually abused in childhood had a tripled rate of heart attacks.[3]
3. Systemic factors like racism can shorten telomeres—tiny DNA structures at the end of chromosomes that shorten with age. One study found that middle-aged Black women were, on average, over seven years biologically older than their white counterparts.[4]
4. A Danish nationwide study found that grieving parents who had lost a child were at double the risk of developing multiple sclerosis.[5]

These findings highlight that trauma is not confined to mental health. It affects our body in tangible, sometimes catastrophic, ways—including, as we will see below, our ability to seek and experience pleasure.

Here's the key point: Our culture rarely remembers and honors what the body has endured. Instead, we focus on advancement and self-mastery over it. We chase quick fixes—prescription medication, lifestyle changes, breathing techniques, health protocols, and the latest longevity science. Yet these pursuits can overshadow addressing the underlying traumas that fuel our desires for such approaches. As Desmond Tutu wisely said, in the context of apartheid, "There comes a point where we need to stop just pulling people out of the river. We need to go upstream and find out why they're falling in."[6] If we find ourselves wanting triumph over our trauma, compulsively stimulating our body, or resisting embodiment, we may be missing the chance to go upstream to experience wholeness.

## Trauma Hinders Pleasure

Trauma's effects go beyond illness. One of the most insidious impacts is seen in our inability to experience pleasure after heartache. When we undergo prolonged stress or pain, our body's capacity to enjoy life's pleasures diminishes. For many, this leads to compulsive behaviors or avoidance, both forms of detachment from the body.

In the aftermath of trauma, we struggle to want even simple pleasures. Whether it's a warm beverage in the morning, a hug from a loved one, or a quiet moment of solitude, trauma can prevent us from being able to fully relax into these experiences. The body becomes so conditioned to tension and vigilance that it struggles to trust or receive alterative realities like safety and peace.

When desire becomes entwined with trauma, the very experience of pleasure itself becomes tainted. Brittany's experience of yearning for connection and sexual pleasure offers a heartbreaking example. The possibility of experiencing goodness creates deep ambivalence: We crave pleasure, yet fear it will set us up for heartache.

Many of my clients who have experienced trauma find their bodies instinctively drawn toward compulsive forms of pleasure. Whether substance use, out-of-control patterns, or unhealthy relationships, these activities return them to the intensity and shame of their original traumas. It might seem like they are pursuing *too* much pleasure, but in reality, they're compiling additional data that reinforces their core belief: *The body cannot be trusted.*

Others react by avoiding pleasure altogether. They fear that any goodness will lead to pain or awaken a monster inside of them. When the opportunity to enjoy something or someone arises, they become deeply suspicious and conclude it's better to stiff-arm those longings. The more this strategy is deployed, the higher the likelihood of experiencing depression, because they've learned to organize their life around resisting desire.

To restore our bodies after trauma, we must learn *embodiment*. Reconnecting to our bodies and accepting even small doses of pleasure helps us learn to trust them again. Just as our bodies can only tolerate simple foods like bananas, rice, applesauce, and toast after the stomach flu, we should aim to gradually offer our bodies gentle experiences of pleasure. A warm bath, soothing music, or movement from dance or yoga are excellent ways to nurture embodiment and restore our belief in the goodness of our bodies.

## BEHAVIORS

As a clinician, I've observed how adverse childhood experiences influence self-destructive behaviors. Here are some examples:

- EMOTIONAL REACTIVITY AND SUBSTANCE USE: As a child, you had an emotionally reactive parent who drew you in with their drama, leaving you emotionally dysregulated. As a teenager, alcohol became a gift to calm your nerves. As an adult, you may find yourself drawn toward or married to an emotionally reactive partner. Even though you feel distressed and used, you also feel an obligation to support them. Consequently, you resort to drinking each night to make life bearable.
- SEXUAL PROBLEMS: As a child, a neighbor introduced you to porn or a sexual experience that initially felt exciting, but later became a source of shame and confusion. Over time, you sought out increasingly intense sexual experiences in an attempt to re-create the original feel. As an adult, you may find yourself caught in behaviors that overstimulate you, preventing deeper connection to yourself or your partner.

### The Link Between Childhood Trauma and Adult Behavior

One telling insight from the Holistic Desire Survey reveals how early adverse experiences shape our adult behaviors:

- A person who answers yes to one or more types of childhood trauma is 3x more likely to engage in a range of sexual behaviors, like porn use, infidelity, and hookups, but is only slightly and insignificantly more likely to report them as "unwanted." This suggests that trauma drives people toward unhealthy behaviors, but over time, they may become resigned to these patterns. When these behaviors feel normal, they're less likely to view them as unwanted, even when those behaviors create consequences in the rest of the person's life.[7]

Childhood trauma leads to a demonstrable increase in a person's desire for various sexual experiences. The question is: Why? One possibility is that these individuals are attempting to transform their trauma into triumph—turning past feelings of powerlessness or disconnection into a sense of power or intimacy. Alternatively, it could be that they are unconsciously reenacting the very trauma that originally caused them harm.

So which is it? Are these behaviors helping soothe the pain of trauma, or are they perpetuating the disconnection and over-arousal that were part of the original wound? As noted in the Introduction, I'm more concerned with the integrity of our motivations than with conformity to any particular school of thought.

The litmus test of a healthy behavior is whether it leads to greater embodiment. Reflect on your life now: Are your behaviors aligned with the hopes of your childhood self? Would that self be proud of you? Do your behaviors foster greater appreciation and kindness for your body? Too often, adult desires are a form of escape or a way to reenact childhood trauma.

Gregory Orr's decision to write poetry is a testament to the impact of his librarian. Brittany's sexual behaviors with older, exploitive men were a continual reenactment of her trauma. The actions and behaviors we are most proud of reflect where we have been loved the most, while the behaviors we struggle with reveal where we are still waiting for love to arrive.

This is why feeling "bad" or defensive of our problematic behaviors is largely beside the point. The behaviors causing the greatest complications in our lives today are a living biography of our past—telling a story of where we come from and how we've learned to navigate the wasteland. When we listen to the message carried in those behaviors, we can begin moving toward a more embodied, passionate life.

### BELIEFS

The more our trauma persists without an empathetic witness, the more likely we are to form negative core beliefs about who we are. When our bodies don't seem to function as they should and the debris of our behaviors and reactions builds up around us, the evidence seems insurmountable: We must be broken or inadequate, no longer worthy of love.

Shame is a masterful but brutal storyteller. Many clients have told me that when they get close to sharing something vulnerable, the voice of shame tells them others will be dismissive or, worse, revolted by their story. When a forty-year-old man thought about going to therapy for his eating disorder, the voice of shame told him that men shouldn't struggle with those types of issues, and even if they did, he should have resolved them by now. Another client told me they hesitated in reaching out to a friend about depression and suicidal ideation, convinced that nothing would make a difference. When the voice of shame is loud, the melody of our belovedness cannot be heard.

The more we try to run from shame, the stronger it becomes. By running from it, we inadvertently legitimize its damaging messages. Instead of challenging its narrative, we internalize that its accusations must be true. Shame carries with it an open-and-shut case of evidence to prove its claims. It meticulously documents every flaw and choice, ready to present this inventory whenever we feel exposed or attempt to change.

Given our trauma-filled world and collective struggle with shame, it's no mystery to me why there is a proliferation of self-help books on productivity and self-validation. Take an excellent book like *Atomic*

*Habits* by James Clear, which has sold over twenty million copies.[8] While its guidance on building small, transformative habits is valuable, I've noticed that my clients with unaddressed trauma often flock to it in hopes of gaining control over their lives. The reader's unconscious and sometimes conscious goal is to avoid feeling surprised, powerless, betrayed, or incompetent in any scenario. This drives people to create sophisticated systems centered on productivity, health, and even mental well-being.

For those who need to hear it: A desire for mastery can be a trauma response. Rather than cultivating systems to sidestep painful beliefs, we should focus on developing systems that allow us to grieve and befriend our inner pain. When we seek wholeness, we realize that the opposite of shame isn't mastery or shamelessness, but vulnerability.

Our desires will flow in the direction of our strongest beliefs. If we believe we are broken, our desires will reinforce that belief. If we believe we are weak or deficient, we will constantly look for strategies and protocols to overcome these perceived flaws. On the other hand, if we believe we are not merely worthy of love and belonging, but also deeply beautiful in our essence, what kind of desires might then fill our imagination?

Take a moment to picture a life where your desires aren't consumed by the need to fix yourself or escape pain. What if healing wasn't about repairing something broken, but about awakening to the deepest truth of who you are and discovering a life beyond pain management and self-improvement strategies? We all have areas that need attention, but the essence of our humanity, the parts that are authentic, beautiful, and strong, can never be erased.

Who are you at your core? What do your deepest desires reveal about the essence of your identity? Don't buy into modern sound bites that confuse self-destructive desires with coping strategies or reduce healing to an endless quest for self-improvement. There is so much more to you than that. While it's natural to want to be free *from* the negative survival strategies of trauma or make improvements, true wholeness comes from asking: What do I want to be free *for*? What kind of life would I be living if I were fully alive?

## BONDS

Trauma leads *to* isolation, but it rarely happens *in* isolation. There is always a relational context. For many of us, trauma first strikes when we are away from the protection and nurture of home or a caregiver—we're bullied at school, abused at a camp, or involved in a car accident. Even in the aftermath, early intervention can make a decisive difference. If we'd had an empathetic witness who was attuned to our pain or a safe relationship where we felt free to talk about our experiences, the trajectory of the trauma could have been far less destructive.

But sometimes, trauma is inflicted by the very people we trust the most. When someone we love or rely on betrays us—be it a parent, partner, or friend—the wound is even deeper. This betrayal creates deep fissures in our ability to trust others. Once trust is broken, it is extraordinarily difficult to mend.

Trauma erodes our ability to feel safe and secure in relationships, which in turn impacts every relational connection we try to form or flee from. The Holistic Desire Survey found that when an individual had a caregiver who was emotionally unreliable or too preoccupied with their own struggles to notice theirs, they were more likely to experience trauma:

- *Women* with high childhood trauma scores were 22 percent less likely to report positive relationships with their mothers and 34 percent less likely with their fathers.
- *For men*, these numbers were even starker: 69 percent and 67 percent, respectively.[9]

This data underscores how the quality of our early attachments to our caregivers shapes our vulnerability to trauma. Without that foundation of safety, trust, and emotional care, we are far more susceptible to harm.

## The Reenactment of Harmful Bonds

The insidious nature of trauma is that it doesn't just damage our relationships; it rewires them. As we've been exploring, this is often most evident in the problems of our adult life. In my research we found the following:

- Individuals with high childhood trauma scores were nearly twice as likely to experience negative romantic relationships as adults.
- Men who had high childhood trauma scores *and* received little support for their desires from their caregivers were 36 percent less likely to experience positive relationships, while women were 19 percent less likely to experience them.
- Survivors of sexual assault were 60 percent more likely to encounter negative romantic relationships.[10]

Most of us desire healthier relationships, yet many of us are unknowingly trapped in patterns that impede our ability to experience them.

One of the key ways trauma manifests is through bonding us to unhealthy people and behaviors. I saw this firsthand when I worked at a psychiatric facility that served individuals with dual diagnoses: a mental health disorder and substance abuse. Many of my clients described their first illicit drug use as a "warm hug" or their first drink as a profound source of comfort, a temporary balm for their emotional pain. What began as a soothing escape became their source of primary attachment.

Similarly, abusive relationships often mimic this dynamic. The abuser positions themselves as a source of attachment, offering what feels like love but is really manipulation. The connection we form with the abuser may offer the touch, affection, or acceptance that we were denied earlier in life. I've heard this tragic refrain countless times from my clients: "The person who abused me was better to me than anyone else in my life." If we fail to extend kindness to ourselves for being drawn into these unhealthy bonds, our self-contempt can drive us to keep reenacting the patterns.

## The Path to Healing Broken Bonds

The paradox of trauma is that while relationships are often the context for our deepest wounds, they also hold the potential for our greatest experiences of wholeness. After trauma, the journey back to relationships feels fraught with risk. We question whether anyone will truly possess the kindness, let alone the skill, to be there for us. Yet deep down, we never stop longing for a compassionate witness—someone who sees us, who can attune to our pain, grieve alongside us, and celebrate our growth, helping us believe that trauma does not have the last word.

## Individual Therapy Isn't Enough

Years ago, Amnesty International launched an initiative to provide individual therapy for survivors of torture, only to find that it did not yield the results they had hoped for. They ultimately found group therapy to be most effective. For survivors, the power of hearing others' stories created a profound sense of solidarity and understanding.

Here's why: In trauma, a region of the brain called Broca's area goes offline, compromising our ability to speak and find language for our experiences.[11] But in community, we begin to hear others share their stories, and slowly, we start to find language for our own.

Community is where shame-based belief systems go to die. In isolation, we often settle for merely "moving on" or hold on to the harshest interpretations of our story. But in a compassionate community, these strategies and belief systems are gently exposed. Many of my clients recognize that they offer far more kindness to others than they do to themselves. As they witness this pattern repeatedly in a group setting (or have it pointed out to them), it gradually leads to the conviction and desire to view themselves with more tenderness. They realize that it's not enough to simply recount or share their story—they must also make sense of how they see themselves as a result.

The stories of Sam, Brittany, Gregory, and Mabel show how powerful an empathetic witness can be, and the consequences that result when those figures are absent. Sam's transformation in particular took place in the context of community. He joined a group therapy program focused on trauma and substance use, and in a pivotal moment, a group member expressed deep upset for Sam's history of neglect and the favoritism shown to his sister. This intense emotion caught Sam off guard. He had grown accustomed to seeing his life through the lenses of neglect and indifference. Now a different way of engaging it was modeled to him. This fiery reaction of his empathetic witness helped change what Sam was willing to settle for in life.

Community offers one of the most powerful antidotes to trauma. When we share our sacred stories in safe spaces, we begin to create new templates for what is possible in relationships. This is the key to healing broken relational bonds after trauma: forming new, compassionate connections. It doesn't happen all at once, but gradually, we find ourselves willing to exchange suspicion for trust, numbing for feeling, and isolation for connection. As we become more in touch with our trauma, the benefit is that it invites us to desire deeper connections and more meaningful conversations than we ever thought possible.

## Trauma Grows Desire

When we learn to study the trauma in our stories—embracing the pain in our bodies, the complexities of our behaviors, the wounds in our beliefs, and the fractures in our bonds—our desires begin to shift. No longer driven by the need to forget, numb, or overly compensate, we start to long for deeper realities. We find ourselves wanting to grow not because we don't like ourselves, but because we hunger to experience more from our lives. We find ourselves moving toward intimacy not because we're lonely or need validation, but because of the profound privilege of knowing another person's story. I wish I could eradicate trauma from the face of the earth, but I am always struck by how it has the potential to lead people to a more embodied and meaningful existence.

## Conclusion

Statistically, it's likely that many of your current problems and desire challenges are rooted in unaddressed trauma. A key step in moving toward wholeness is developing a story bank of traumas you've experienced. The process of recalling these adverse childhood experiences will be different for each of us. Some people have vivid flashes of memories etched into their minds. Others may sense that *something* happened, but they can't quite put their finger on it. For many, their memories may only surface after therapy or a triggering experience that helps them recall experiences they haven't thought about in years. If memories don't surface for you immediately, give yourself time.

Memories are most likely to emerge when they are welcomed. To do this, revisit old photos or yearbooks, go back to your elementary school or middle school on a weekend, or use the internet to look up the top movies, television shows, or songs from a particular year in your childhood. If possible, call a sibling or childhood friend and ask them what they remember. Another option is to reflect on your primary or most difficult caregiver and write three adjectives you would have used to describe them (angry, distant, charming, etc.).

If recalling specific events is difficult, start by identifying a current situation that triggers feelings of shame, anger, or anxiety. Embedded within your emotional reactions are clues to past wounds. Once you've identified a present-day challenge, allow your mind to float back to a time in childhood when you might have felt similarly. Flashes of memory might emerge. If they do, write these down, along with your approximate age at the time.

The goal isn't just to remember the events, but to understand the context in which they occurred and the meaning you assigned to them. Many people mistakenly equate retelling their trauma stories as "processing" the trauma. While remembering and sharing your story is important, real transformation happens when we address the negative core beliefs that we formed during times of powerlessness and shame.

For example, someone who was bullied might believe they were targeted by a parent or sibling because they were "annoying" and "deserved it." Upon deeper reflection, they might realize that their childhood self was actually very buoyant, filled with curiosity, or willing to boldly challenge rigid people in their life. This updated perspective can shift the meaning of why they were attacked—perhaps it wasn't because they were annoying, but because others envied their vitality or tried to shut down conflict by making them feel small. The fruit of effective trauma care is that our negative core beliefs start to break up, allowing us to see ourselves not only with compassion but also with greater dignity.

The accompanying *Desire Workbook* is full of questions and exercises to help you further process the meaning of your traumas, experience greater embodiment, and determine what to look for when choosing a supportive community of witnesses. Restoring your relationship to desire after trauma is possible, and the exercises in the workbook will show you how to do so.

• • •

Part One of this book may have been illuminating, and maybe even painful, in ways you did not expect. I hope you have found a more informed and gentler understanding of the origins of *you*. The totality of your childhood experiences and roles you learned to play served as your functional map of desire. The American novelist William Faulkner once wrote that the past is never dead; it's not even past.[12] The problems, complexities, and emotional reactions we experience today show us that our past is alive and well in us. Learning to be curious about our life and responding to triggering experiences with kindness is how we become whole.

While Part One revealed the wounds of your past, Part Two will highlight the ways your relationship with desire might be underdeveloped as a result. For most of my clients, this is often the point where fatigue settles in. Acknowledging the pain of our past is difficult enough, but to confront the person you've become as a result can be even more disconcerting.

Even still, remember that *integrity is a muscle that strengthens the more you use it.* The honesty you've developed with your story will now empower you to examine what a desire for growth truly requires. In time, this muscle will allow you to create a future you are deeply proud of.

# PART TWO

# A Desire for
# *Growth*

——

## CHAPTER 5

# Welcome to the Crucible

*To love someone else is easy, but to love what you are,*
*the thing that is yourself, is just as if you were embracing a*
*glowing red-hot iron: it burns into you and that is very*
*painful. . . . You cannot stay away from yourself forever,*
*you have to return, have to come to that experiment, to know*
*whether you really can love. That is the question—whether*
*you can love yourself, and that will be the test.*

—CARL JUNG[1]

## The Modern Search for Growth

Paul is the epitome of modern man's search for personal growth. He reads all the bestselling personal improvement books, listens to the latest podcasts, and builds his life around optimizing his physical and mental well-being. It all began after the birth of his first child. His marriage began to fray as his wife's attention shifted to their newborn—and even more when she experienced postpartum depression. Paul felt rejected, sensing that years of investment into their relationship had been for nothing. Simultaneously, his career became more demanding. No matter how hard he worked, he was falling short on something. Overwhelmed, he became increasingly careless with his food and alcohol intake, which negatively affected his self-image and sleep. At his lowest point, Paul felt unwanted and unfulfilled. He completely despised the person he'd become.

Desperate for change, Paul dove headfirst into radical self-improvement. He transformed his mornings with new routines: cold plunges, infrared saunas, and meditation. He adopted intermittent fasting, took up trail running, bought a sophisticated sleep system, and made a standing date night with his wife. Slowly but surely, Paul's physical health and mental clarity began to improve. His colleagues even started calling him "The Growth King" because of his relentless drive to live his best life. By many standards, his life was better than it had ever been.

But beneath his gains, there was a persistent ache—a sadness that no amount of self-mastery or health protocols could resolve. Inside, it felt like there was a cavern, empty and painful. Other unwelcome guests surrounded his life, too: constant bickering with his wife about feeling undervalued; envying his friends for having more money, more free time, or a more attractive spouse; a dread that one day his desire to improve himself would fade and he'd spiral to a faster, more dramatic fall. When these dark thoughts surfaced, Paul would scan the world around him for rescue. Maybe a trip to Costa Rica to try Ayahuasca, or another round of therapy.

This is when we met. In our first sessions together, it became clear that Paul's desire for growth was rooted in a desperate—and at times contemptuous—attempt to fix himself and bypass pain through self-mastery. According to the modern metrics of personal growth, Paul was a success. But each step he took toward progress was moving him further from his heart and story. Sometimes, what looks like growth isn't growth at all.

## Understanding Our Story Is Not Enough

The summer Paul turned ten years old, he remembers being tasked with mowing the lawn. When his father—a former military man turned businessman—got home from work, he'd ask Paul to walk with him to inspect the imperfections in his work: the blades of grass left uncut and the clumps of grass that hadn't been properly bagged. Whenever Paul enjoyed a popsicle or ice cream cone with his mom or sisters in the evening, his father would comment on how "soft" his body was getting or compare him to the boys down the street, who were developing their basketball skills and their physiques through consistent effort.

Paul eventually recognized a painful truth in our work together: It didn't matter if he cut the grass perfectly or strained to build his body as an athlete. There was no way to succeed in his father's world, because what the man enjoyed most was the power derived from criticism. Making people feel small and anxious was the delight of his father's heart.

In Part One, we would have analyzed Paul's relational challenges and endless striving as a reenactment of the world his father set him up for. No doubt, his father had inflicted him with an indelible, all-consuming wound, and therapy was helping Paul gain insights into that. But he remained unaware of how these dynamics were impacting his marriage and career. At home, he gave his wife a laundry list of emotional needs that she felt exasperated by. Meanwhile, he relied on his physical health and his job as props to validate his worth. Paul had a habit of slipping into self-contempt whenever he allowed his body to experience comfort, and no amount of late nights at the office or early mornings at the gym seemed to quiet his anxiety. Whether he worked or rested, there was hell on earth.

Paul's search for growth shows us what happens when we are disconnected from our story: We create, or even appoint, a taskmaster to live inside of us. Too often, our efforts at personal development are driven by a longing to escape vulnerability or compensate for a perceived lack. But genuine growth, rooted in a longing to experience wholeness, allows us to offer self-compassion for our inadequacies, grieve the stories that harmed us, and approach the future with wisdom, playfulness, and imagination.

The more we lean on superficial growth strategies, the more we set ourselves up for relational or professional struggles down the road. When a crisis inevitably hits, the false sense of self inside of us will plummet, and our ability to tolerate distress will be exposed.

Yet, as fourteenth-century mystic Julian of Norwich wisely said: "First there is the fall, and then there is the recovery from the fall, and both are the mercy of God."[2] This reminds us that all our efforts to grow or escape growth must lead to a fall if we are ever going to recover and build something beautiful, good, and true within ourselves.

## A Desire for Personal Growth

The second core longing—which we'll cover in this part of the book— is about developing an authentic desire for personal growth. We all arrive in adulthood underdeveloped in some way, limping from a core wound and dealing with complications from how we've learned to survive. To grow requires that we welcome these ongoing conflicts and listen to what they're trying to teach us. Instead of outsourcing our healing or growth to external sources, we commit to becoming the person we've always needed.

At some point in life, we will encounter an experience that will crack us open. Whether we call it a crisis, a crucible, a thorn in our flesh, or a dark night of the soul, these moments ask, or even demand, that we finally confront the dynamics we've spent our life avoiding. The process can feel both miserable and freeing. We begin to acknowledge our unhealthy patterns to ourselves and to others. We shed the persona we developed to survive, and we become increasingly curious about the formative stories of pain and heartache that set everything in motion. But before we truly surrender to this process, we typically exhaust all other strategies.

Let's take a closer look at the three most common ways most of us sidestep growth.

## Three Ways We Sidestep Growth

Before my clients are ready for authentic growth, they typically avoid the process through one of three ways: self-mastery, resignation, or seeking external validation.

I. **SELF-MASTERY: ATTEMPTING TO OPTIMIZE OUR LIVES AND EXCHANGE TRAUMA FOR TRIUMPH**

This was Paul's story. His desire for growth was centered around mastering his body, following health protocols, and looking outside of himself for rescue. Instead of offering hospitality to his wounds, he sought to evade them through the pursuit of continual progress. Rather than caring for his vulnerabilities, he sought to triumph over them.

2. **RESIGNATION: SETTING OURSELVES UP FOR DEPRESSION AND SELF-SABOTAGE**

Growth is often painful and unpredictable. As a result, some of us resign ourselves to disappointment, choosing it over the difficult, uncertain work of change. This resignation can lead to depression, which is often the soul's way of telling us that we are not truly living. When we settle for less than what we're capable of, our mental health suffers.

Another outcome of resignation is self-sabotage. Think of it like a force majeure, the French legal term for natural disasters, public health crises, or other scenarios that prevent someone from fulfilling their work obligations. Self-destructive behaviors force a personal crisis upon us, alleviating us from the burden of hope and the hard work required to cultivate goodness in our lives.

3. **EXTERNAL VALIDATION: PINING FOR SIGNIFICANCE**

External validation is when we use relationships, careers, or material success as mirrors to our self-worth. Instead of growing beyond the need for external approval, we chase after accomplishments and relationships because we believe they will fill the void inside. We use the world outside of us as a mirror, determining our value based on how we are seen by others. Yet the more we depend on external validation, the more we use others and stall our growth into becoming an authentic self.

For some this will look like a desire for self-mastery, but for others it will be a tendency toward self-deprioritization. This often happens when we come from families or communities that view personal growth as synonymous with "selfishness." In these environments, we deprioritize our own development to avoid criticism and remain in good standing in the eyes of others. Unfortunately, this too is a form of external validation, where we find our identity through becoming what others expect from us.

When we try to sidestep growth, our desires will get hijacked or never fully develop. In avoiding growth, we unwittingly necessitate one of the most painful and transformative experiences of adulthood: the crucible.

### The Crucible: The Gateway to a Desire for Growth

A crucible is a difficult and transformative experience through which a person comes to a new or altered sense of identity. It often manifests as an intense, traumatic, and unplanned experience that pushes us to grow in ways we never would have imagined. We rarely volunteer for such a developmental task. Instead, we are summoned against our will. Crucibles come in many forms: an existential crisis, significant relational conflict, personal illness, the death of a loved one, professional failure, or even succeeding beyond one's expectations.

If we choose to remain in the crucible and develop a true sense of self, it's usually only after we've exhausted all other options and attempted to excuse all our less-than-mature attributes. For example, I've witnessed many parents enter therapy after they realize that they are repeating some of the patterns of harm they experienced as children. In the past, they might have dismissed their behavior as "not a big deal," blamed their child's disobedience, or used their lack of sleep as a way of avoiding self-confrontation. Now they see the heartache they're causing, and an inner defiance rises inside them to change.

When you learn to stay in the crucible without escaping it, some considerable benefits begin to emerge:

- You develop a willingness to tolerate difficulties.
- You develop curiosity for problems.
- You develop a capacity to confront the parts of yourself that are false.

- You develop a desire to deeply know and be known by others.
- You develop a strong container (yourself) for the next season of life.
- You develop an identity you are proud of rather than a persona you put on.

Each of us carries a formative wound that leaves us limping for a lifetime. We don't know what to do with our wounds because all our attempts to heal them, evade them, and hate them do not work. Only when we recognize that our wounds drive us toward a more authentic existence does our attitude toward them begin to shift. The paradox is that our woundings are not healed so much as they become the very foundation for our deepest joys and most vulnerable connections. In our honest wrestling with them, our true identity, tenderness, and growth are forged.

*If you realize you're struggling in this area and could use some guidance on examining how childhood stories influence the ways you show up as an adult, the accompanying* Desire Workbook *has several questions and exercises to help you go deeper.*

## Before Entering the Crucible

To grow from a crucible, you will need to commit, to the best of your ability, to cease destructive behaviors, unhealthy patterns, and cyclical attempts to bootstrap your way to growth. There is no shortcut to becoming you. The distance between the person you are and the person you want to become can only be closed when you fully surrender to enter the crucible.

Consider a baby chick learning to poke its way through an eggshell. The chick's struggle fosters an essential developmental task that prepares it to encounter the outside world. Escaping the shell too early, disliking the shell, or blaming its parents for not genetically modifying the shell to be thinner would all be attempts to avoid the necessity of struggle. The shell is the crucible that prepares the chick for life on the other side. Similarly, the problems we encounter in our lives and relationships are developing us into the type of person who is strong enough to face difficulties with humility and kindness.

As I worked with Paul through his crucible, he agreed that his adult life had become a reenactment of his childhood but had a harder time seeing how he was burdening his marriage and career with his need for validation. "I know I have some work to do," he told me, "but I really think my wife is the one deficient in intimacy. If I didn't sustain our connection, we wouldn't have any. She never chooses me."

I responded, "For her to choose you, there must be something authentic in you. At this point, her choosing you would be a form of palliative care. It's going to take time to cultivate your identity and expand your imagination for growth. That way, when you ask her to choose you, it will be an invitation to an adventure, not to a hospice for your reluctance to grow."

Paul took a moment to let the invitation settle in. He reflected, "It's hard to hear, but I think there's truth in that. I've been putting a lot of pressure on my wife to notice me and my career to fulfill me. Maybe the reason I continue to feel miserable is that I've never been responsible to notice and care for myself. I don't know why I can see it now, but that way of life isn't good for me and sets up my wife to feel miserable, too." This was a seismic shift for Paul, and one all of us must experience: He connected to the story of his past *and* recognized how those wounds were impeding his growth and emotional bonds in the present. We study the past not to find excuses for who we are, but because we want to grow into the healthiest, most authentic version of ourselves as an adult.

Part Two of this book will offer a vision for how you can intentionally cultivate personal growth. As we end this introduction, I invite you to consider something counterintuitive: What if your loneliness, relational conflicts, and professional struggles are doing exactly what they are designed to do? By design, problems reveal the limitations of our development and push us toward authentic personal growth. The most important thing you can do for yourself and others at this stage in your journey is to undergo the crucible that awaits you.

As you move through this part of the book, be prepared for resistance. Growth always sounds lovely until we look at the price tag and see pain. You will find yourself saying things like, "Do I really have to take *that* path?" or "I know I have some things to work on, but have you met my significant other? *They* need to read this, not me," or "Surely we're not as screwed up as these people described in this book."

But deep down, you know that your current life is uninhabitable. To experience more meaning and beauty, you must renovate your heart to make room for all that is to come. The crucible is the process that enables our soul to finally say no to patterns of escape and yes to cultivating an identity that is ready to embark on the wild and beautiful journey of desire.

To help guide you in this personal renovation, we'll explore two core questions:

1.  *Do I have hospitality for the struggles I face?*
2.  *How am I burdening others with my need for validation?*

These two questions are closely intertwined. When we can show hospitality toward our struggles, we are less likely to burden others with our need for validation. Conversely, if we avoid facing our struggles with kindness—if we despise our bodies or intellect or feel lost when we're alone—we will project our needs onto others, creating pressure that weakens their desire for us and diminishes the connection we seek.

We all long for an authentic identity. And the questions that guide the next two chapters—hospitality toward adversity and awareness of how we are burdening others—are key to fulfilling that longing. Let's now explore how we can cultivate this hospitality for the struggles we face.

CHAPTER 6

# Do I Have Hospitality for the Struggles I Face?

*May you find in yourself*
*A courageous hospitality*
*Toward what is difficult,*
*Painful, and unknown.*[1]

—JOHN O'DONOHUE

## Kate's Dilemma

Kate was a twenty-nine-year-old consultant living in the Northeast. She had fond memories of playing and baking with her mom as a girl, but as she entered adolescence, Kate developed a growing sense of pity for her mom. As far as she could tell, her mother had few hobbies, zero career aspirations, and never put anything in her personal calendar that did not involve her role as a mother and wife.

In high school, Kate had a pivotal moment when her best friend left school early to travel with her mom on a business trip to a big city. Kate was taken aback. She couldn't imagine what it would be like to have a mom who had desires and talents outside of domestic duties. That year, she made a vow to leave the suburban life behind. This freed her from her mother's world, but also threw her into a new set of problems she was unprepared to navigate.

Kate started therapy with me because she was facing a major relational bind. She really liked the guy she was dating, and she sensed that their deeper attachment could lead to marriage. The prospect of nuptials, however, flooded her body with a nervous disgust. She could not tolerate any path that might lead her to being a wife and stay-at-home mother. Citing the need for self-preservation and a fear of consumption, Kate had ended more than six relationships in the past two years. Her friends celebrated her for being an independent woman, but something in her knew there was more to the story.

Kate, like many of us, felt caught between a desire for deep connection and a dread that her independence would be compromised in the process. When her partner expressed a desire to meet each other's families, or when he asked how many kids she might want to have in the future, a visceral claustrophobia overwhelmed her. Kate's operating belief was that deeper romantic intimacy was a slippery slope to domestic banality. Counseling Kate felt like treating someone with a broken finger who wanted their hand amputated.

A few sessions in, I asked Kate if she knew when and why her mom chose the domestic path. She believed it started when her mom got pregnant as a junior in college. She dropped out of school and attempted to re-enroll two years later, only to discover she was pregnant with Kate. This was her second and final attempt at finishing college.

Aside from the enormous burden of believing her own birth stalled her mother's advancement, Kate felt upset that her mom "never chose to move through difficulty." She had a similar sentiment toward her grandmother, who stayed with an alcoholic and abusive man to the detriment of the family's psychological and physical well-being. In her formative years, Kate learned to see marriage and family as unnecessary detainments.

I suggested to Kate that while she'd chosen a very different path from her mother and grandmother, all three of them shared a resistance to authentic growth. Caught off guard, yet engaged, she said, "What do you mean? How am I anything like them? I hate the paths they chose, and I am doing everything in my power to grow beyond them."

I pointed out that her mom allowed domestic roles to hinder her desire for self-development, but Kate was allowing her need for independence to limit her capacity for intimacy. Her mother used enmeshment to sidestep individuation, but Kate was using independence to escape the crucible of letting herself be known by a man she loved. Although she had been resolute in avoiding enmeshment, she lacked the same resolve to be hospitable to the relational challenges that stood before her.

Kate's story raises important questions for all of us: What if our most fervent desires are motivated by something underdeveloped within us? What if we are aiming our growth at the wrong target?

In our modern age, there's a real danger in chasing growth that gives us the illusion of progress yet distracts us from grappling with the civil wars that wage within. Our society's obsession with health protocols, atomic habits, and optimizing life often masks our refusal to confront the messy, anxious, and even most beautiful aspects of our existence. We may succeed in the metrics of modern growth, but never recognize how small we've allowed our lives to become.

True growth—the kind worth dedicating your life to—comes from a willingness to be hospitable to the deepest parts of ourselves: our shame, our questions, and our unspoken desires. Hospitality, at its most basic level, is a willingness to welcome where we are, without distraction or manipulation to change. It's about learning to become gracious hosts, gently restoring ourselves to greater health.

Because our lives are unfolding stories, it's essential to view ourselves as protagonists on a journey of transformation. Without this perspective, we risk falling into the trap of viewing ourselves as mere bodies to be maximized for strength, utility, and earning potential. Through the lens of narrative, we understand that growth, especially through the hardest chapters, isn't about achievement, optimization, or mastery. It's about respecting the character we are becoming and elevating the quality of the story we're choosing to live.

In this chapter, we'll explore how to develop a healthy and sustainable desire for personal growth. This process involves two essential tasks: embracing our challenges with hospitality and adopting a growth mindset when setbacks arise. We'll also cover best practices for increasing our tolerance for distress, taming our fiercest emotions, and honing our awareness of the internal sensations within our bodies. All of this ensures that our desire for growth and our connections with others are grounded in a deep, authentic place, rather than a superficial pursuit.

## Developing Hospitality for Challenges

When we find ourselves in a personal or relational crucible, our natural longing is to eliminate or reduce the discomfort we're experiencing. We might visit a psychiatrist and ask, "Doctor, I'm so anxious. Is there anything you can prescribe to make it go away?" Or in prayer, we might plead, "God, please change this terrible situation I'm in." While the desire to alleviate heartache is completely natural, it often diverts us from a more crucial task for our development: learning hospitality. When unwelcome guests arrive, as they always do, they do not need to be shunned. They need a place to be loved.

Imagine you were in a car accident that left you with significant neck pain. We tend to get frustrated with our pain symptoms rather than recognizing they are trying to serve us. If our goal is only symptom relief, we will find ourselves seeking out painkillers or distractions. But if we see the problem of pain as a truth teller, then we might be more willing to work in collaboration with it, bringing our body to treatments like physical therapy that address the root cause of the pain. In the same way, personal growth comes not from repressing or banishing painful emotions or relational experiences, but in learning to extend as much kindness toward them as we can muster.

Crucibles are not trying to destroy us as much as remake us. They form us into more compelling people, filled with an ambition for a more meaningful life than we've settled for. Therefore, the best way to engage with problems is to practice an inner hospitality toward them. Pain can eventually become one of our body's most valuable collaborators, but only when we stop scapegoating it for the message it brings.

## What a Restaurant Can Teach Us About Hospitality

One of the best modern examples of hospitality comes from restaurateur Will Guidara, who ran Eleven Madison Park, the world's number one restaurant at the time. One day, while clearing dishes from a table of four, he overheard one of the guests say, "What an amazing trip—we have been to all the best restaurants in the city." Then another guest added, "Yeah, but the only thing we didn't get to try was a New York City hot dog!"

In that moment, a lightbulb went on for Guidara.[2] He dropped the dishes in the kitchen and ran out to the nearest hot dog cart to purchase one. Returning to the kitchen, he asked the chef to plate the hot dog for the guests. The chef was naturally perplexed by the idea of serving a cheap, processed piece of meat while he was working on the party's main dish: a honey-glazed Muscovy duck that had been dry-aged for two weeks, utilizing a technique that had taken years to perfect. But seeing Guidara's desire for unreasonable hospitality, the chef agreed. He cut the hot dog into four perfect pieces and plated it with a swoosh of ketchup, a swoosh of mustard, and a quenelle of sauerkraut and relish.

Guidara brought the dish to table and said, "To make sure you don't go home with any culinary regrets, a New York City hot dog." The table was ecstatic. Each person said it was not just the highlight of their meal, but of their entire trip to New York.

Guidara's decision to bring a humble hot dog into a three-star Michelin restaurant has become a beloved story in the hospitality industry. It was a simple yet creative act that defied all expectations. It offered the guests something we all long for: someone who hears our longings and offers us something better than we could ever ask for or imagine.

When we reflect on the best experiences of our lives—whether at a restaurant, a hotel, or a friend's home—we remember the simple gestures that made us feel seen and valued. It's why we'll spend significant sums of money to procure a great experience, only to feel cheated or deflated if hospitality is missing. No matter how lavish the setting or exquisite the service, if we don't feel a genuine sense of welcome, the experience falls flat. Hospitality always gives us something that can't be bought: the feeling that, even if for a few moments, there is somewhere on the earth we belong.

## *Hospitality for the Soul*

When a dear friend was facing a significant illness, the writer John O'Donohue sent a letter that included the words "May you find in yourself a courageous hospitality toward what is difficult, painful, and unknown."[3]

What we need the most amid personal challenges is hospitality. We often believe that personal change will come through persistence—by pushing harder, seeking insights, and doing more. But often, that persistence is actually leading us further away from the core issues we need to address. Outsourcing our needs to others and relying on willpower are tenuous solutions. The more sustainable option is to teach ourselves that, even in our deepest vulnerability, we can become the soothing, safe, and secure presence we need. Without personal hospitality, we risk using other people as sanatoriums and seeking quick fixes to profound questions that, if given the space to be processed, could transform us. Hospitality may feel slower, but the healing and growth it fosters are far more profound—and in the long run, faster.

To begin the practice of personal hospitality, set aside at least fifteen minutes to intentionally listen to and respond to a difficulty you're facing. Start by scanning your body, just noticing what you're feeling without judgment. Is there pain, pressure, or confusion swirling within? Spend a few minutes journaling about what these symptoms might be trying to convey to you and how you might respond compassionately to them.

Next, create a ritual to directly address the difficulty you're feeling. For example, if you're bombarded by anxiety, make a cup of herbal tea or step into the sunlight, imagining the warmth as a soothing elixir designed to ease your anxiety. Take several breaths to reinforce the calming sensations. Or, if you've identified tension in your body, draw a warm bath and bring that area of your body into the healing waters. If those ideas don't resonate with you, ask your body what it needs—it typically has great wisdom to offer.

One hour of intentional self-compassion can accomplish more

than a thousand nights of prayerful despair or years of persistence. By creating these mindful prescriptions, you teach your body that there is a host within you, ready to listen and restore you for the journey ahead.

## *Adopting a Growth Mindset with Desire*

When my clients find themselves stuck in the ruts of significant problems, they often say things like, "I will *always* struggle with my body image." "The conflict with my partner will *never* go away." Or "My career has *completely* plateaued." Dr. Carol Dweck famously refers to this thought pattern as a "fixed mindset": the belief that our problems are carved in stone. When we have a fixed mindset, Dweck says, it sets us up to feel deficient in most circumstances. "Every situation calls for a confirmation of [our] intelligence, personality, or character. Every situation is evaluated: Will I succeed or fail? Will I look smart or dumb? Will I be accepted or rejected?"[4]

A fixed mindset does not have to be our default. Dweck offers a powerful alternative: "There's another mindset in which these traits are not simply a hand you're dealt and have to live with, always trying to convince yourself and others that you have a royal flush when you're secretly worried it's a pair of tens. In [a growth mindset], the hand you're dealt is just the starting point for development. This growth mindset is based on the belief that your basic qualities are things you can cultivate through your efforts."[5]

Below is a chart that identifies fixed mindsets that may be impeding your growth across the five core longings, the consequences of those beliefs, and how you can shift to a growth mindset.

| CORE DESIRE | Beliefs That Limit Our Growth Sound Like: | Consequences of Limiting Beliefs | A Growth Mindset Sounds Like: |
|---|---|---|---|
| Wholeness | "I was such an awkward and sensitive kid." | You see your childhood vulnerabilities with judgment and spend your life managing shame. As a result, you lead a small, safe, and predictable life. | "I had to develop armor to survive, but now I have the privilege of becoming the empathetic witness I lacked. My vulnerabilities are not liabilities, but the foundation for growth and connection." |
| Personal Growth | "I should be over this by now." | You're unable to tolerate discomfort. You end up escaping your problems or attempting to find mastery over them. Either way, you reinforce your worst fears— you are undesirable to others unless you're constantly proving your value. | "I haven't learned how to move through this challenge yet. Instead of berating myself, I will be kind. I'm curious what this experience will develop in me." |

| CORE DESIRE | Beliefs That Limit Our Growth Sound Like: | Consequences of Limiting Beliefs | A Growth Mindset Sounds Like: |
|---|---|---|---|
| Intimacy | "If my relationship is struggling, it must mean I picked the wrong person." | You may abandon relationships or become emotionally hardened, avoiding the work necessary for relational connection. | "This challenge can teach me more about myself and deepen my understanding of someone I care about. It's an opportunity to grow together." |
| Pleasure | "I should be over this sexual difficulty by now." | Sex becomes a source of shame, escape, or validation. Rather than a bridge to connection, sex becomes a barrier to it. | "Sex is a window into some of my deepest desires and vulnerabilities. I wonder how this sexual difficulty can help me to know myself or my partner more deeply and passionately?" |
| Meaning & Purpose | "My job is a dead end. I'll never find purpose in my life." | You squash your hope for a meaningful life and seek ways to escape the challenges you encounter. This leads to an apathetic life. | "I'm learning about what I don't enjoy in my career. This experience is guiding me toward what is truly meaningful to me." |

Fixed mindsets are dangerous because they set self-fulfilling prophesies into motion. Growth mindsets are powerful for the exact same reason. If we believe we're deeply flawed, we will inevitably find, or even create, evidence to confirm this belief. But if we see ourselves as individuals on a journey to becoming more courageous, more creative, and a valuable contributor to others, we'll find ourselves pursuing desires that align with those beliefs. Our desires always flow in the direction of our strongest thoughts about who we are.

### The Powerful Combination of Hospitality and a Growth Mindset

When combined, hospitality and a growth mindset create the conditions for the breakthroughs we've longed for but haven't yet experienced. Just as children thrive when they feel secure—when their parents act as a safe base of protection and a launching pad for adventure—hospitality and a growth mindset function in the same way for adults. Hospitality teaches us that we are loved exactly as we are, and with this assurance, we feel empowered to take life-defining risks. Whether we succeed or falter, we trust there is a welcoming host within, ready to extend kindness and delight when we return.

When we view our lives as an unfolding story, we can shift our perspective on our challenges. Rather than seeing them as signs of inadequacy or mere fate, we come to recognize them as crucial thresholds on our journey toward becoming our truest selves. If we learn to offer hospitality to ourselves in our crucibles, we may find the symptoms of our struggles alleviated, clearing the path to pursue a more meaningful story. But if we only seek to eliminate distress, we risk wandering through life, not in search of meaning, but of distraction.

The next section will explore practical ways to cultivate both hospitality and growth for your journey ahead. These practices are not about making small, incremental changes for self-improvement. Instead, think of them as scaffolding that will support the more profound renovations you desire to make in your personal and relational world.

### *Three Practices to Increase Our Ability to Experience Hospitality and Growth*

#### 1. INCREASE YOUR WINDOW OF TOLERANCE

The first practice to develop greater hospitality and foster growth is learning how to dramatically increase our capacity to tolerate distress. Understanding this concept is essential for personal transformation, as it allows us to engage with life's challenges without being overwhelmed or shutting down. Dan Siegel, a renowned author and clinical professor of psychiatry at UCLA, coined the phrase "window of tolerance" to describe the range of emotional states we can experience. In his book *The Yes Brain,* he breaks this concept down into three distinct zones: the Green Zone, the Red Zone, and the Blue Zone.

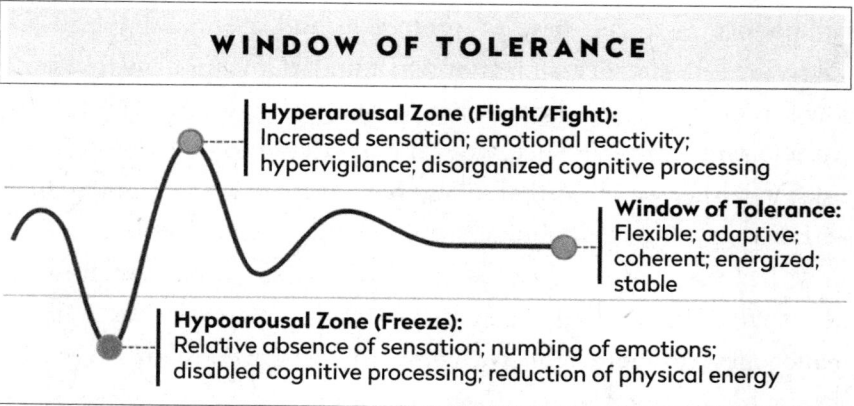

**WINDOW OF TOLERANCE**

**Hyperarousal Zone (Flight/Fight):**
Increased sensation; emotional reactivity; hypervigilance; disorganized cognitive processing

**Window of Tolerance:**
Flexible; adaptive; coherent; energized; stable

**Hypoarousal Zone (Freeze):**
Relative absence of sensation; numbing of emotions; disabled cognitive processing; reduction of physical energy

#### *The Green Zone (Window of Tolerance)*

The Green Zone is the ideal zone for human flourishing. In this range, we feel emotionally flexible, resilient, and grounded. Our desires are fully present. We can savor the world around us and engage our emotions without being overtaken by them. It's the feeling of a springtime walk through cherry blossoms, a delightful meal with loved ones, or a guttural laugh with friends. In this self-state, stress feels manageable, and the days of sorrow or anxiety seem miles behind. We're adaptable, energized, and even find inspiration in the face of relational or developmental challenges.

Our goal should be less about finding the perfect set of circumstances that put us in the Green Zone and more about expanding our window of tolerance so that we can more comfortably engage with both the difficulties and joys of life. When we are operating in the Green Zone, we accept life as it is—without demanding that it change or fearing that it will remain the same. Rather than constantly trying to alter our external world, we shift our internal world to live with greater maturity and presence.

### The Red Zone (Hyperarousal)

The Red Zone is a state of hyperarousal in which emotional reactivity takes over. Our desires become compulsive, entitled, or intensely reactionary. In this self-state, we might feel under duress, experience a racing heart, or feel consumed with the urge to eviscerate someone who is frustrating us. The hallmark of this zone is heightened arousal: increased physical sensation, hypervigilance, the feeling of being "triggered," and disorganized cognitive processing.

While the Red Zone can sound like a state to avoid, it's designed to help us survive a crisis by initiating a fight-or-flight response. The problem is that when we face non-life-threatening problems, our nervous system can still react as if we're in immediate danger and respond in ways that exacerbate the situation. The Red Zone can save our lives in emergencies, but it can also make us, and those around us, quite miserable.

Are you aware of when you're operating in the Red Zone? This awareness is essential, because we tend to make some of the worst decisions in our lives when we're in this state. Rather than trying to eliminate stress, we need to develop awareness and tolerance for it. In cultivating a kind and resilient host within, we teach our nervous system that we have the internal resources to calm ourselves and approach challenges from a more grounded place.

### The Blue Zone (Hypoarousal)

The Blue Zone is characterized by hypoarousal, a state of emotional shutdown or numbness. It's the feeling of being disconnected from ourselves, apathetic toward life, and disengaged from the world around us. This "blue" state often follows an intense fight with a loved one or the morning after we've indulged in an unwanted behavior. When shame blankets us and powerlessness defines our existence, we've entered the Blue Zone.

It's important to understand that the Blue Zone is a protective response from our body. It's designed to numb us to emotional overload, allowing us to cope with intense heartache or anxiety that would otherwise feel unbearable. This "freeze" state can help us survive difficult situations, but prolonged stays in the Blue Zone can lead to a sense of soul deadness, diminishing hope that real change is possible.

As we grow into hospitality for our problems, we learn to attune to these emotional states without overidentifying with them. We need to approach our Blue Zone with the same gentleness and compassion a good mother would offer to a crying baby or a troubled adolescent—acknowledging the distress but also providing a kind, restorative presence. As adults, we need to grow in our ability to connect with ourselves in the Blue Zone, offering both compassionate presence and healthy self-care practices that can bring us back from the brink, and into a more vibrant, resilient state.

Take some time to reflect on a difficulty or crucible you're currently undergoing. It's likely you've experienced moments where you've slipped into the Red or Blue zone—feeling reactive, overwhelmed, or exhausted. In those moments, we look down at the cup of suffering before us and dread what the journey ahead will require of us. Soon, we begin to tell ourselves that these experiences will never change and the difficulties ahead are insurmountable.

It's all too easy to view our emotional distress, apathy, or unhealthy choices in these self-states as the problem. More often than not, I've found, the emotions and behaviors that seem the most problematic are a continuation of an unresolved story that needs our hospitality.

This means that your window of tolerance is inextricably linked to your life story. If we were raised by caregivers who lacked emotional strength and kindness to deal with our biggest emotions, we will inevitably enter adulthood with a narrower window of tolerance. This makes us more susceptible to anxiety, depression, emotional dysregulation, and a host of problematic behaviors.

In my research, individuals who struggle with harmful coping behaviors, such as the overuse of screens, alcohol, drugs, sex, food, or work, are more likely to have childhood experiences marked by:

- A needy or emotionally unavailable mother
- Unkind parents
- Childhood trauma (especially sexual assault)

Our window of tolerance tells the story of the challenges we've faced and how we've learned—or been unable to learn—to respond to them. The good news is that we can expand our window of tolerance. Each time we calm our body when it's in the Red Zone or engage our Blue Zone with hospitality, we're offering ourselves corrective experiences. (We will explore some specific practices later in this chapter.) Increasing our window of tolerance is how we become the adult we needed as children and become ready to move into greater challenges in the future.

## 2. NAME EMOTIONS TO TAME EMOTIONS

Once we've learned to expand our window of tolerance, the next step in building hospitality and a growth mindset is learning how to effectively name our emotions in the moment. Dan Siegel's simple and eloquent phrase captures this practice well: *Name it to tame it.*[6] When we can accurately identify what we're feeling, we take away its power to sideline us. Instead of being controlled by the wild emotional reactions within us, we name them. And when these feelings are acknowledged, they have a way of calming down.

This practice of naming and taming is not just a philosophical idea. It's grounded in science. Psychologist David Rock, co-founder of NeuroLeadership Institute, has found that we can reduce stress by up to 50 percent by simply noticing and naming our emotional states. Why? Because emotions are processed in a part of our brain called the limbic system. Studies show that when our prefrontal cortex (the thinking brain) accurately labels what we're feeling, our brain releases soothing neurochemicals like oxytocin down into the limbic system. When we accurately name distressing emotions, we simultaneously begin to tame them.

Unfortunately, most of us respond to emotional distress by either reacting impulsively or trying to escape our feelings. But if you want to shift to a growth mindset, here are some ways you can practice "name it to tame it" in your own life, beginning with the naming:

- "I feel *ashamed* of how I reacted in that situation."
- "I feel *scared* to make this change because of the disruption I anticipate."
- "I feel *intimidated* and *powerless* when I'm around that person."
- "I never thought I'd feel this *lonely* in my marriage."

By naming the emotions we're experiencing, we create a healthy separation between our thoughts and our experience. This space allows us to process the feelings more thoughtfully and respond with wisdom. After this step, take a moment to reflect how you want to respond to those emotions with kindness and authority.

To make this practice even more effective, combine it with grounding techniques to further calm your nervous system. One simple exercise involves focusing on your breath:

- Inhale for five seconds.
- Exhale for five seconds.

- Repeat this cycle five times.
- Now, scan your body for any areas of tension.
- Ask yourself: What might this tension be trying to communicate?
- Name the emotion: "I feel sad," "I feel overlooked," etc.
- On your next inhale, imagine expanding your capacity to be compassionate toward those emotions. You can visualize a cozy fire, the warmth of the sun, or a soothing breeze to enhance the feeling.
- On your next five-second exhale, imagine releasing any judgments, fixed mindsets, or negative energy you may be harboring. Let it go; it no longer serves you.

Repeat this process, especially the last two steps, until you feel more grounded.

This practice helps you recognize your body's remarkable ability to soothe and empower you. It works because slow, deep breathing activates the parasympathetic nervous system, which is responsible for calming and grounding us. While you may not always immediately reach your desired emotional state, you'll learn to trust your body's natural ability to gently restore itself.

### 3. DEVELOP INTEROCEPTION

Interoception is the ability to notice and respond to the subtle sensations within our bodies. In time, we can tune into our heartbeat, breath, muscle tension, hunger, and other internal cues—and this awareness helps us understand both our emotional and physical states. Interoception is crucial for developing healthy, grounded desires, as it prevents us from being preoccupied with escaping or ignoring the body's signals.

For many of us, especially those whose bodies have been a source of danger, shame, or neglect, developing interoception can be particularly challenging. Dissociating from our bodies may have been necessary for survival or easier than grappling with complexity, but we can't experience flourishing until we reconnect with it. For personal growth to truly flourish, we must care and listen to our bodies.

Self-care is having a moment right now. Spa days, chocolate cake, wine after a long day, and high-intensity workouts are just a handful of our culturally celebrated prescriptions for making life feel better. But not all self-care practices truly nurture interoception. Many popular practices—like excessive exercise, indulgence, or an overconsumption of comfort—reinforce dissociation from the body rather than promote embodiment. As the language and practice of self-care spreads, we need to decipher how some of these rituals might be hurting us more than truly caring for us.

Take Sam, a client who came to me struggling with anxiety and low self-esteem. Though she had started a running routine and mindfulness practices, old patterns of anxiety and self-hatred resurfaced.

One day she came into my office gloriously sweating after running on her lunch break. I asked how her workout went. "Amazing! I crushed it," she replied. I knew the phrase *crushed it,* but as her therapist, I'm paid to be hypervigilant about word choices. I asked her to clarify how many miles were necessary to crush a workout. She said she'd run seven miles in under an hour. When I asked her what happens if she doesn't get to seven miles, she playfully said, "That wouldn't be good. My body would not feel calm."

I knew endorphins played a role in this, but I inquired again about why so many miles were needed for rest. One of my graduate school professors, Dr. Dan Allender, used to say that change doesn't happen in abstraction, but only in the dirt, when we enter the particularities we'd prefer not to name. In earlier sessions, Sam had spoken generally about her body shame, but no particularities had been offered. So I asked her now, "What part of your body most benefits from being crushed?"

Sam hesitated for a moment, looking down. In shame, she said, "It's always my thighs." I thanked her for her vulnerability and asked when this conflict began.

In eighth grade, she related, she was at a department store with her mom trying on bathing suits for a spring break trip. She found a suit that she liked, but her mom pointed out how her thighs were touching each other. Her mom then suggested she'd benefit from buying a pair of shorts to wear over the suit. On the way home, her mom continued to demoralize her, telling Sam that all the women on her dad's side had thick thighs and the only way to manage it as she got older was daily exercise.

On the surface, going to the gym and running seemed like healthy lifestyle choices. But in reality, Sam had adopted them as forms of self-punishment. Her story raises an important question for all of us: At what age did you become aware that you had a body? And when, and in what context, did you first feel a sense of shame for it?

Some of us militantly sculpt our bodies into compliance, while others neglect them to the point of cruelty. Still others nurse them with substances or screens to silence the stories of heartache our bodies are trying to tell. Healing and growth require not only that we identify the wounds we carry in our bodies but also that we recognize how our present-day habits might be unintentionally reinforcing them. This is where interoception comes in.

### Interoception, Emotional Flexibility, and Sex

The practice of interoception can help with a common issue that affects 9–25 percent of men and 6–16 percent of women: sexual performance anxiety.[7] In my clinical practice, I frequently hear from men plagued by premature ejaculation and women discouraged by their inability to sustain pleasure or experience orgasm. These anxieties don't just exist in our minds; they are rooted in the body. Too often we try to resolve these problems through forcing our bodies into compliance or neglecting them altogether, both of which widen the chasm between mind and body.

Interoception helps us bridge that gap by using our mind to deepen our awareness of our physical body. In part, this is thanks to a process called myelination. Imagine the nerve fibers in your brain and nervous system as highways, with myelin being the smooth road surface that allows signals to travel faster and more efficiently. The more we practice interoception, the more myelin forms, making communication between your brain and body quicker and more effective. The better this connection, the more sexual satisfaction we experience.[8]

A simple yet effective way to practice this is by doing mindful breathing during sex. Start by noticing your breath. You may find yourself unconsciously holding your breath or breathing too rapidly. If you feel anxious, rushed, or tense, take a moment to slow down and deepen your breath. Let each inhale bring you into a deeper sense of embodiment, and let each exhale release tension, worry, or energy that isn't serving you. By focusing on your breath, you'll shift toward a state of relaxation and heightened awareness, enabling you to experience greater connection. It may take an extra minute or two to slow down before or during sex, but this small adjustment can lead to a more meaningful and prolonged experience of intimacy.

Another helpful practice is synchronized breathing with your partner. By matching your breathing patterns, you create a rhythm that fosters unity and body connection right from the start. This synchronicity not only demotes anxiety but also promotes shared pleasure and emotional closeness.

Afterward, take a moment to reflect on the sexual experience. How did your body feel throughout? Did you notice any fears or insecurities? Were there moments when you lost connection to yourself or your partner? Conversely, were there moments when you felt deeply connected? Reflecting on these questions can help you identify areas where you might bring more interoception into future sexual experiences.

Rather than allowing fear, shame, or insecurity to dominate our lives, interoception enables us to slow down and enjoy a more embodied experience. The more you practice it, the more quickly you'll be able to connect to yourself and the one you love. The benefits of mindful sex are powerful: increased self-esteem, improved romantic relationships, and greater sexual satisfaction.[9] Why not give interoception a try?

## *Putting It All Together: The ALARM Approach*

A helpful framework for putting all of this into action is the ALARM approach.

A—AWARENESS. The first step is to notice the distress signals your body is sending. Tune into the physical sensations like tightness in your chest, your heart rate, and how fast or shallow your breathing has become. Each of these provides clues into what zone you are in—Blue, Green, or Red.

L—LABEL. After you become aware of your distress, take a moment to label what you're feeling emotionally. Are you anxious? Sad? Angry? Defeated? Then consider how you can serve as an empathetic witness to this distress.

A—ACCEPTANCE. Accept your feelings without judgment. Remind yourself that you can feel anxious or distressed without becoming too overly identified with these self-states. For example, you might feel bad inside, but that does not mean you are a bad person. Accept that we can feel discouraged and hold on to ourselves in the process.

R—REFRAME. Challenge the negative story you're telling yourself. Float back to a time in life where you may have felt this way before. What did that younger version of yourself need to know or experience? How might this situation offer you a chance to grow through a significant threshold on your journey?

M—MOVE. Physical movement is essential for emotional regulation. Whether it's a short walk, deep breathing, or stretching, movement will release tension and improve the collaboration between your mind and body. If possible, move toward water. If that's not available, find a green space, as these environments can amplify the calming benefits.

By integrating interoception into your daily life, you'll improve your ability to handle distress while becoming more attuned to the messages your body is sending you. As you grow in this practice, you'll find more flexibility not just in your body, but in your relationships and responses to the difficulties of life.

## Self-Assessing the Quality of Your Practices

As we conclude this chapter, here's a brief self-assessment to help you reflect on your hospitality toward life's problems. If you're in a romantic relationship and feel solid enough in your connection to your partner, consider asking them for their feedback as well. While it can be difficult to receive feedback from loved ones, this is an important part of growth: learning to hold on to your sense of self while integrating others' perspectives.

For each statement, circle T for *true* or F for *false*. Each "true" answer scores one point. Reflect on your results and how they can motivate you to greater hospitality and growth.

### FROM YOUR VIEWPOINT, HOW DEVELOPED IS YOUR WINDOW OF TOLERANCE?

1. I daily notice when I am emotionally dysregulated. T F
2. When I am distressed or feeling down, I can consistently return to the Green Zone. T F
3. I focus on calming down my body before reacting to a stressful situation. T F
4. I can consistently self-regulate when there is disruption in my primary relationships. T F

### FROM YOUR VIEWPOINT, HOW DEVELOPED IS YOUR ABILITY TO NAME AND TAME EMOTIONS?

1. I have a regular practice of naming and befriending my emotions. T F
2. I have a growing vocabulary to name the complex emotions I experience. T F
3. I can consistently tame difficult emotions when they arise. T F

4. I trust myself to handle a stressful or alarming situation in the future. T F

**FROM YOUR VIEWPOINT, HOW DEVELOPED IS YOUR INTEROCEPTION?**

1. I daily notice the sensations running through my body. T F
2. I can label and respond effectively to my body's experiences in various contexts, including work, friendships, sex, and solitude. T F
3. I am growing in my ability to engage problems mindfully. T F
4. I consistently use breath and other self-care practices to establish grounding. T F

## Reflection and Next Steps

If you scored 6 or higher, you're well on your way to practicing hospitality and growth. If you scored below 6, that's okay. It's just your starting point. Low scores might be indicative of childhood attachment wounds or emotional compulsivity, but remember, these are not fixed traits. With continued practice, you can develop daily habits that foster hospitality in distress, leading to greater emotional resilience.

For additional recommendations and practices to help increase your emotional tolerance, check out the accompanying *Desire Workbook*.

In this chapter, we explored how to offer ourselves hospitality as we face various crucibles and difficulties. But be prepared, the next chapter is going to push you even further. We'll examine differentiation, a concept that's critical to understanding why we burden others with our need for validation. We'll learn how prioritizing others' desires and opinions over our own can undermine our growth and hijack our authentic longings. Let's face this issue head-on and learn how to outgrow it.

## CHAPTER 7

# How Am I Burdening Others with My Need for Validation?

*Our connection with other people
is only as solid and deep as our
connection to ourselves.*

—BRENÉ BROWN[1]

## Peter's Costly Need for Validation

Peter and Charlie had been dating six months when everything hit the fan. Charlie worked as a photographer. One night while editing photos, he made a comment about how attractive the man from his recent shoot was. Immediately, Peter erupted in anger. "You haven't told me I'm attractive in months. You don't even seem to care about me anymore!" He stormed out of the apartment and went to a bar, where he quickly drank a martini and two vodka cranberries. By the end of the night, Peter had hooked up with someone who was completely mesmerized by him. The next morning, he texted Charlie to officially end their relationship.

Peter's story is an intense example of how desperately we seek external validation from others when we don't have a secure sense of self. As long as the IV drip of Charlie's affirmation flowed, Peter felt okay. But once it was removed, something in him crumbled. Where did this need come from? To understand Peter's behavior, we need to understand his origins.

Peter grew up in the Midwest, where he always felt like an outsider. While the other boys were playing sports, he was chasing butterflies in the fields. In high school, he found his niche in theater, which made his mother proud but sent his father running for the hills. By the time Peter reached college, his relationships with other men had been marked by rejection, and his connection with his mother had become a hybrid of support and enmeshment.

Peter knew he was gay, but without any safe places to process his feelings, he found solace in romantic fantasies. His internal sense of self was steeped in weakness and undesirability. Yet, in his fantasies, those inadequacies were temporarily eclipsed as he imagined being with a man who embodied everything he believed he was not: physically strong and emotionally secure.

Something changed during his senior year of college. Tired of feeling weak, he decided to transform himself through weight training. Several months later he was in the gym when a strong and kind man complimented his stylish hair and trim body. The affirmation was intoxicating. The more his physical appearance improved, the more attention Peter attracted. External validation became a drug for Peter, fueling a new sense of confidence to start dating.

In his romantic relationships, Peter gravitated toward strong, muscular men. The more masculine the partner, the more secure he felt in all areas of his life. His identity, once marked by vulnerability, was now mirrored to him by the strength and admiration of the man at his side.

We're all a bit like Peter. Whether it's the need to merge with someone attractive, the craving to be admired, the accumulation of material possessions, or the desire to be the most accomplished person in the room, we tend to look outside ourselves to feel secure. The kindness of our crucibles is that they expose the false foundations we've built our life upon and push us to exit the validation treadmill in search of the deeper, transformational work of differentiation.

## *What Is Differentiation?*

*Differentiation,* a concept developed by Dr. Murray Bowen, refers to the ability to maintain emotional closeness with others while staying true to one's sense of self. It's the ability to express ourselves authentically and be emotionally present in relationships without losing our individuality. For any individual, relationship, or organization to be healthy and strong, each part must be highly differentiated while also meaningfully connected.

Think about the human body: All of our cells start from the same genetic material but gradually *differentiate* into unique, specialized functions. Our eyes, ears, nose, mouth, and brain perform distinct roles, yet they work seamlessly together to keep us alive. Relationships function much the same way. For a partnership or friendship to thrive, each person needs to develop their unique identity while building a deep emotional connection. Without differentiation, problems arise, and intimacy suffers.

To better understand differentiation, it's important to recognize how our need for individuation and connection evolves as we grow. We're born hardwired for relationships, continuously looking for the delight and collaboration of others. This never stops. As infants, we're so dependent on our caregivers that our heart rate and body temperature are regulated by their warmth and love. But as we mature, we're intended to develop our ability to self-soothe and give the people around us more than just our needs. For example, a child eventually learns to put on a jacket when it's cold instead of crying for a parent to warm them up. Yet so many of us remain young in our emotional development, setting up our relationships, careers, and addictions to be on call whenever we need soothing.

## *Differentiation and Desire*

When we lack differentiation, our desires become distorted. We objectify not only the world around us but also our own identities. Desire becomes a transaction, a way of filling the emptiness we feel within. We chase lifestyles defined by others as meaningful and search for status symbols that affirm our worth. Intimacy becomes less about authentic connection and more about finding someone who can alleviate our loneliness. Careers become the ultimate measure of our self-worth. In short, we desire the whole world and yet lose our soul.

Authentic personal growth can only emerge when we pursue differentiation. If our desires for growth aren't grounded in a strong sense of self, they're not worth our investment, because they will only pull us away from our true self, keeping us stuck in a cycle of postponing our transformation and burdening others with our need for validation.

Earlier chapters have laid the groundwork for building a differentiated life. Integrity through our crucibles, hospitality for our distress, and a growth mindset are all building blocks in becoming a differentiated person. As we grow in these qualities, we become less dependent on the opinions and mirroring of others, allowing an inner wisdom and drive for authenticity to become our preferred guides. But before we can develop into the best versions of ourselves, we need to examine the places in our life where our sense of self still relies on external sources.

## Consequences of a Lack of Differentiation: A Reflected Sense of Self

Dr. David Schnarch believed most people have poor differentiation and therefore operate from what he called a *reflected sense of self.* This happens when our identity is constructed too much on external feedback. Imagine this reflected sense of self as a "dependent" or "needy" version of yourself that is constantly scanning the world for contact, validation, consensus, and confirmation of its desirability.[2] The reflected sense of self does not know who it is or what it wants, and it may not really like itself. So, it needs to be defined and desired by something or someone outside of itself.

The complexity is that, as children, we all needed healthy mirroring. My research shows that if we were enjoyed, invited to cultivate our longings, and encouraged to take risks in our formative years, we are more likely to have a healthier relationship to desire as adults. But when healthy mirroring isn't available, we find ourselves seeking symbols of success or objects of security. Job titles, social media followers, how many people text us each day, and material possessions become mirrors that soothe us in the short term. But in the long run, we end up exchanging an authentic self for the symbols of a self that we can gather around us.

How can you tell if you're living from a reflected sense of self? If you fall apart when you're alone, find yourself angry when someone doesn't come through for you, grow angsty when people disagree with you, or feel insecure about the amount of money, power, or attraction you possess, these are all signs that your sense of self has room to develop. The insecurities we feel in our external world are always a reflection of the insecurities we feel within. We think the solution is to attain or achieve more, but it's not. The antidote is a desire to develop greater intimacy with the self.

When we live from a reflected sense of self, we burden those around us by expecting others to validate our worth, affirm our desirability, or bend to our need for control. This can strain relationships, making them more about our needs than genuine connection.

Here are some common beliefs that burden others, their consequences, and how you can shift to a differentiation mindset if you find yourself in that scenario.

| Belief | Consequences of a Reflected Sense of Self | Differentiation Mindset |
|---|---|---|
| "My relationships should consistently affirm that they desire me." | We withhold the best in ourselves from our friends and family because we're waiting for their validation. The quality of our relationships diminishes, since people can't desire us while also feeling the pressure to soothe us. | "Even when I feel inadequate, I will bring my most authentic self to my relationships." |

| Belief | Consequences of a Reflected Sense of Self | Differentiation Mindset |
|---|---|---|
| "I shouldn't feel alone in my marriage." | We pick fights rather than taking responsibility for our own emotional needs. We also might stay busy to avoid the necessary work of transforming loneliness into solitude. | "When I feel forgotten, I can still choose to remember myself. Loneliness doesn't mean incompatibility—it's an opportunity to deepen my connection to myself." |
| "I need you to agree with me." | A relationship without separateness is enmeshment. | "I can be curious about the conclusions you've arrived at. I can share my perspective without being preachy or needing you to agree with me." |
| "I need to become who you want me to be." | We lose ourselves by trying to become what others want. | "If I fit in for you, I may no longer belong to myself.[3] I'm learning to stay rooted in authenticity while also deepening my connection to others." |

As you can see, individuals with low levels of differentiation can present in vastly different ways. Some can't tolerate separateness and become overly dependent on others, while others may appear outwardly confident, even as they struggle to form meaningful, intimate connections. Regardless of outward appearance, the issue is the same:

Individuals at low levels of differentiation can't maintain a strong sense of self in proximity to others.

As you pursue growth in differentiation, you will find your connection to others deepening. This is why I have placed this part of the book, "A Desire for Growth," before "A Desire for Intimacy." People tend to show up in their relationships as emotional orphans. They may be yearning for the validation they never received, or they may be so committed to hustling through life that they've never allowed themselves to be fully known. Without differentiation, the quality of our intimacy will suffer, and our longing for it will be highly suspect. While there are many other significant obstacles to developing intimacy, none are as fundamentally problematic as a person who doesn't truly know or like who they are.

Differentiation is how you shape yourself into a vessel capable of traveling deeper into the heart of desire. While it takes considerable time and resources to differentiate, the quality and longevity of your journey ahead depend on it.

## *Differentiation in Conflict*

Differentiation reveals itself most dramatically in how we handle conflict or tension. Imagine two people who hold differing opinions on sensitive issues related to politics, ethics, or religion, yet still manage to respect and seek out each other's perspectives. Conversely, imagine another couple in the same scenario who can't handle differences. One partner might succumb to anxiety, suppressing their own beliefs, while the other person demands a faux sense of unity. The first couple reveals the power of differentiation, while the latter highlights its absence. According to Dr. Schnarch, differentiation allows us to engage with "a difficult, emotionally charged problem and not feel compelled to preach about what others 'should' do, not rush to 'fix' the problem, and not pretend to be detached by emotionally insulating oneself."[4]

Reflect on how you approach or shy away from relational tension. Do you rush in with certainty, convinced that you already know the other person's motivations? Does conflict make you anxious, leading you to avoid it at all costs? Do you wait for someone to strike first and then fight dirty from a place of victimization? Do you take time to reflect on yourself before engaging, acknowledging to the other person where you may be emotionally hardened or underdeveloped?

Often, the more certain we feel about another person's faults, the less likely we are to recognize our own contributions to the conflict. Differentiated individuals don't seek to "win" in a conflict. For them, their desire is to better understand what's motivating the other person, fostering collaboration and growth in the relationship. Differentiation is foundational to the flourishing of all relationships, but especially romantic partnerships.

## Differentiation and Romantic Relationships

If a romantic relationship does not have two distinct persons, a *me* and a *you*, intimacy will stall. A classic example of this is when one partner dominates the relationship, dictating everything from how the dishwasher is loaded to the frequency of sexual intimacy, while the other person's needs are disregarded. While these partners may seem like opposites, the underlying issue, as we've been learning, is the same: low differentiation.

In fact, this is why those "opposite" personality types often end up together. The dominant partner can't handle emotional closeness and therefore defaults to rigidity. But the more passive partner struggles to hold on to themselves or move into conflict. Dominant partners take up considerable space and passive partners become emotionally detached and harbor deep resentments. Whenever there is a breakdown in love or collaboration, the lack of differentiation is a major contributing factor.

At low levels of differentiation, recurring problems are viewed as signs that someone else is the problem. When our partner doesn't change fast enough, or to the extent we desire, we make them pay by becoming overly critical, contemptuous, or unfaithful. For example, a study found that when men feel invalidated by their female partner, their chance of turning to infidelity increases.[5]

A note of caution: This is not to be confused with cases of domestic violence or emotional abuse, which require a different level of intervention. However, for the rest of us, reducing our partners to labels like "narcissist" or "borderline" whenever the relationship hits gridlock does little to mature us emotionally. Instead, it displays our own low differentiation.

In a differentiated relationship, each partner expresses their own desires while remaining open to mutual influence. Maybe one partner hasn't ever enjoyed dancing, but they are willing to learn their partner's passion for Argentine tango to deepen their connection. They may have differing opinions on certain topics, yet they deeply respect and learn from each other's perspectives. For a differentiated person, authenticity is of far greater value than being on the same page with the other person.

The more differentiation partners have, the more confidence they will gain, and the better their relationships will become. The Holistic Desire Survey measured confidence scores by asking respondents eight questions about the degree to which they liked who they were: Did they recognize their positive qualities, feel comfortable with themselves, feel like their life was going in a healthy direction, etc.? When individuals had high confidence scores, they were more than 25 percent less likely to have negative relationships. High confidence was also linked to more positive relationships: Men were 2.8 times more likely and women 2.3 times more likely to report being in a healthy relationship when they had high self-confidence scores.

## *Differentiation vs. Attachment: A Fundamental Distinction*

Dr. Schnarch's approach to relationships, rooted in differentiation, diverges significantly from more traditional marriage advice, such as that found in Dr. Sue Johnson's book *Hold Me Tight*. The late Dr. Johnson was a prominent expert in helping couples see their marriage from an attachment-based perspective. She believed that much of marital conflict stems from "a desperate attachment cry, a *protest against disconnection*" (her italics). She argued that this cry could "only be quieted by a lover moving emotionally close to hold and reassure. Nothing else will do."[6]

Notice the difference between these two approaches to emotional distress. Differentiation-based theory suggests it's quite possible— even essential—for individuals to calm themselves, manage their reactivity, and handle tension independently. In contrast, some attachment-based theorists argue that relational distress cannot be soothed without emotional closeness between partners.

While both perspectives recognize the essential need for emotional regulation, the differentiation approach places the responsibility for soothing squarely on the individual. Though co-regulation can be valuable, it's important to ask: What happens when co-regulation isn't available? While it might feel intuitively right to prioritize emotional connection with a partner in times of distress, my concern is that we aren't considering the ramifications of two individuals who are unable or unwilling to calm down their bodies independently. Relying on a partner or friend for reassurance can lead to a kind of emotional hostage situation: "You need to reassure and hold me because nothing else will do."

It's natural to desire a supportive partner, but without growth in differentiation, we risk demanding codependency. The most effective way to navigate disconnection is to first connect to ourselves. This includes calming our distress, learning to respond rather than react to conflict, and committing to greater collaboration than we've ever shown our partner before. Many of us want our relationships to change, but we often lack an equal level of desire to transform ourselves.

At times, pursuing differentiation may temporarily reduce emotional closeness with your partner. But that's okay—you're playing the long game. Time apart can be an investment in the flourishing of both individuals and the relationship as a whole.

When I ask couples about the moments they have felt the most attracted to their partners, they rarely talk about connection in terms of emotional closeness. Instead, they describe their partner's uniqueness or a time when they saw them fully in their element. One client shared how he becomes transfixed when he sees his partner sing and play guitar. Another client spoke of how she finds her partner most attractive when he's captivating a room with his storytelling at a party. It's not that intimacy is overrated; it's that differentiation is under-pursued.

Becoming differentiated is one of the most loving things you can do for your friends, family, and yourself. When we develop a strong sense of self, we can enjoy solitude without feeling lonely or relying on unhealthy coping mechanisms. And when you are near others, you can engage in a way that allows for mutual influence—without the fear of losing your identity or militantly controlling others to align with your views.

## Questions for Self-Reflection

To assess how well you can differentiate yourself in relationships and situations, ask yourself the following questions. These aren't meant to be diagnostic but can offer insight into behaviors that may indicate a lack of differentiation.

1. Do you hide how you really feel about things?
2. Do you feel anxious when someone expresses a different opinion or perspective?
3. Do you suppress your feelings until they explode?
4. If you're in a committed relationship, do you tend to see your partner as the primary problem?
5. Do you soothe yourself through substances or other self-destructive behaviors?
6. Do you pursue relationships primarily when you're feeling empty or need validation?
7. Do you care for the needs of others but disregard your own?
8. Do you commit to doing things you have no desire for?
9. Do you feel anxious or purposeless when you are alone?
10. Do you gossip about your problems with others instead of talking directly to the person involved?

Differentiated individuals tend to answer no to most of these questions. They can express themselves authentically and navigate relationships without excessive anxiety, emotional reactivity, or entitlement.

If you found yourself answering yes to more than two or three of these questions, it may indicate that you're relying on external validation or have difficulty managing your emotions in a healthy way. But remember, a reflected sense of self doesn't have to be permanent. In the pages ahead, we'll explore three concepts that can help you develop your true self and stop practicing inauthenticity. While there is no singular formula for achieving this, these three concepts will provide a strong foundation for your desire to live authentically.

## *How to Satisfy Your Desire for an Authentic Self*

### 1. CONFRONT YOUR SHORTCUTS

Building an authentic self requires considerable effort and introspection. We all know this on some level, which is why we're often drawn toward shortcuts. A shortcut is anything we use to evade the difficult work of personal and relational growth. These shortcuts are evident when we rely on others' opinions to define us, use unhealthy behaviors to numb discomfort, or look to external symbols, like a logo on our clothes or an emblem on our car, to feel confident. Shortcuts seduce us with superficial desires, but hinder the emergence of our true selves.

One of the most common shortcuts in our world today is narcissism. In high school, I understood narcissism as a condition in which someone was *full of themself.* It was the jock who needed to have the most attractive girlfriend, the fastest car, or the most fashionable wardrobe. As I got older, I saw narcissism in politics, sports, and celebrity culture. These individuals had exaggerated self-importance, needed to be admired, tended to lack empathy, and exploited people for personal gain. What I learned in my clinical training, however, is that narcissism is not a fullness of self, but a profound *absence of self.* In this sense, we all have some measure of narcissism within us.[7]

The narcissistic option appeals to individuals and societies that are lacking in love, leading them to derive their worth from external symbols and displays of power over others. One study found that narcissists may look grandiose, but they are actually insecure.[8] Their characteristic hunger for accolades, excessive goal-setting, attractive partners, external appearances, promotions, personal networks, and obsession over the best brands all function to distance them from the pain of lacking an authentic identity.

One of the insidious aspects of narcissism is that it damages healthy desire. Narcissism convinces its prisoners that they will not be loved or important outside of the idealized self they can project and the objects they can attain. This leads them to desire sex, money, and power—initially to avoid shame, but eventually to dominate and control others. Here are a few common narcissistic shortcuts many of us fall into:

- Letting our identity be defined exclusively by our work or family, because we don't know who we are outside of our roles or relationships.
- Having an affair or pursuing fleeting excitement to feel "alive," rather than doing the necessary personal and relational work to cultivate lasting passion.
- Turning to entertainment or substances when we're stressed or lonely.

Beyond individual expressions of narcissism, our culture is also becoming increasingly narcissistic. Social media platforms amplify these tendencies by encouraging us to broadcast idealized versions of our lives for public admiration. Likes, shares, and followers all become imitation versions of being known. Narcissists sell a lot of products and experiences, and merging with their brands and attending their events provides a shortcut to feeling like we're living a meaningful life.

Though narcissism has become a derogatory buzzword in our culture, I hope to reframe it as a concept that leads us to grief. It may appear as a towering tree of self-indulgence, but its root system is *shame*. The core motivation isn't initially to be better, richer, faster, stronger, smarter, or more beautiful than someone else. It's to avoid feeling weak, poor, slow, dumb, and unattractive. A narcissist is someone who has learned to hedge against future encounters with embarrassment.

The antidote to narcissism is to grieve the genesis of all that is false within us. As we develop a more authentic identity, we might feel shame for the shortcuts we put our trust in, but the invitation is to sorrow. The narcissistic option appealed to us because we lacked love and guidance in significant moments of pain and confusion. Once we recognize these origin stories, we will be more likely to experience grief over the ways we used others or relied on external mirrors to define us. Narcissism dies through sorrow.

## 2. CHOOSE GRIEF

As we descend deeper into personal growth, we will inevitably become more aware of our shortcuts, inadequacies, and unresolved issues. The best response to this awareness is to choose more grief. Tears have a powerful way of helping us exchange our underdeveloped desires for healthier, more authentic longings. Through sorrow, it's easier to confront our past choices and awaken a greater defiance to live differently today.

Think about how a seed grows into a plant. When the casing cracks open, at the right temperature and moisture conditions, the root first grows downward, anchoring the plant. Only then can the shoot emerge above the soil. There is immense metaphor in this process. To grow upward, we must first descend.

In our culture, however, we are obsessed with celebrating visible success. We are loquacious about the surface-level aspects of growth—what can be easily measured and admired. But an authentic person is equally captivated by what happens beneath the surface. To "wake up" to personal growth, we need to become like seeds. Just as a seed germinates in dark conditions, we must face difficult, uncomfortable truths about ourselves if we are to grow.

There is so much to grieve: the roles we were asked to play in our families and communities, adverse experiences we survived, the pain of loneliness, and the ways we've hurt others. When we choose grief, we allow the root of our true self to descend, anchoring us for all that lies ahead. In time, the shoots of passion, purpose, and joy will rise. But only if we have first descended into grief can we trust that our desires are emerging from an anchored place.

Many of my clients resist grief, because they fear their tears will never stop. Truth be told, I've never met someone who drowned in a pool of sorrow. What I have seen, however, is the damage done by individuals who avoid grief, inadvertently passing down generational trauma and prolonging emotional and physical health problems, all because they never found tears for their story.

Choosing grief allows us to connect more deeply with our story, our body, and our relationships. If we want our desires to flourish, we must learn to plant the seeds of grief. When the false self dies, we will descend into the depths of sorrow. But this descent is working to anchor us, allowing for the shoots of an authentic life to rise.

### 3. LISTENING TO THE BELLS WITHIN: HONORING THE CALL TO PASSION AND AWE

Annie Dillard, author of the Pulitzer Prize–winning book *Pilgrim at Tinker Creek,* wrote, "I had been my whole life a bell, and never knew it until at that moment I was lifted up and struck."[9]

These are the moments in life when a deep, often sudden recognition rings within us—that we are alive and connected to something vast. Maybe it's a conversation with a friend that stirs a knowing deep within you, a powerful piece of music that resonates so strongly it brings tears, or standing in awe before the vastness of a breathtaking landscape. These moments don't merely spark passion or awe; they remind us of truths we've always known. They invite us to remember who we are and to awaken to a wilder, more beautiful existence than we ever dared imagine.

In contrast, superficial desires arise from scarcity or imitation. They appeal to a part of us that is disconnected and desperate, which is why they never satiate. But when we're connected to our true selves, our desires arise from a place of fullness. In them, we realize that we are the proud owners of everything that can't be bought.[10]

A significant part of personal growth is learning to honor these moments by investing significant time and resources into nurturing them. One of the best practices is to dedicate two of your most productive hours each day or week to cultivating these desires. Whether it's sitting down to write the screenplay, learning how to make a butter block and laminate dough, planning an adventure, or simply setting aside time to listen to vinyl records, we must give ourselves the permission both to cultivate passion and to increase the likelihood of experiencing awe. These aren't just hobbies. They are vital pillars in the foundation of an authentic life.

These bell-like moments of passion and awe offer profound benefits to our mental and physical health. Research from psychologist Dacher Keltner at the University of California, Berkeley, shows that beauty quiets our negative self-talk by deactivating the default mode network, the part of the brain involved in how we perceive ourselves.[11, 12] Awe also calms down our nervous system and triggers the release of oxytocin, the "love" hormone that promotes trust and bonding.[13] When negative self-talk is reduced and we feel inspired by beauty, our confidence grows, and we are empowered to pursue our desires with greater clarity.

Most of us understand that pain makes us hunger for what we want the most in life, but we often underestimate the extent to which beauty can reshape our desires. Keltner's research shows that we are deeply moved when we witness what he calls "moral beauty"—when we see others living with courage, compassion, or selflessness.[14] When we see a friend endure great suffering with grace, or hear a story of a soldier who risked their life to pull a comrade to safety, it creates a transformative awe that can shift our desires in profound ways.

Sometimes the best way to pursue personal growth is by recognizing that it's not all about us. When we can experience awe and gratitude for the beauty of others, we break through to a significant stage of growth. Without the capacity to deeply appreciate and honor others, our journey toward the remaining desires of intimacy, pleasure, and purpose will remain limited.

## *Conclusion to Part Two*

In Part Two, we explored how the difficulties in our lives and relationships are invitations to enter the crucible of growth. True growth occurs when we choose to say no to shortcuts and yes to tolerating the discomfort that stretches us into the people we are meant to become. Within each of us lies a life-giving route that will only be revealed when we're willing to let go of every other option.

Many people struggling with desire think they need to do a better job managing or suppressing their longings. My suggestion is to do the opposite: Release yourself to desire again. Let yourself be seduced by the flight of an eagle, the fragrance of peppermint, or the rejuvenating waters of a local river. Live in awe of the physical and moral beauty that exists all around you. The bells are ringing. Are you listening?

As you move forward, remember that each moment of integrity, hospitality, grief, passion, and awe you experience is helping shape you into the person you need to be for the travels ahead. Your authentic self is the vessel you are building for the journey. I hope you're beginning to enjoy what is taking shape within you. And if not, remember: It's just the starting point.

Each part of this book builds on the one before it, and the next is no exception. In Part One, you were invited to understand your story and the origins of your desires and gain clarity about the patterns influencing your life today. In Part Two, you were asked to confront some of the toughest dimensions of your life, learning to approach them with both hospitality and a growth mindset. In Part Three, you will take what you've discovered about the power of differentiation and apply it to your romantic relationships, dramatically opening the door to deeper intimacy.

As I wrote earlier, we all arrive in committed relationships unprepared and underdeveloped in some fundamental way. Part Three will invite you to see these challenges as clarion calls to develop intimacy and learn the skills necessary to love well, especially when it's difficult. I hope you're ready. Intimacy requires you to have the courage to recognize both the best and worst in you. Are you ready for it?

# A Desire for
# *Intimacy*

———

## SATISFYING
## OUR NEED
## TO LOVE AND
## BE LOVED

CHAPTER 8

## *Clarion Calls*

> *Nobody's ready for marriage—*
> *marriage makes you ready for*
> *marriage.*
>
> —DAVID SCHNARCH

WENDY AND PHIL, BOTH ON THEIR SECOND MARRIAGE, HAVE been together twenty-six years. "Twenty-two of them happily," Phil jokes with classic dad humor. Once a power couple, both were successful, ambitious, and always in motion. Now in their sixties, they're empty nesters with a nine-month-old puppy. Phil, a partner at a Washington, D.C., law firm, feels pressure from Wendy to retire, but the thought of staying home doesn't excite him. Wendy wants to travel the world but admits she rarely plans trips and has bought her dog to escape the emptiness she feels. This never would have been the future they imagined for themselves at the beginning of their marriage.

Over the years, Wendy and Phil have learned to get along. Phil makes Wendy's coffee most mornings, and she often texts him when running errands to see if he needs anything. They occasionally make dinner together and host holiday parties for friends. But words like "passion" and "friendship" would never be used to describe their relationship. While their puppy provides a mild distraction, they both know retirement would ask them to confront years of prioritizing stability over passion.

Phil, driven by his love of learning and his desire to make a meaningful impact, dreams of moving to a city, becoming a professor, and cultivating thought leadership in his field. Wendy thinks cities smell, wants a slower-paced life, and tells Phil that she'd like them to think about moving to Tennessee, near her sister and best friend. Phil joked about him getting an apartment in D.C. and her a condo in Nashville, which made Wendy laugh, but led to a more somber conversation about how little desire they have in common.

Wendy has always wanted more from Phil, but has been conditioned to acclimate to his meager portions. Early in their marriage, she sought greater intimacy—more time, deeper sexual connection, and shared values. But the more she wanted, the more Phil withdrew, and in turn, the more rage she unleashed on him. Fifteen years into the marriage, she learned from a renowned marriage therapist that 69 percent of relationship problems are unsolvable.[1] This statistic deeply resonated with her and led her to question whether Phil or her first husband were capable of intimacy. Eventually, she stopped asking for something Phil didn't seem capable of or willing to give. Now, standing at a crossroads, Wendy wonders if either of them even want to save their marriage.

Wendy and Phil are facing an issue that's common in long-term marriages, when the frenetic pace of career and parenting begins to ease. They've reached a disruptive, but necessary, inflection point where a stability-focused marriage no longer satisfies. Phil's primary gripe about Wendy is that she wants comfort and ease at the expense of personal growth. He feels she's lost interest in challenging herself intellectually, something that initially drew him to her. Wendy resists this interpretation, seeing it as a convenient excuse for Phil's failure to prioritize building intimacy with her. Like many couples, they've become masters at conditioning one another to expect less. In all marriages, this mutual dissatisfaction can either become a harbinger of renewal or set the stage for the termination of the relationship.

Here's the thing about intimacy problems in marriage: They don't tend to go away until they've taught us what we need to learn. When we face relational difficulties, we often assume there's something broken in the relationship. But I'd like you to consider a radically different perspective: Your relationship is actually functioning quite well when intimacy issues arise. These moments ask us to lean in and understand ourselves in ways we tend to avoid. The intimacy couples seek often lies in the very problems they've been avoiding or unable to resolve.

In this chapter, we will explore what intimacy is and begin building the foundation for the marriage you want. While there will be hard work ahead, the reality is that marriage is also working hard on us. In the upcoming chapters, we'll focus on developing two key traits to dramatically increase your ability to give and receive love. But first, let's explore some essential concepts that will help you understand the challenges you're facing on your journey to connection.

## *Only Marriage Prepares Us for Marriage*

A brief author's note: When I refer to "marriage" in this book, I mean more than its legal definition. I'm including lifelong romantic partnerships and committed, monogamous relationships. While my examples and research come from my work with married couples, the core concepts in this section are relevant to a broad spectrum of relationships. Even if your specific challenges are not addressed, my hope is that this part of the book will offer an interpretative lens that you can apply to your own situation.

Marriage is a crucible. While this concept was introduced in Part Two, it's worth revisiting here: No amount of personal development can fully prepare us for the work of sustaining intimacy with another person. As the late Dr. David Schnarch, founder of the Crucible Approach Therapy, aptly said, "Nothing prepares you for marriage. Marriage prepares you for marriage."[2]

Personal growth is essential for building healthy intimacy, but in this realm marriage itself is the master teacher. It's within the day-to-day experiences of delight, conflict, anxiety, monotony, and hope that we are crafted into the partners we need to become. There is no resource or amount of preparation that can fully equip us for the universal challenges of intimacy, let alone the one-of-a-kind issues that arise from our individual pairing with our partner.

The hardest years of marriage will vary from couple to couple, but no love story is immune from a crucible. Couples who stay together over the long haul will often navigate many different versions of them-selves and their relationship. In this way, we aren't just married to one person, but to many different people who evolve out of the same per-son as these various seasons unfold. While some of these shifts will be linear, the particular years and dynamics are influenced by factors such as age, personal growth, life circumstances, and external pressures. Here's a look at four common crucibles couples in my practice often find themselves experiencing.

In the early stage of marriage, typically years one through five, cou-ples face a crucible marked by considerable adjustments. This is not just a time of getting to know each other, but a time of learning how to stay *with* and *for* one another. Partners begin reconciling and pro-testing expectations with reality, discovering whether they're more afraid of being alone or becoming consumed. These formative years lay the foundation for the power dynamics and ingrained patterns that will shape the trajectory of the marriage in the years to come.

As the marriage enters its second stage, around five to ten years in, desires outside of the relationship, or external pressures such as parent-ing or career, become more pronounced. It's common for one partner to feel neglected while the other is focused on the responsibilities of work or caring for the family. In this stage, each partner may make distinct contributions—one might pour energy into nurturing the re-lationship itself, while the other may invest in the broader connections or responsibilities of life in their community. This dynamic can breed resentment or inspire a deeper honor for each other's contributions. Though romantic passion might seem difficult to find, the crucible of this stage pushes couples to develop a more collaborative and compan-ionate love—one that can sustain them for decades.

The third stage, often spanning from ten to twenty years, is the midlife period. This is a time when couples face a profound reckoning. Each partner is likely to reevaluate their lives, reassess their values, and recognize how life has reshaped them into people who may no longer resemble the individuals they were when they first met. Empty-nest syndrome, a midlife crisis, or the first signs of health challenges may emerge, leading to intense disillusionment with the relationship or the meaning of life. Yet, through the crucible, an opening is created for a deeper connection to forge. When this occurs, partners grow in gratitude for one another and find great meaning in bearing witness to who they are becoming.

The final stage of marriage, twenty-plus years in, can bring both a sense of rest and heartache as the realities of death come into focus. The couple may enjoy more time together—traveling, reconnecting with friends or family, and deepening their bond in ways that were difficult during their busier years. But this stage brings inevitable crucibles: health issues, the loss of loved ones, changing dynamics with adult children, and the heartbreaking mathematical reality that one partner will eventually become widowed. Although vulnerability intensifies, the value of the investments they've made in each other and in their extended relationships becomes clearer. Couples learn to surrender to the inevitable, finding beauty in their shared history and leaning on the strength of their bonds as they face life's final chapters.

The journey of marriage cultivates an intimacy that cannot be learned in any other way. Each of these crucibles is intended to eventually serve us—to stretch us, confront us, awaken us, and surrender us to the preciousness of our days. While there are certainly stages couples will simply want to survive, the hope is that, over time, they come to see one another as beloveds—privileged to walk together through both the craggy and the verdant terrain of life.

## *The Purpose of Intimacy*

Several years ago, I found a compelling illustration of intimacy—though it came from an unlikely source. In *The Simpsons Movie*, an ominous dome descends over the fictional town of Springfield, trapping the residents inside. As it descends, one character is torn between staying inside or going outside the dome. He runs back and forth between his two apparent options, exclaiming, "If I stay, I am trapped. If I leave, I'm all alone!" Unable to choose, and stuck in his ambivalence, he is squashed by the dome.[3]

Many of us experience this dilemma in our romantic relationships. We feel trapped by our partner's need to remain connected, but if we leave, we fear being alone or hated. Thankfully, we don't have to choose between being confined, isolated, or crushed. Marriage, unlike any other relationship on earth, pushes us to learn how to remain authentic to ourselves while also belonging to the one we love.

The purpose of intimacy is to transform us into people more capable of giving and receiving love. For this transformation to occur, we must allow marriage to simultaneously soften and strengthen us. Without a growing desire to be tender with one another, past heartaches or frustrations will callous our hearts. But if we don't also grow in strength, we'll settle for enmeshment or avoid hard topics instead of becoming bold in our love for each other.

Most couples who are struggling to develop intimacy constantly flip what I call the "Marriage Illusion" coin. On one side of the coin is the expectation that marriage will be easy, or that if you pick the right person, a passionate and mysterious connection will naturally evolve between you and your partner. The other side is the belief that your difficulties are evidence of irreconcilable differences. Unfortunately, both sides of this coin will lock people in a cycle of disconnection.

Again, contrary to popular belief, marriage is working quite well when it encounters problems. It's through these challenges that unhealthy traits, intimacy illusions, and our deepest longings come to the surface, giving both partners the opportunity to engage with them. At its core, intimacy is meant to be more than cozy companionship, an anesthetic for loneliness, or an outcome of passionate sex. In a marriage grounded in healthy intimacy, smooth sailing is less important than transformation—challenging both partners to become the best version of themselves.

In this way, marriage problems are not just inevitable; they serve as clarion calls: clear signals to urge couples to deepen their understanding of and desire for intimacy. These issues may range from disagreements about how to load the dishwasher to more significant conflicts around sexual-desire differences, family dynamics, or conflicting values. Until *both* partners are willing to value these clarion calls and recognize the deeper stories embedded within their conflicts, intimacy will plateau. Problems in marriage are normal, but growth is optional.

Blame and compromise are the two most common ways couples avoid responding to clarion calls. Blaming our partner may provide a temporary sense of stability, but it prevents us from acknowledging our own role in the relationship's decline. Instead of looking inward, the focus shifts outward, fueling a destructive cycle of blame and withdrawal. One partner feels justified in their accusations, while the other emotionally distances themselves to avoid further scrutiny, only to be blamed again for retreating.

Some couples see compromise as the antidote to relational tension, but it often acts as an opiate, numbing both partners to the painful truths they need to face about themselves before the relationship can thrive. Think about conflicts over sexual frequency or how much time to spend with in-laws. Many couples try to compromise on these issues—agreeing on a particular frequency of sexual intimacy or splitting holidays between in-laws. But what if these compromises overlook deeper dynamics? Perhaps one pushes for more frequent sex because they haven't learned to self-soothe or connect with their partner without an orgasm. Or maybe both partners are avoiding the anxiety of disappointing their families, so instead, they prioritize their parents over their marriage. While accommodation can be valuable, relying on it too heavily over time will eventually lead to cowardice and stall intimacy.

The third, more effective option is to listen carefully to the clarion calls, seeing conflict as an opportunity to deepen intimacy. These calls are rarely as obvious as a bullhorn. They're often subtle, akin to the persistent beep of a smoke detector with a low battery. No one enjoys the sound, but its purpose is to irritate you into action. Here are a few ways clarion calls drive couples to greater intimacy:

- *Loyalty to parents:* If one partner's loyalty to their parents overshadows or competes with their commitment to their spouse, the other partner may initiate conflict to address this imbalance, ultimately strengthening the marriage.

- *Imbalance of power:* Research shows that when a man is not willing to share power with his partner, there is an 81 percent chance that his marriage will self-destruct.[4]
- *A lack of teamwork:* A significant disparity in managing the responsibilities of home and family life is a primary reason why people's marital satisfaction goes down, particularly for women. One study found a 31 percent drop in marital satisfaction when a spouse does virtually none of the housework, compared to when they do half of it.[5]
- *Fear of risk:* If one partner struggles with being alone, shies away from risks, and bemoans their partner's desires, the other partner may feel forced to suppress their desire for adventure to comply with their partner's demand for stability.

Marriage has a way of exposing aspects of ourselves that we might not see—our control, the selfishness in others or ourselves, unspoken loyalties, and fears. Responding to these clarion calls requires curiosity, humility, and a strong sense of self. If we are too rigid in our ways, too fragile to confront the shortcomings of others, or too proud to admit where we've failed, intimacy cannot deepen. To thrive in marriage, we must teach our egos the lost art of embracing our imperfections and acknowledging our need for mercy.

## WE'RE ALL UNDERDEVELOPED IN INTIMACY

One of the kindest and most freeing things you can do for your marriage is to recognize that we all come into the relationship underdeveloped in our ability to experience true intimacy with our partner. The dynamics that bonded us early on often seem endearing, but that doesn't necessarily mean we were experiencing healthy intimacy. For example, one partner's need for emotional support may have aligned with the other's childhood role of providing reassurance to a needy parent or sibling. In this case, the couple thought their initial intimacy was strong, but they were unable to see how their provisional identities brought them together—one needing to feel seen and the other needing to feel useful.

Alternatively, a hidden, deceptive part of your partner may have felt deeply familiar to you because it mirrored a trait from one of your parents. But when you allow yourself to see these dynamics for what they are, the illusion of intimacy or peace begins to break down, leading to necessary conflict. In this case, intimacy is not eroding; it's finding its true potential.

We often find ourselves drawn to partners who not only tolerate but also accommodate the underdeveloped parts of who we are. It's these personal weaknesses—more than love itself—that initially bond us to one another. The longer a couple stays together, the more their once suppressed dynamics become glaringly obvious. As we grow and evolve, our tolerance for these underdeveloped aspects of ourselves and of our partner begins to fade, and this is a good sign. The next time you fear your intimacy breaking down, consider that the undoing might be clearing space for a new story to unfold in your relationship.

## Confronting Sabotage and Cultivating Love

A strong marriage doesn't form naturally. It's intentionally built over time, shaped by consistent effort and conscious choices that break through the dynamics that lead to plateaus in connection. To deepen your capacity for intimacy and lay a solid foundation for a lifetime of love, we will explore two core questions in the remainder of Part Three:

- *How Am I Sabotaging Intimacy in My Relationship?*
- *How Can I Learn How to Love and Be Loved?*

These questions function like an if/then statement: If we honestly confront the ways we're sabotaging intimacy, then we create the conditions for love to thrive. Too often, couples express a desire to love better without first examining how they consciously and unconsciously undermine that goal. For relationships to flourish, we can't leave their development to chance. We need to actively cultivate relational skills, especially the ones we never saw modeled in the past. And when we learn how to love, we also strengthen our resolve to protect that love from sabotage.

In the next chapter, you'll learn three common ways couples sabotage intimacy and how you can effectively outgrow those unhealthy patterns.

## CHAPTER 9

# How Am I Sabotaging Intimacy in My Relationship?

*Your task is not to seek for love,*
*but merely to seek and find all the*
*barriers within yourself that you*
*have built against it.*

—RUMI

## Chris and Michelle

Chris and Michelle were high school sweethearts on the precipice of divorce. They married after their senior year of college, and children followed shortly after. Six years in, Chris became a dentist and opened a small practice. Michelle felt a considerable bind between her desire to be a consistent mother and a feeling that she was sacrificing her career aspirations on the altar of domesticity. In college she majored in psychology, but she foreclosed her desire for graduate school when she started having children. As Chris's dental practice grew, Michelle took over the management and accounting roles. She didn't receive an official paycheck because, as Chris said, "The money all goes to the same place." The job provided life outside of children, which she enjoyed, but her ache for meaning persisted.

After years of putting her desires on hold, Michelle shared with Chris how much she wanted to go back to school to earn her master's in counseling. He pushed back, citing his large student loans, their young children who needed a mom, and the suggestion that counseling others might not be her thing.

That same year, Chris began an emotional and eventually sexual affair with a periodontist in a nearby city whom he met at a conference. Michelle discovered the affair after noticing recurring business credit card charges every Friday at a local restaurant. When she confronted him about the charges, Chris froze, then tried to deflect by claiming he ordered a cocktail as a weekly reward. He then flipped the situation, insisting that she stop trying to micromanage his expenses.

Suspicious, Michelle followed her instincts and drove to the restaurant two Fridays later, where she saw Chris having lunch with a woman she had never seen. She confronted Chris that night, and details of his six-month affair emerged. After a month of *staggered disclosure*—a process in which the injuring partner gradually reveals the full truth of their actions—she was devastated and pursued a counseling intensive with me for betrayal trauma.

## *Marriage Reveals Our Destructive Roles*

For Michelle, the affair was a painful clarion call, exposing unresolved issues that had been festering for years. As she surveyed her life—not just her marriage with Chris—she realized that she felt used in nearly every significant relationship. Her mother, who lived in town, consistently stopped by unannounced to drop off random treats and share her latest gossip. Her friends confided in her about their problems, but rarely took the time to ask about hers. As a mother she mostly adored her children, but their magnetic need to be linked to her body began to grate on her. And then there was her marriage: She felt Chris was using her for her business acumen rather than freeing her to pursue the life she truly wanted.

The affair devastated her, but clarity ripped through her soul like lightning. No longer would she allow her mom, her friends, or her husband to use her. She wanted to fundamentally alter how she existed in relationships.

On the third day of our intensive, Michelle came in and said, "I realized last night that I need a divorce, or at least a year of separation." While I understood this conviction, especially after her betrayal trauma, my sense was that there were several other dimensions she had bypassed to get to that conclusion. I asked her to share more.

"I am tired of spending all my time mothering, serving his practice, and letting my desires rot," she said. "We were only seventeen when we started dating. How can an adolescent make a lifelong decision like that? I didn't know what I was choosing. Leaving him might be the most empowering thing I can do."

I reflected to Michelle that I heard her desire for separation and divorce, but maybe not in the way she was conceptualizing it. Her urge to leave seemed less about Chris himself and more about escaping a role she'd taken on. While she might eventually choose to end her marriage, leaving him without separating from a provisional self that denied her own needs wouldn't solve her intimacy struggles. The deeper work would be to address why she so often suppressed her desires and overly accommodated the exploitive expectations of others.

Though agonizing, Michelle's marriage problems were doing exactly what marriage problems are designed to do: reveal the patterned and destructive ways two people have learned to make their life work.

Chris and Michelle were operating from different, but equally damaging, models of intimacy. Michelle's model was rooted in emotional fusion and codependency. She felt anxiety if Chris wasn't pleased with her and consistently sacrificed her own desires to support him. Inadvertently, this enabled him to avoid confronting the deeper implications of his choices as a husband and business owner. Though it looked like love, it was a dangerous counterfeit, a cycle that prevented both of them from growing.

Chris, on the other hand, had developed a model of intimacy that involved using Michelle to fulfill his desires and make his life easier. When Michelle sought more from him, he found escape hatches: denying her expressed desires in order to avoid disruption to his way of life and beginning an affair with someone who didn't have to live for years under the weight of his manipulation.

The cost of not engaging these negative dynamics is a growing risk of infidelity and divorce. In the Holistic Desire Survey, we examined the correlation between the ratio of support-to-negativity and the likelihood of extramarital affairs. We found that when men's relationships were marked by more negative interactions than positive experiences, they were 65 percent more likely to cheat. Similarly, the likelihood of infidelity increased by over 88 percent when the ratio of positive to negative interactions was low.[1]

Of course, infidelity is just one of the most obvious signs that a couple has stopped caring for one another. Many couples will stay married and sexually faithful long after their hearts have strayed far apart. Intimacy thrives when our desire for connection matches our willingness to confront the patterns that get in the way of it.

## *Three Marital Habits That Sabotage Intimacy*

Do you ever feel like there is some mysterious force that prevents you and your partner from experiencing consistent intimacy, even when you're both trying hard to connect? You're not alone. Many couples unwittingly sabotage their intimacy through three marital patterns that we will explore in this chapter. While it may seem more productive to focus on how to build intimacy instead of addressing its obstacles, my work with couples has taught me that we tend to long for deeper connection more than we're willing to address the ways we sabotage it.

In this way, we're a lot like someone who wants to get in better shape, commits to running three miles a day, but sabotages their progress by consuming a day's worth of calories in their recovery meal. They're doing many of the right things, but without addressing the patterns that derail their efforts and desires. Similarly, couples can try to build intimacy, but their progress stalls because they don't address underlying patterns of sabotage.

If I were to craft a recipe to ruin your relationship, it would include these three ingredients:

1. Emotional Immaturity
2. Dysfunctional Conflict
3. Escape Hatches

The chart below highlights why we choose these patterns and how we can begin shifting them. I'll offer a brief description here, and we'll spend time examining each of them in the chapter ahead.

| Unhealthy Pattern | Why We Employ It | How to Shift It |
|---|---|---|
| EMOTIONAL IMMATURITY<br>• Emotional Fusion<br>• Codependency<br>• Counter-dependency | Provides a surrogate feeling of closeness and/or separation. | Divorce yourself first from the pattern, not the person. |
| DYSFUNCTIONAL CONFLICT<br>• Contempt<br>• Avoidance | Helps us sidestep emotional difficulties like vulnerability, rejection, or anger. | Create a demilitarized zone for exploration and collaboration (more on this later). |
| ESCAPE HATCHES<br>• Sexual Disconnection<br>• Distractions | We are unable to tolerate pain or navigate complexity. | Confront and outgrow avoidance behaviors together. |

Though one of these saboteurs may resonate most deeply with you, most couples will encounter each of them at some point in their relationship. As you begin this work, recognize that your primary stance might be one of resistance. It takes considerable integrity to acknowledge and actively address the specific ways in which you undermine intimacy. By doing so, however, you clear the path for a lifetime of love.

**INTIMACY SABOTEUR 1:**

**EMOTIONAL IMMATURITY**

We're all familiar with emotional immaturity in its most obvious forms—like dramatic outbursts or blatant selfishness. But it can also be present when the relationship appears to be running smoothly or feels just slightly distant. In this section, we'll look at three common forms of emotional immaturity that sabotage intimacy: emotional fusion, codependency, and counter-dependency. While distinct, they all share the same core issue: a couple's inability to maintain a healthy balance between differentiation and belonging.

The challenge in identifying these patterns is that they often masquerade as healthy dynamics. Fusion can look like harmony, codependency can appear as mutual care, and counter-dependency can present as emotional strength. In reality, these dynamics are harmful imitations that undermine connection and hinder growth. Our desire should be to root them out, not stabilize them.

### Emotional Fusion

Emotional fusion occurs when two people's feelings and identities become so intertwined that they lose their sense of self. In this dynamic, partners struggle to differentiate their emotions, needs, or desires. The relationship's primary purpose becomes mutual reassurance—and when this is threatened, anxiety or conflict takes over. While it may feel comforting in the short term, emotional fusion creates a fragile foundation that can't support genuine intimacy because it is based on reassurance rather than anxiety tolerance.

### Codependency

Codependency takes emotional fusion a step further by conditioning one partner to sacrifice their needs and desires to care for or enable the other. Often, one partner will adopt a caretaker role—deprioritizing their well-being for the sake of the other. While this may look like sacrificial love, it's an immature pattern that undermines the emotional health of both partners. One partner settles into a familiar role of being the ongoing project or family liability—often due to substance abuse, financial recklessness, or chronic irresponsibility—while the other derives a sense of worth through rescuing, being needed, or staying in control. The relationship "works" because they are united in their abdication of emotional growth.

## Signs of Fusion and Codependency

Surrogate intimacy in enmeshed relationships will become most apparent when one partner chooses to grow—they resist being used as an emotional prop or express frustration at the patterns in the relationship. In these moments of rising tension, emotionally immature partners might feel that their "intimacy" is deteriorating. However, as we saw with Michelle and Chris, what's really happening is that the fragile, unsustainable foundation of their fused relationship is being exposed. When problems arise in these types of relationships, the critical question to ask is not, "Is our intimacy suffering?" but rather, "Is our emotional immaturity finally being unveiled?"

Here are some signs that you and your partner might be dealing with emotional fusion or codependency:

1. **LACK OF BOUNDARIES:** Do you feel responsible for your partner's emotions, often acting as their "fixer" rather than allowing them to face and solve their own problems?

2. **DIFFICULTY MAKING INDEPENDENT DECISIONS:** Do you frequently rely on your partner's approval for decisions, big or small, rather than trusting (or being allowed to trust) your own judgment?

3. **GUILT, BLAME, OR RESENTMENT WHEN APART:** Do you feel anxious, guilty, or resentful when your partner is away or spends time with others?

4. **LOSS OF INDIVIDUALITY:** Do you feel lost or adrift when not with your partner? Is it difficult to pursue your own activities without feeling guilty?

5. **ENABLING NEGATIVE BEHAVIOR:** Do you make excuses for your partner's destructive behaviors to keep the peace or strategize to prevent others from seeing their flaws?

### Counter-dependency

At the opposite end of the spectrum lies counter-dependency, an arrangement in which one or both partners have a strong aversion to

relying on others. They might insist on solving everything alone, shut down when their partner expresses a need, or be unable to ask for help, even if they genuinely need it. At first glance, this may appear as healthy independence, but it conceals a deeper struggle to connect without losing their sense of self.

Counter-dependent partners often view their emotional detachment as a sign of strength, especially when they are married to someone who seeks emotional enmeshment (a common pairing). What they fail to recognize is that their need for emotional distance actually exposes a weakness in their differentiation. Unable to stay grounded in themselves while in close proximity to their partner, they become triggered or frustrated when faced with bids for greater intimacy. They are often more comfortable being perceived as angry, distant, or aloof than facing the deep fear of being truly known.

This desire for rigid independence can stem from disillusionment with the demands of modern love, from feeling overwhelmed by life's pressures and reluctant to take on an additional emotional load, or from past experiences with a caregiver who dismissed their emotional needs. Regardless of the cause, these partners develop rigid, emotionally disengaged patterns in their relationship that leave the other emotionally starved. Marital conflict will inevitably arise; the emotionally malnourished partner voices a complaint, which the counter-dependent partner conveniently frames as neediness.

Here are some key signs of counter-dependency:

1. **RELUCTANCE TO CREATE INTIMACY:** Do you withdraw when emotional conversations arise? Are you uncomfortable with emotional closeness? Are you unwilling to bring vulnerable fears to your partner?

2. **STRONG NEED FOR EMOTIONAL SEPARATION:** Do you often prioritize personal interests or activities over spending time with your partner? Do you feel suffocated by emotional closeness or resentful of your partner's desires for connection?

3. **FEAR OF LOSING YOURSELF:** Do you resist relying on your partner, or do relational needs feel like impositions?

### Divorcing Ourselves from the Pattern,
### Not the Partner

Couples caught in emotional dysfunction often get stuck in a binary mindset: *Should I stay in a bad marriage or leave?* But a more constructive approach is to focus on divorcing yourself from the unhealthy patterns, not the person. I refer to this as lowercase "d" divorce, distinct from the uppercase "D" that involves the legal dissolution of the marriage.

This paradigm shift might seem counterintuitive, and valid objections are likely to arise. What about situations involving domestic violence, relentless gaslighting by a narcissist, or repeated betrayal trauma? In such cases, legal divorce may not only be prudent but essential for safety. No partner should ever be expected to endure an emotionally, physically, or sexually violent relationship. If you are in this type of marriage, work with a licensed professional or a trusted member in your community to come up with a plan to break free from the cycles of abuse.[2] This process is anything but easy. Tragically, it takes a half dozen attempts or more for most people to leave an abusive marriage.

However, if you're in an imperfect marriage, but one with a baseline level of safety, respect, and mutuality, it's worth investing time and effort to identify the patterns that you need to be divorced from. This shift is most effective when both partners collaborate to address dysfunction. But even if your partner isn't on board with therapy or personal growth, all is not lost. If one partner refuses to tolerate or look away from dysfunction in themselves or the relationship, the entire marriage system must adapt. The other partner is confronted with a choice: to grow or risk the loss of connection.

I've seen many marriages resuscitate after they appeared to be on their last breath. Initially, I thought the renewal was due to a miracle or my clinical expertise. But the better explanation is that both partners intuitively knew they had been colluding rather than collaborating in their relationship. One partner's unilateral commitment to change can serve as a wake-up call for the other, pushing them into a transformative space of growth. We'll explore this in greater detail later in this chapter.

INTIMACY SABOTEUR 2:
DYSFUNCTIONAL CONFLICT

Conflict often carries a stigma in relationships because it's seen as a sign of incompatibility. But let me be clear: Incompatibility is a natural part of relationships. As clinical psychologist and marriage therapist Dr. Dan Wile put it, "When choosing a long-term partner . . . you will inevitably be choosing a particular set of unsolvable problems."[3] This means we will never marry the "right" person. Instead, we *become* the right person through developing integrity within our conflict, learning how to manage it, and, eventually, committing to fight for one another, especially when it's difficult.

In every relationship, moments of tension trigger a predictable set of responses, creating a choreographed dance of conflict. Over time, each partner develops signature moves to navigate these dynamics, either confronting the problem head-on or avoiding it. In this section, we will examine three conflict moves and their role in eroding intimacy: *aggression, avoidance,* and *emotional neutrality.* If you're feeling emotionally distant or trapped in your relationship, these conflict styles may be part of the culprit.

### *Aggressive Conflict: Anger Gone Awry*

Anger itself is not inherently destructive; it is a natural and necessary emotion for all of us. Even within relationships, research shows that anger is not a predictor of negative outcomes, unless it can be classified as contempt or criticism. This has led researchers to the conclusion that anger is an *approach* emotion that couples use to connect and engage important themes in their relationship.[4] Anger, properly approached, is an act of love, a way of signaling, "I want to connect with you."

However, when anger shifts into criticism and contempt, it becomes a destructive move. Criticism occurs when we attack our partner's character rather than addressing the issue at hand. Instead of saying "I'm upset that you didn't call me," it becomes "You're so inconsiderate; you never think about anyone but yourself." Contempt goes a step further, turning criticism into a character assassination. It involves mocking, belittling, name-calling, and taking sadistic pleasure in adding to the other person's pain.

An aggressive conflict style eventually sets up cycles of hiding and blame. Hiding occurs when one partner withdraws or disengages, retreating into silence rather than addressing the issue. This leaves the other person feeling alone and unheard. Blame, on the other hand, becomes both a weapon of offense and a means of counterattack. It deflects responsibility and projects all the negativity and dysfunction of the relationship onto the other person.

### Normal Marital Sadism

If these patterns remain unaddressed, the desire to hurt one another intensifies. Dr. David Schnarch coined the term "Normal Marital Sadism" to describe couples who intentionally hurt one another through cruelty or emotional disengagement.

Most of my clients initially struggle to admit that they would choose to hurt someone they love. However, with deeper reflection, they recognize that their actions are not merely reactions to feeling wounded. Instead, they sometimes derive a sense of satisfaction from seeing their partner in pain or in feeling a sense of superiority that comes with having power over their partner.

Normal Marital Sadism can manifest in several ways in your marriage. Here are some common scenarios:

- You are mean to your partner but justify it as "helpful" or "candid" feedback.
- When your partner achieves something, you make a snide remark about how much time it took them to accomplish it.
- You emotionally withdraw from your partner to make them pay when they don't meet your expectations.

- You play mind games, like changing plans without inform-
  ing your partner, then accuse them of being overly sensitive
  when they react.

Many marital approaches focus heavily on developing a secure attachment and healing wounds. While these are undeniably important,
they often fail to challenge partners to address the worst in themselves.
When a spouse lies, emasculates their partner in front of friends, or
fails to collaborate, another discussion about childhood wounds or
building a secure attachment isn't likely to create the lasting change
needed.

If we want real transformation in our marriages, we need integrity
for the ways we manipulate, undermine, and avoid one another. It is
through taking responsibility for the worst in ourselves that we show
the best in ourselves to our partner. Only then can a deeper, more secure attachment grow.

### Conflict-Avoidant Couples

Conflict-Avoidant Couples trade true intimacy for an artifice of
peace, prioritizing comfort and stability over the transformative,
often messy work of navigating tension. These couples generally fall
into two styles: those I refer to as "Cozy Couples," who maintain
warmth and closeness by avoiding confrontation; and those researchers identify as having a "Neutral Affective Style," where their emotional involvement diminishes over time, leading to a quieter, more
detached relationship. While these couples successfully avoid conflict, they forfeit the connection that comes from working through
discomfort effectively.

On one end of the avoidant spectrum are Cozy Couples. These
partners focus on creating an atmosphere of intimacy through shared
routines—quiet moments together, watching their favorite shows, or
engaging in familiar activities like going out to dinner or walking
around the neighborhood. Getting along becomes one of their highest
values, and they become experts at avoiding land mines that could
disrupt their equilibrium.

Cozy Couples expect intimacy to be like butter—smooth, easy, and effortless. But real intimacy is more like sandpaper—it requires both partners to stay in the tension, not to hurt one another, but to refine each other. It's through the friction of respectful conflict that our desire for intimacy is built. The real question for these couples is: Do we want a relationship that glides along, comfortable but shallow, or one that challenges us to desire something deeper, one that could alter the trajectory of both of our lives?

On the other end of the spectrum are couples who have what psychologists refer to as a Neutral Affective Style. In these relationships, couples make the unspoken agreement to avoid not only conflict but connection as well. From the outside, the couple may seem stable or independent, but a closer look reveals a retreat from the more vulnerable dimensions of being deeply seen, heard, or enjoyed.

Emotional detachment can be just as damaging as active conflict in the long run, because it removes the valuable opportunities that conflict provides for us to learn how to collaborate and solidify what matters. Research shows that contempt-based marriages are the number one predictor of divorce in the first six years of a relationship. But in long-term marriages, the Neutral Affective Style takes over as the best predictor.[5]

Whether it's the warm avoidance of conflict in Cozy Couples or the cold detachment found in a Neutral Affective Style, both dynamics deprive partners of authentic intimacy. These patterns inevitably set the stage for a crisis or provocation. (For example, one partner might disrupt the stagnant status quo with a reckless decision, such as a financial gamble or an affair.) While the fallout of these actions requires engagement, it often becomes the Kafkaesque axe that breaks the frozen sea of their marriage, forcing them to confront reality.

For Conflict-Avoidant Couples seeking to avoid crisis, alternatives do exist. Intimacy grows in proportion to our dissatisfaction and our bold acknowledgment—both to ourselves and our partner—that we want more. While it would be ideal if both partners desired this change equally, even one partner's unilateral decision to introduce consistent, respectful honesty can trigger the conversations and conflicts necessary for transformation. Beneath the surface of marital frustration lies a deeper wish for intimacy.

### The Outcome of Dysfunctional
### Conflict Styles: DMZs

Regardless of which dysfunctional pattern a couple falls into, they often will end up creating what psychologist Dr. Dan Allender has referred to as a "marital demilitarized zone (DMZ)"—areas of conflict that partners avoid at all costs.[6] In geopolitics, a demilitarized area is a location that serves as a buffer between two or more military powers or alliances—the most famous being the strip of land between North and South Korea. Although DMZs remain free of active conflict, both sides know they hide miles of resentment and fear.

Marriages operate in a similar way. The couple establishes a DMZ, where conflict is suppressed, but contempt and fear simmer beneath the surface. One couple might agree to have sex once a week or month just to avoid the vitriol around sexual frequency. Another couple might look away from each other's consumption habits—maybe one partner drinks too much while the other loves their Netflix, and they both agree not to poke their respective bears. Or one partner is enmeshed with their family of origin or adult children, but that provides cover for the other partner to devote unlimited hours to their career. The unspoken motto for couples entrenched in a DMZ becomes: "I won't bother you, and you don't bother me."

On the surface, a marital DMZ may appear civil, even peaceful. But make no mistake: It buffers miles of unprocessed tension that could quickly escalate into a costly war. The key question to ask of your marriage, especially if it leans toward passivity or avoidance, is: Is my marriage thriving, or is our DMZ just functioning well?

### Shifting from DMZs of Avoidance
### to DMZs of Exploration

DMZs aren't just buffers for conflict; they can also be spaces for exploration and discovery. Think of Antarctica or outer space. They are both remote, inhospitable places that become frontiers for discovery. In the same way, couples can transform their conflict zones into areas of deeper connection and understanding.

One couple I worked with learned to use their sexual difficulties as a space for exploring their individual sexual narratives. For years, they blamed each other for their sexual disconnect, but after a major fight, they experienced a moment of mutual recognition: They both dreaded sex. This wasn't so much a breakthrough of maturity as it was a shared exhaustion from their constant cycle of blame and frustration. In response, they made a pact to take thirty days off from criticizing each other's sexual energy. Instead, they would focus on learning the backstories that shaped their understanding of their bodies and sexual intimacy.

Establishing this DMZ allowed one partner to uncover that he had always felt intense pressure and scrutiny around his body: His father insisted he play piano, his piano teacher pushed him to become an advanced pianist, and his conservatory of music demanded excellence. Sex, like piano, had become a place of pressure and performance. Meanwhile, his partner grew up in an emotionally distant home. In high school, her first sexual experience ignited a deep desire for connection and pleasure. From that moment on, she placed immense pressure on her partners to make her feel both desirable and alive.

These collective revelations allowed the couple to see how their individual histories had shaped their sexual challenges. One partner confronted how he tended to withdraw under stress, while the other recognized that she needed sexual validation when she felt anxious of being alone. With this newfound awareness, they began to rewrite their sexual narrative together—acknowledging how the confluence of their respective patterns was compounding the pain they faced.

DMZs of exploration show couples how their individual histories set them up for problems in marital intimacy. Instead of avoiding or becoming aggressive with one another, couples can ask themselves two questions:

1. What is this problem teaching me about my story?
2. How is this problem helping me better understand and care for my partner's story?

Answering these questions can help your relationship uncover the deeper meaning of recurring conflicts and outgrow unhealthy dynamics. The goal of conflict is not to win or prove a point, but to produce a desire to learn what truly matters to one another. Ultimately, conflict resolves when it draws us into deeper attunement with the stories that lie beneath the surface, inviting us to see and love one another more fully.

Though a part of us longs to be loved, we've also learned that this isn't always the case. Aggression, avoidance, and neutrality often feel easier than—and, in many cases, preferred over—the desire to be kind, generous, and curious with one another. To reflect further on your conflict dynamics and learn how to shift to a loving approach, turn to the corresponding chapter in the *Desire Workbook* for more guidance.

## INTIMACY SABOTEUR 3:
## THE ESCAPE HATCH

When faced with intimacy challenges and persistent difficulties with our spouse, we tend to revert to the escape mechanisms we developed earlier in life. On a purely physical level, relational tension burns tremendous calories, which is why marriages so often flow to the path of least resistance and easiest reward.

While it's easy to bemoan the typical distractions from intimacy (work, social media, parenting, screens, compulsive behaviors, an overcommitment to extended family), we need to recognize that these escape hatches, despite their negative consequences, can also serve a purpose in the relationship. What would you and your partner be forced to confront if there weren't all those hours sacrificed to screens, extended family, and work?

At its core, every escape hatch is a form of dissociation—a process where we intentionally or unintentionally separate from unpleasant feelings or dynamics. These behaviors may seem harmless or even comforting at first, but over time, they rot the foundation needed to sustain a healthy marriage. In this section, we'll explore two common escape hatches that couples use to avoid intimacy: sexual escape and compulsive behaviors, such as substance use and excessive screen time.

### The Sexual Escape Hatch

Sex plays a vital role in marital intimacy. It's a space for couples to experience love, desire, vulnerability, and erotic passion. However, it's also one of the most common and powerful areas where relational distress can manifest. Approximately one in three marriages experience infidelity,[7] the majority of men (and an increasing number of women) use pornography,[8] and at least 15 percent of couples report having not had any sex for over a year.[9]

Here's what the Holistic Desire Survey found about extramarital sexual behavior:

- Twenty-eight percent of men reported a desire for sex outside their marriage, nearly twice the rate of women.
- Men were 1.7 times more likely to have an extramarital affair when they experienced their relationship as negative. Similarly, women were 2.1 times more likely to pursue an extramarital affair under comparable negative relationship conditions.
- A woman's sexual satisfaction was more influenced by the ratio of positive to negative experiences she had with her partner.[10]
- A man's sexual satisfaction was more closely linked to his overall anxiety levels than to his relationship rating (which ranked second in the results). The higher a man's anxiety, the lower his sexual satisfaction.

These statistics underscore a crucial point: When emotional connection to our partner and to ourselves erodes, our desire for infidelity and sexual escape rises. Yet when women feel emotionally supported and connected to their partners, and when men manage anxiety effectively, sexual satisfaction improves and the drive toward extramarital sex decreases.

### The Rise of Non-Monogamy

While cheating has existed as long as marriage itself, there is a growing trend toward open and non-monogamous relationships. According to a 2021 YouGov poll, a quarter of Americans are now open to trying these alternative relationship structures.[11] Furthermore, Pew Research shows that one-third of Americans now believe open marriages are somewhat or completely acceptable.[12] This shift raises an important question: Is non-monogamy increasing our potential for healthy intimacy, or is it creating yet another escape from the inherent challenges of traditional relationships?

Let's examine what research shows is driving this growing desire for non-monogamy. A 2021 study found six key motivations:[13]

1. AUTONOMY: the desire to make one's own sexual decisions.
2. BELIEF AND VALUE SYSTEMS: the belief that monogamy is an artificial construct that can also cause harm.
3. RELATIONALITY: using polyamory as a healthy way to have more experiences of belonging.
4. SEXUALITY: exploring one's sexual needs and sexual identities.
5. GROWTH AND EXPANSION: widening one's personal experiences.
6. PRAGMATISM: when one's primary partner is long distance or can't offer the connection they are looking for.

While these motivations vary, they reveal two core themes we've been exploring: a desire for greater authenticity and a search for deeper connection. For some, non-monogamy offers a powerful context in which to express their desires more authentically or feel a deeper sense of connection than they have in monogamous relationships.

### Jess's Story: The Complexities of Non-Monogamy

Jess's story is a window into the challenges and complexities of non-monogamy. After six years in a monogamous marriage, she had an interaction with a captivating man at a New Year's Eve party in Manhattan that left her feeling energized in a way she hadn't felt in years. While it stirred feelings of guilt, Jess spoke honestly with her husband the next day about the connection she'd felt. To her surprise, he responded with understanding. This led to a longer discussion in which he suggested opening their marriage. Neither of them wanted a divorce, but they both craved something more than what their relationship had become. It was one of the most powerful conversations she had ever had with him.

Within six months, Jess had started a relationship with the man from the party, while her husband began seeing a former colleague. They continued finding additional partners over the next decade. At first, Jess was exhilarated by the highs of non-monogamy, likening each new relationship to the rush of a mighty waterfall. But she also found herself experiencing levels of ambivalence, jealousy, and emotional turbulence she hadn't anticipated.

Reflecting on her journey—six years in a monogamous marriage and eleven in a non-monogamous one—Jess said, "We solved one problem, but created seven more. It was an exciting time, and I learned a lot about what I wanted sexually and relationally. But I wasn't prepared for the drama and emotional demands of those additional relationships. They distracted my husband and me from addressing the real issues in our marriage and robbed me of meaningful time with my kids during their formative years. Looking back, I wished I had asked more of my marriage, but at the time, I guess I didn't believe my marriage could meet my deeper longings."

By the time of this writing, Jess and her husband had decided to stop pursuing non-monogamy. Although they acknowledged the vitality it initially brought to their relationship, they realized it was sidestepping the issues that needed attention. The more they faced the crucible of marriage, the more their appreciation grew for one another. They came to understand that the relationship they were searching for wasn't "out there"—it was in the work they had been avoiding together.

Opening a relationship does not transform the underlying issues a couple is facing. In many cases, it may exacerbate them. Sex therapists generally advise that opening a marriage should only be considered when a couple already has a strong foundation of intimacy and trust.

An important relational principle to consider in this conversation is: Whatever we resist will persist. If we avoid pursuing the personal and relational growth necessary for building intimacy in a monogamous relationship, those unresolved issues will inevitably persist in new romantic and sexual connections.

### *The Transformative Possibilities Within Monogamy*

The rise of non-monogamy should serve as a wake-up call for those who champion traditional marriage. It highlights long-standing critiques—rigid gender roles, male-centered sex, the significant orgasm gap between men and women, and power imbalances—that have pushed many to question or even reject the traditional model. If we're not honest about the shadow side of traditional marriages, we fail to allow it to reach its true potential. Non-monogamy isn't eroding traditional marriage nearly as much as our collective refusal to address the intimacy and power gaps that contribute to its decline.

That said, I believe the crucible of a monogamous marriage offers just as much excitement, tension, risk, and potential for dismantling harmful gender norms as any non-monogamous relationship. The increasing interest in non-monogamy may, in part, reflect a diminished imagination about the transformative potential within monogamy itself—along with the financial privilege that enables non-monogamous arrangements, including maintaining separate households and managing the added costs of multiple partners. It's often only when we have the courage to say no to all other exits, suitors, and unhealthy patterns that the real work of intimacy-building begins. Through this integrity, we find ourselves waking up to new partners—not because our names or Social Security numbers have changed, but because the marriage is pushing each partner to become someone different from who they were when they began.

Every type of relationship faces its challenges: How do we balance erotic passion with domestic stability? How do we cultivate personal growth alongside relational intimacy? How do we find adventure while staying anchored in companionship? These paradoxes are inherent in romantic love. The key isn't to escape these dilemmas, but to hold the tension. The obstacles we overcome today lay the foundation for deeper, more resilient connections tomorrow.

### The Distraction Escape Hatch

Our world has no shortage of escape hatches. It's all too easy to lose ourselves in distractions like alcohol, digital screens, or other habits that promise temporary relief from the challenges of life. While these activities may seem harmless, or at least personal, they quickly become relational issues. My phone can track how many hours I personally spend scrolling, but it can't calculate how many hours of intimacy I've denied my partner by choosing distractions instead.

Consider these concerning statistics:

- Worldwide, the average person spends 6 hours and 38 minutes looking at a screen each day,[14] and as much as 9 hours per day for American children between ages eleven and fourteen.[15]
- The average American watches 3.1 hours of television daily.
- Men once outnumbered women 3 to 1 in drinking and binge drinking. Today those numbers are approaching parity.[16] Substance abuse is also a key driver of divorce.
- More than 2 in 5 adults have obesity (42.4 percent).[17] This often leads to greater self-contempt, and when we loathe ourselves, intimacy will always suffer.

These statistics reveal a troubling trend: We're becoming more intimate with our screens and other coping mechanisms than with our partners. As our attachment to quick and easy gratification grows, our capacity and desire to engage in the slow, meaningful work of real intimacy diminishes.

One of the best ways to outgrow distractions is to collaborate with one another. One couple I worked with felt paralyzed by their financial situation, claiming it was the primary saboteur of their intimacy. Early in their relationship, they tried various choreographed dances, from aggression—sharp remarks like "We're drowning in debt, and you're buying new clothes *again?*"—to avoidance, where they simply ignored finances: no investment plans, no budget, and an overreliance on credit. These patterns only amplified their distress.

Instead of letting money continue to divide them, they decided to allow finances to become a DMZ of exploration. They partnered like never before, committing to regular meetings with a financial advisor, creating a family budget, and educating themselves on effective debt-repayment strategies. Each month, they set aside time for a date night at their favorite brewery, where they celebrated their progress and shared new insights. Over time, they eliminated their debt, allowing them to purchase an Airbnb property for extra income.

This couple's story offers hope to us all: Through intentional effort, couples can transform intimacy barriers into intimacy builders.

### The Distraction, Not Your Partner, Is the Enemy

Each one of us has our own set of habits that distract us from intimacy. That's why it can feel futile to point out our partner's compulsive use of social media, only for them to counter with criticism about our on-line shopping habits. Blaming each other or moralizing about who has the worse distraction leads nowhere. Instead, both partners can take the higher road by acknowledging their own areas for growth. When we confront our individual patterns, we create the space necessary to work together in overcoming these proclivities.

To break free from distractions that inhibit intimacy, couples can identify specific areas to work on individually and together. Some possibilities include:

- *Improving physical health:* Commit to making healthy meals or doing regular workouts together.
- *Managing finances:* Work together to pay off debt, create a budget, and set financial goals.
- *Pursuing a creative project or shared goal:* Whether it's home improvement, community service, or planning a trip, a joint project fosters teamwork.

- *Increasing self-care:* Ask your partner if they have the time they need to feel rested and connected to themselves. Then establish regular rituals to ensure that happens.
- *Supporting personal growth:* Share your individual goals, learn the backstories that inform those desires, and establish systems to accomplish them.
- *Intentionally doing something that's outside the norm for your relationship:* Surprise your partner with a spontaneous weekend away, or ask them if there's a new activity they've been wanting to try.

Once you've identified one or two areas for marital or individual growth, create a system to achieve your goals and set regular check-ins, like monthly meetings, to assess progress and address roadblocks. Holding each other accountable in the process of outgrowing old patterns is an overlooked but immensely valuable way to deepen intimacy.

### Responding to the Call, Tolerating Tension, and Avoiding Sabotage: A Marriage Case Study

Now that we've explored the saboteurs of intimacy, let's look at how these dynamics unfolded once Chris and Michelle sought help for their marriage. After completing my intensive, Michelle asked if I would be willing to work with her and Chris in a couples intensive.

In the initial hours of our session, Chris was visibly remorseful for the heartache he'd caused. He demonstrated a deep understanding and responsiveness to Michelle's anger over his affair. Research shows that the ability of the injuring partner to tolerate and respond to the betrayed partner's anger and pain is crucial to the forgiveness process.[18] Chris's acknowledgment of his escape hatch and the pain it caused was a promising start to our work.

However, as the session progressed, it became clear that Chris was addressing only the surface-level form of betrayal, the affair itself. He was committed to avoiding a legal divorce, but he showed little interest in divorcing himself from the underlying patterns that led to the affair—specifically, his tendency to manipulate Michelle into emotionally fusing with him, and then resorting to aggression and sexual betrayal when she didn't comply. Chris wanted things to go "back to normal," a normal where he called the shots and Michelle was more involved in managing his business.

One of the most important questions after infidelity is: *What meaning are we making out of the affair?* Too often, couples oversimplify their explanations. The betrayed partner might conclude that their spouse is simply a "cheater" or, worse, internalize feelings of inadequacy, believing that it happened because they just weren't good enough. The offending partner might justify their affair as a result of the lack of passion or excitement in their marriage or the longing to be desired by someone. While these explanations may contain partial truths, they don't go deep enough. (See this section of the *Desire Workbook* for Betrayal Trauma exercises.)

As we explored Chris's story, a crucial piece of his past emerged that helped explain both his affair and his manipulative behavior. His father had owned a landscaping business, and he hoped that Chris would one day take over. But Chris had different aspirations. He wanted to become a doctor or dentist. When he shared these desires with his dad, he was met with the same disdain he experienced when he told him he didn't want to play high school football. His dad mocked him and told him he didn't have the discipline needed to complete a rigorous program.

Chris described this as his "Robert Frost 'The Road Not Taken' moment." Two roads diverged in the woods of his life, and he chose the path to becoming a dentist, even if it meant possible failure, rather than staying in his father's world. But when it came to his marriage, he seemed stuck in the pattern of following his father's playbook and blocking his wife's desire to travel the road not taken in her own life.

When I brought this up, Chris became defensive. He explained that the overwhelming student loans from medical school had made supporting Michelle's career nearly impossible. I responded, "Do you remember how it felt to have your dad pressure you to stay in a field you didn't want, insinuating you'd never make it as a dentist?" He nodded, and I continued, "In your marriage, you're following his playbook. You planted seeds of doubt about Michelle's potential as a counselor, and you've used her skills to build your own practice. To date, she hasn't received a paycheck from you."

Like many people I counsel, Chris could have stopped having affairs while never confronting his habit of conditioning his partner to want and expect less. Long before the affair, he had become to Michelle what his father had become to him—a figure of control and manipulation. To increase intimacy in his marriage, he needed to divorce himself from the pattern of using his wife to make his life easier.

Chris had been operating under a common misconception: that intimacy was about being on the same page with his spouse, about Michelle aligning with his goals and desires. Michelle, on the other hand, had always viewed intimacy as self-sacrifice, a belief that led her to suppress her desires in favor of her husband's. The two of them had created a marital DMZ: When both partners operated out of these underdeveloped modes of intimacy, their marriage went smoothly. But when Michelle started pushing back against these expectations, tension increased.

Though challenging, Michelle began to realize that she couldn't build intimacy with someone and remain disconnected from her own desires. This shift also changed her perspective on the struggles in her marriage: One of the reasons this season of life was so difficult was that it was pushing her to own her desires with greater integrity, a choice she had never been able or invited to make before.

### The Role of Marital Integrity

Michelle crafted a thoughtful and playful plan to engage Chris. She sent him an email announcing her resignation from her unpaid internship, offering to stay on for a few hours a week to help with the transition. She also shared her excitement about pursuing freelance writing opportunities with their city's local paper and a regional magazine. In her email, Michelle expressed how much his support would mean to her.

Although Michelle was unsure how Chris would respond, she felt a deep sense of relief in finally voicing her desires and not being trapped in emotional fusion, a toxic mimic of intimacy. This was a huge step in reclaiming her sense of self and setting the stage for greater intimacy with others.

Unfortunately, Chris's response was not what Michelle had hoped for. He became more stressed, griping about the money they were spending on babysitters. Like many manipulative partners, he'd learned that showing distress was one of the best ways to induce his partner to foreclose her desires.

As Michelle's differentiation and authenticity grew, so did Chris's desperation. He brooded, accusing her of disrupting the family with her "little writing dreams." In the past, Michelle would have backed down in the face of his intimidation, but this time she chose to work through her anxiety and stand firm. She asked for his collaboration in solving *their* problem, telling him that her dreams were no less important than his. "I loved how you pursued your longings in the face of your dad's disdain," she told him, "and I'm asking you to extend the same respect to me."

This conversation was a pivotal moment in Michelle's journey— a courageous act of marital integrity. She invited Chris to join her in rewriting the script of their relationship. For Michelle, this meant developing a deeper sense of desire and selfhood, while encouraging Chris to confront how his unresolved issues with his father were shaping his behavior.

In the end, Chris refused to respond to the clarion call. His drinking intensified and he became more threatening toward Michelle and their children. Despite Michelle's repeated requests for him to confront these patterns, he remained steadfast in his unwillingness to change.

Michelle made the painful decision to pursue a legal divorce. But this time, the decision was not driven by the same fears and insecurities that had kept her trapped in her marriage for so long. Although her marriage ended, a result that some might interpret as an "intimacy fail," her commitment to authenticity and genuine connection was laying the groundwork for healthier relationships in the future.

## Conclusion

Emotional immaturity, dysfunctional conflict, and escape hatches are all powerful saboteurs of intimacy. Although most of us claim to want more closeness and connection in our lives, we underestimate the depth of work necessary to truly experience it. Marriage exposes the limitations of our current models of intimacy and consistently pushes both partners to grow into the best, most compassionate, and empowered versions of themselves. It's through learning to tolerate discomfort and friction that true intimacy can deepen and flourish.

Michelle's journey exemplifies this painful yet transformative process. She chose to excavate her past, embrace the crucible of personal growth, and respond to the clarion call in her marriage. Even though it ended in divorce, her marriage did what marriages are designed to do: reveal the imitation forms of intimacy that both partners operate under. This process opened the door to a new vision of intimacy for her. Instead of "use and be used," it became "know and be known."

If we've done the work to dismantle the barriers to intimacy and committed ourselves to the journey of differentiation, the path will begin to clear for us to build the marriage we desire. While this work has been challenging, our commitment to approaching it with kindness and integrity enables us to expect more in our marriage than we ever thought possible. When we are no longer driven by fear or hindered by immaturity, we become far freer to give and receive one of life's greatest, but most misunderstood, gifts: love. As the next chapter will reveal, love isn't something we stumble into; it's something we build.

CHAPTER 10

# How Can I Learn to Love
# and Be Loved?

*The act of loving itself becomes a
path of humble apprenticeship.*

—DAVID WHYTE

### Brad and Samantha

Six years into their marriage, Brad and Samantha hit gridlock. Brad
had struggled with porn off and on, but it wasn't until he got married
that it became a persistent issue. When he made bids for sex at night,
Samantha would unleash all the ways he wasn't coming through for
her. "How can you want sex when you don't even ask me about my
day? You leave all your dirty clothes on the floor and never empty
the dishwasher, and then you want me to want you? You are like a
toddler with a sex drive." Emasculated, Brad would retreat to the
couch feeling powerless. Unable to self-regulate or sleep, he'd watch
porn.

Brad believed that if Samantha really loved him, she would prioritize sex. Samantha believed that if Brad truly loved her, he would
be more helpful around the house. They both claimed to want more
love from one another, but neither had any idea of how to give or
receive it in a meaningful way. They each tied love to the fulfillment
of expectations. This narrow, transactional view of love kept them
stuck, unable to see how it was sabotaging the potential for greater
intimacy.

## UNMET NEEDS AND HIDDEN HURTS

Samantha had once desired Brad deeply. Over time, however, she began to view his carefree spirit as selfish, even piggish. When she learned Brad was watching porn, she asked him to stop, but he didn't. She couldn't believe she was married to someone who would do that. But beneath her devaluing of Brad was a deeper hurt: She felt unseen. No one—least of all Brad—seemed to care about her needs. For his part, Brad, too, felt unchosen and unacceptable. He had been bullied in seventh grade and still carried deep insecurities about his body and intellect.

Both Brad and Samantha wanted love to mend their wounds. Instead, their relationship was working to deepen them. Samantha's life experiences had convinced her that no one would ever care about her. Brad wasn't as driven as her father, which she hoped would offer her more potential for connection, but what she wasn't able or willing to see was that he was just as focused on himself as her father had been. Brad's story, meanwhile, had convinced him that he would never be good enough. Samantha initially offered him the hope that someone beautiful and competent would choose him. But now he shared a bed with someone who daily reminded him of his inadequacies. Their marriage had devolved into a competition over who was overlooked the most.

They sought out therapy with me as a last resort, wondering if their marriage had any shot before they pursued divorce. In the middle of our first session, their contempt for one another intensified and Brad moved into the Red Zone. "I'm done with this marriage. I can't do this anymore." This (as predicted) set up Samantha to say, "*You're* done? I've been married to someone who has never loved me!"

These moments of exasperation can be a critical turning point for couples. As we learned in the previous chapter, every couple must learn how to divorce themselves from their patterned way of relating to one another before intimacy can grow. The central question Samantha and Brad needed to answer was not who felt the most overlooked, but whether they were willing to learn how to love one another, even when their relationship seemed beyond repair.

When you think about love, what comes to mind? Many couples equate love with feeling supported, getting along, or having warm, affectionate feelings. When marriage leads them through valleys of loneliness or sorrow, they become disillusioned with their relationship, thinking it's a sign that they've fallen out of love, or never were compatible in the first place. Like Brad and Samantha, many of us think of love as something fixed—a quality we either have or don't. In reality, love is a skill that must be learned and put into practice.

## *Three Intimacy Skills Needed for a Lifetime of Love*

As we look around, it might seem that some people are simply better at love. Maybe they have a genetic predisposition for affection, or a personality trait that makes connection easier. They effortlessly remember the little details that make others feel deeply known and radiate a compassionate warmth that makes people feel valued. While it's true that some of these individuals may have grown up with more secure attachments or faced immense challenges that necessitated their growth in love, this doesn't mean that the rest of us are doomed to struggle. Love is a skill and, therefore, we can grow and catch up.

Knowing how to give and receive love are two of the most fundamental abilities that we need in order to thrive. Yet, these essential skills are rarely taught. Our education system prepares us to solve math problems, write essays, and punctuate sentences, but it does little to teach us how to truly know and be known by another person—skills that could transform our marriages and even our society. We end up leaving our development in love to chance, assuming we'll figure it out as we go. And then when relationships stall or fail, we call it fate.

It doesn't have to be that way. We can turn our marriages into training grounds for learning how to love. In this chapter I'll introduce you to three key skills that will help you increase your capacity for love. While each skill is powerful on its own, their real impact comes when they're combined into a tool kit for lasting intimacy. We will start with foundational skills to lay the emotional groundwork for your relationship, and gradually move toward deeper levels of trust and intimacy.

## SKILL 1:
## EMOTIONAL REGULATION

Marriage brings us face-to-face with another person's deepest desires and greatest fears. We enter the relationship with hearts full of longing, but we are rarely prepared for the emotional turbulence that follows when those desires are unmet. In the ongoing tension of marriage, some people suppress their hope for love as a way of avoiding the sting of disappointment; others lash out in anger when needs go unmet; and some simply give up, allowing themselves to be physically present but emotionally absent.

But what if we could hold on to our hope for love through the difficult moments we experience together? What if, instead of allowing tension to fracture us, we could learn to regulate our emotions, repair the ruptures, and grow stronger together? If we want a good marriage, full of hope and trust, it will depend on our ability to develop emotional regulation.

### *Expanding Your Marital Window of Tolerance*

Building on what we learned in Part Two, every couple has what I refer to as a Marital Window of Tolerance (MWT). In moments of stress or conflict, couples naturally fluctuate between emotional zones—Green (well-regulated), Red (high stress and fight/flight), and Blue (emotional withdrawal and freeze).

Some couples hover in the Red Zone during tension, characterized by intense arguments and emotional drama. Others hover in the Blue Zone, marked by emotional withdrawal and disengagement, an emotional environment that could be summed up as "Let's be depressed together." Some couples shift between the two, where one partner becomes flooded with anxiety or anger (Red) and the other descends into the abyss of despair (Blue).

Reflect on your own relationship: Do you and your partner tend to default to one of these zones, or perhaps a mix of two? Either way, your dynamic is likely shaped by your past experiences. Think back to how your mom or dad responded under stress. What would cause them to shift into the Red or Blue zones? For example, maybe your dad had a narrow window of tolerance and could only remain in the Green Zone when he was watching TV or when family life was easy. When something more was required of him, he would become angry and fly into the Red Zone. In response, your mother and the rest of the family might have felt humiliated and retreated into the Blue Zone of despair. In your own marriage, which of your parents' traits are you most likely to mirror?

The emotional patterns of our childhood homes tend to shape how we react in the pressures of our own marriages today. Let's explore three different ways couples struggle with emotional regulation.

### Couple 1. Stuck in the Red Zone

Sam and Peyton both gravitate to the Red Zone when tensions arise. Sam's high-pressure career in commercial real estate leaves him emotionally dysregulated. When he comes home, he has rigid expectations around how the apartment needs to look and how much sex they should be having. Peyton hates Sam's entitlement. She yells at him for his attempts at control, and Sam becomes defensive, insisting he's under pressure and needs support. This often escalates into a shouting match where they both feel angry and overlooked. Even when the emotional storm passes, they remain one comment away from another eruption.

### Couple 2. Stuck in the Blue Zone

Connor was once full of passion, but a college heartbreak left him emotionally numb. Mei, raised in an immigrant family, focuses on hard work but has never been invited to explore her deeper needs and desires. When Connor expresses a desire for more, like wanting to travel or start a family, Mei dismisses it as selfish and indulgent, a violation of her environmental values. Under tension, they both become emotionally distant, sinking further into silence and isolation.

### Couple 3. One in the Red, One in the Blue

Terrance and Liv have opposite emotional responses. Liv, quick to anger, pushes Terrance for more involvement at home. She wonders how a man can be so competent in his career and so irresponsible at home. Terrance responds by withdrawing emotionally, spending time with the kids or leaving the house to go for a jog. This infuriates Liv at first, but if he withdraws for too long, she will switch to the Blue Zone and spend hours in front of the TV, drinking wine and disconnecting from the family. Terrance will then become anxious and overwhelmed (Red Zone) and try to counter this by taking on more tasks to bring Liv back from the brink of despair.

#### *Connor and Mei's Expansion*

To move beyond these emotional stalemates, couples must first identify their Marital Window of Tolerance and then intentionally work to expand it. This requires becoming more emotionally aware and learning the skills of self-regulation and co-regulation.

In therapy, Connor and Mei discovered that they both defaulted to the Blue Zone under pressure. But awareness alone was not enough. For the dynamic to shift, one partner must often take the first step toward emotional expansion. In this case, Connor, tired of folding under Mei's criticism, committed to staying connected to his desire for children, even when Mei dismissed it. Rather than retreating into the Blue Zone, he held on to his longings and learned to tolerate her disapproval.

When Connor showed no sign of folding under pressure, Mei had to confront why his desire made her so dysregulated. She realized that her resistance wasn't only about protecting the planet; it was also a way to avoid addressing her deeper fears of raising a child—fears tied to unresolved trauma from her childhood as an immigrant. Growing up, her parents were under significant financial strain, forcing them to work long hours. At school, Mei felt a deep sense of alienation and endured racist comments about her eyes. She learned to survive and support her family by being a smart, resilient, and financially independent daughter. But the thought of having a child triggered a wave of Red Zone panic. Would she be able to protect her own child from the same pain and demands she had faced?

As Connor grew more emotionally resilient, he was able to empathize with Mei's fears, offering her the space to process them. He was surprised by his ability to hold on to his desire for children while also connecting to Mei's anxieties. Mei, in turn, experienced a similar shift—she longed for Connor to experience fatherhood, yet she could also be hospitable to the panic within herself. For both of them, expanding their Marital Window of Tolerance didn't just help them work through a big decision or avoid simmering conflict; it allowed them to connect in a way they'd never done before.

### Practical Ways to Improve Emotional Regulation

Staying in the Red Zone during an argument is like running a car without oil—it will overheat and eventually break down. When you feel your emotions spiking or plummeting in a conflict situation, it's essential to take a brief step back to ground your body before continuing the conversation. Taking just one to five minutes to calm your body and mind can make a significant difference. Here are some effective self-regulation techniques:

- *Breathing exercise:* Slow, deep breathing helps activate the parasympathetic nervous system, which calms the body's stress response. Try the 4-7-8 technique. Inhale for 4 seconds, hold for 7 seconds, and then exhale for 8 seconds to slow your heart rate.
- *Physical movement:* A short walk, stretching, or gently shaking out your arms and legs can help release tension and shift your nervous system toward a more regulated state.
- *Smell, taste, and feel:* Seek out something fragrant to smell, like lavender, peppermint, or citrus. Drink a soothing beverage or

take in some protein to feel more grounded. Wash your face and apply something soothing like rose water or oil.

While autoregulation is about taking responsibility to manage your own emotion, co-regulation is about calming your emotional state in tandem with your partner. Rather than letting conflict escalate, co-regulation involves creating a safe space for both partners to de-escalate and connect. Here are some of the best techniques for co-regulation:

- *Physical touch:* Touch releases oxytocin, the "bonding hormone," which can reduce stress and increase feelings of safety when practiced with care. Hugging until relaxed, experiencing skin-to-skin contact from holding hands, or resting a hand on your partner's arm can return you both to a calm and connected state.
- *Take a break together:* Go for a walk, play a game, listen to dance music or your favorite comedian. After twenty minutes or so, you will be in a much better self-state to resume the conversation.
- *Mutual kindness:* Begin the conversation with a shared commitment to kindness, acknowledging your desire to be *for* one another rather than against each other. Phrases like "I want to understand you" or "I'm here to work through this together" set a collaborative tone.

Emotional regulation is not just a tool for avoiding conflict; it's a fundamental skill for deepening intimacy. Couples who understand their emotional patterns and know how to regulate their distress are more likely to experience greater emotional health and relational satisfaction. Emotional regulation creates a solid foundation that allows couples to withstand their most significant storms.

### Repair Ruptures

We fail our partners all the time in marriage. We can be harsh, deliberately withhold intimacy, or simply be too preoccupied with our own worlds to notice the other's needs. But the strength of a good marriage isn't measured by the absence of harm; it is defined by the willingness to repair it. Each act of repair is a deposit in the bank of relational trust.

### Acknowledge the Impact of Your Harm

The first step in repairing any rupture is acknowledging the harm you've caused. This involves taking full responsibility—not just for the action itself, but for the emotional impact it had on your partner. It's easy to hide behind phrases like, "That wasn't my intention," deflecting responsibility. But intentions don't undo harm. Just as a car accident leaves damage regardless of intent, we must own the consequences of our actions.

Sometimes harm is intentional. Dr. David Schnarch points out, "Realize you're living with an emotional terrorist. Someone who occasionally (or frequently) does things knowing it will hurt someone else and feels entitled rather than guilty. Someone who can be vindictive, punitive, and withholding. After you realize you have to deal with this kind of person day after day, you can turn your attention to your mate's flaws too."[1] While it's hard to face how cruel we can be with one another, doing so can build significant trust. Instead of saying something like "I'm sorry if it made you feel bad when I yelled," it's more effective and honest to say, "I yelled at you because something in me wanted you to feel belittled. I know I really hurt you, and I'm sorry."

### Getting Curious About the "Why"

Once we've acknowledged the harm, the next step is understanding *why* we acted the way we did. This involves getting curious about our underlying motivations. Was it out of fear, powerlessness, unresolved resentment, or the enjoyment of making someone suffer? The most meaningful repairs require time and honest reflection.

To engage this reflection, we need to create intentional space. This can take many forms: Perhaps we connect with a trusted friend, see a therapist, or sit in quiet contemplation. We allow the feedback and insights from these experiences to guide us toward greater integrity as we address the harm we've caused. When you're ready, return to your partner and say, "I've been thinking about why I was so mean to you. After reflecting, I realize what it's connected to. I want to share that with you, but first, I need to fully acknowledge the pain I caused." Self-awareness helps us to understand our behavior and reduces the probability of repeating it in the future.

### Ask Your Partner What They Need

Once we've acknowledged the harm we've caused and reflected on why we acted the way we did, it's time to ask our partner what they need for a meaningful repair. How did our actions affect them? How can we help them feel seen and supported in their healing? When they share, it's crucial to hold space for their emotions—whether sadness, anger, disgust, or despair—without becoming defensive or shutting down.

Apologies and conversations are important, but they are not sufficient. A meaningful repair is incomplete without visible change. Here are a few concrete actions to deepen the repair process:

- Attend individual or couples therapy to address underlying dynamics.
- Provide financial restitution or seek accountability if the harm was related to money or dishonesty.
- Establish a ritual or renewal ceremony to honor the pain and allow something new to emerge.

After a rupture is repaired, the best practice is to check in regularly to ensure the repair is holding. Some useful questions might include:

- "Do you feel more connected now?"
- "Is there any lingering resentment or mistrust?"
- "Have you noticed any old patterns resurfacing?"

Brief, consistent check-ins during the weeks or months that follow will allow both partners to stay connected and will reinforce trust.

broken their heart, and imagine where they have the greatest potential to become fully alive.

If you do not know your partner's story—*really* know it—you cannot love them in a meaningful way. Only through intentional sharing and attunement of each other's dreams, hurts, and the forces that have shaped our hearts can we learn to love each other in a way that could truly transform us.

One of the best ways to grow closer is to better understand each other's heartache and joy. Let's look at two actions you can take to build intimacy through sharing stories.

### Action 1: Identify Three to Five Formative Stories of Heartache in Your Partner's Life

Begin by expressing your desire to learn more about the formative stories that have shaped your partner's life, particularly those marked by heartache. These narratives might include experiences such as parental neglect, emotional abuse, childhood trauma, body shame, or discrimination. Ask if they're open to sharing a few of those, and, if so, schedule a time and place for them to do so.

When the time arrives, your role is to be an empathetic witness. Avoid offering advice, suggesting relevant resources, or trying to act as their therapist. Instead, focus on offering empathy and being curious about how these experiences might be impacting them today. There may be stories you've already heard portions of, or there could be entirely new stories they haven't shared before.

The *Desire Workbook* includes space for both of you to write detailed accounts of one or more of the stories on your respective lists. After writing, you and your partner can decide whether to read your stories aloud to each other or silently. To enrich the experience, gather photos and/or video clips from the age(s) at which the stories took place.

Finding someone who listens and engages with stories of shame and pain is rare, whether in romance or friendship. While our closest relationships can indeed be the source of our greatest wounds, they also hold the potential for the deepest intimacy. By showing compassion for your partner's heartache, you demonstrate that pain can be a bridge rather than a barrier to intimacy.

### Action 2: Identify Three to Five Formative Stories of Joy and Purpose in Your Partner's Life

The next step is to ask your partner to share stories that have ushered in great beauty or meaning in their life. These could include simple childhood joys, like the carefree delight of riding their bike around their neighborhood, cherished moments with a beloved grandparent, or significant achievements that showcased their creativity. You might also recall times when you saw them laugh with delight or lean into love, especially when others might have given up. Your role is to be a witness to these stories, too—offering your delight and joining them in their joy.

### Reflection

In the weeks and months that follow, set aside time to reflect on how these stories have shaped your partner's journey. Schedule another time to connect and share with them that you've been thinking about the major themes in their life. Ask for their permission to share your reflections during your next intentional conversation.

Together, these stories serve as treasure maps (and gift-giving guides), revealing valuable patterns and insights into your partner's essence and potential. Many of us come from backgrounds where honor and praise were overlooked or withheld. By actively supporting your partner through both their pain and joy, you help break this cycle and create a space where they can feel deeply loved and seen.

As you learn more about their story, you'll begin to recognize recurring themes and relationships that have defined them. Often, this includes wounds from their family of origin and the ways they've remained loyal to those people and dynamics, despite the harm those relationships may have caused. For example, your partner may have had a parent who belittled their body or intellect, and although they hated the experience, they remain loyal by conditioning their body or mind to be impenetrable. To experience a deeper connection in marriage, both partners need to leave these old loyalties behind and weave together new ones as a couple.

## Leaving External Loyalties

In one of the most influential sentences about marriage ever written, Genesis 2:24 (KJV) states, "Therefore shall a man leave his father and his mother, and shall cleave unto his wife: and they shall be one flesh." In the context of the ancient Near East, this was not merely a physical departure but a radical separation from emotional and familial ties. Although newlyweds typically lived on or near the groom's family property, the true meaning of *leaving* was not about geographic distance but about making an emotional and psychological break from old family allegiances.[3]

Marriage was not intended to blend or extend the family systems of each partner's childhood family. It was about creating something entirely new—a union in which the emotional bond to one's spouse displaces all other family loyalties.

One reason why so many couples flounder in love is that they have not fully left the roles, expectations, and family dynamics from their youth. Instead, they remain tethered to their families, and this emotional entanglement keeps them from fully investing in one another. When a couple's loyalty is divided—whether between parents, siblings, extended family, or the roles they learned to play—the quality of their relationship inevitably weakens.

## Why Leaving Is So Difficult

In my clinical work, I've observed three main reasons why people hold on to family-of-origin loyalties. The first is that they can serve a functional role in the marriage, despite their consequences. If one partner becomes absorbed in their work, for example, it's common for the other to remain enmeshed with a parent or sibling. Without the buffer of family enmeshment, their emotional void would be exposed, and the other partner's emotional distancing would need to be confronted. In this situation, enmeshment keeps both people from experiencing emptiness and tension.

The second reason leaving external loyalties is challenging is because love can become entangled with obligation. Many people feel a deep sense of debt to their family for the love, care, and sacrifices they received growing up. This sense of indebtedness can make it feel morally wrong when they sever emotional loyalties as a natural step in developing their own life. As a result, they might feel more comfortable disappointing their spouse than their family of origin, an obvious signal of misplaced loyalty. The question here is: If our loyalty remains with our family of origin, do we have the freedom and energy to build a passionate marriage with our spouse?

Finally, some partners remain loyal to their family system precisely because it's dysfunctional. They might feel overwhelming responsibility for a family member's well-being. If they don't care for their parent's or sibling's needs, they worry, no one else will. Other parents condition their children to remain emotionally dependent, setting them up to seek approval, validation, or emotional reassurance for decisions that should be made independently or within their marriage. In these situations, the child's self-worth may be contingent on meeting the needs and expectations of their family.

## *Obvious and Subtle Forms of Loyalty*

We remain loyal to our family of origin in both obvious and subtle ways, and this loyalty often holds us back from experiencing intimacy with our partner. It's unhealthy—and unfair—when we allow our desires to be shaped more by a parent's or sibling's needs than by the person we took vows to support and love. Or when we spend our days trying to overcome our childhood wounds, yet never truly allow our partner to see and love us through them. Left unchecked, these past loyalties don't just rob our partner of the best parts of ourselves; they trap us in old, painful cycles that unwittingly sabotage marital intimacy.

One of the most obvious ways this loyalty to our family of origin plays out is by prioritizing old family traditions over creating new rituals with our spouse. I saw this firsthand when one of my clients wanted to spend the winter holidays at a warm beach instead of their hometown in Minnesota. Her spouse refused, citing concerns that his parents would feel lonely if they didn't get to spend time with the grandchildren. This led to years of emotional depletion, as their relationship was continually sacrificed for external family loyalty.

We can remain loyal to our family system even when we strongly dislike them or are no longer in relationship with them due to conflict or death. Take the case of JT, a former soldier who struggles to open up emotionally to his wife. Growing up, JT's parents forced him to sleep in a shed if he wet the bed or picked a fight with his younger brother. When he turned eighteen, he left for boot camp at Fort Moore (formerly Fort Benning) in Georgia, and never returned home. To survive the traumas of childhood and the pressures of the military, he learned to seal himself off emotionally.

JT's pattern of emotional detachment was more than a simple coping mechanism; it was an unconscious loyalty to the very family system that traumatized him. JT hated his parents and physically separated from them, but his emotional world was still governed by the harsh patterns his parents created. Although his wife wanted to know him more deeply, he refused to let her in, which led to significant conflict that necessitated couples therapy.

As JT began to recognize this pattern, he took a courageous risk and cried to his wife, telling her how humiliated and cold he'd felt when he was thrown into the shed as a child. His wife's response was beautiful—she held his face in her hands with deep compassion. When the two of them told me this story the following week, he summarized it like a tender soldier: "I'm learning that the ultimate defeat of my parents is not to hate them, but to allow myself to experience the care I never received."

## Loyalty Findings

We are most likely to be loyal to our parents when we come from either a supportive family or one that was considerably unhealthy. In my research, we found that compared to individuals with low enmeshment scores, those with high enmeshment scores were nearly three times more likely to say they had a good relationship with their mother and more than two times more likely to report a good relationship with their father. Interestingly, even individuals with a negative relationship with their parents were still more than twice as likely to have high enmeshment scores compared to those with lower scores. Both the warmth of a supportive family and the challenges of a difficult one can bind us in ways that are hard to break free from.

So, what was the consequence of high enmeshment scores? These individuals were 22 percent more likely to struggle with desire problems and 14 percent more likely to have high anxiety. When we feel overly loyal to our family of origin because of how much they have done for us or how much we need to do for them, the result is that we deprioritize our own desires.

Enmeshment doesn't just affect the individual; it significantly burdens our spouse. When we're entangled with our family and distracted by anxiety, how can we give our partners the best in ourselves? Moreover, how can we prioritize our spouse's needs and desires when we've never learned how to prioritize our own? Our partners end up carrying the weight of our unlived lives and unresolved tensions.

The benefit of leaving external loyalties is that, even if it feels costly in the short term, it frees us up to spend our emotional energy on the marriage itself. Until we do so, our marriage will consistently highlight our divided loyalties and the provisional identities that are getting in the way of intimacy.

### SKILL 3: EXPANDING AND SUSTAINING LOVE

The final intimacy skill we will explore is how to expand and sustain love over a lifetime. This is accomplished both by cultivating a life outside of your marriage and by creating meaningful routines within it. While these principles may seem contradictory, they complement each other beautifully. When partners maintain individual passions and interests outside of one another, they bring greater vitality back into their marriage.

### Expand Your Relationships

One challenge of modern love is the tendency to rely too heavily on our partner for all our emotional and social fulfillment, something a broader community is meant to provide. In a healthy marriage, partners are comfortable sending the other out to pursue their growth and outside passions, knowing that when they return, they will show up as fuller versions of themselves.

Relationships have undergone an astounding metamorphosis in recent decades. In 1990, 75 percent of adults in the United States reported having a best friend. Today, that number has dropped to less than 60 percent, with 40 percent of people saying they have no one they consider a best friend at all.[4] The situation is even more alarming: One out of four of us are estranged from a family member, and middle-aged loneliness is the single greatest health risk facing American men. Studies show it is linked to a 29 percent increased risk of heart disease and a 32 percent increased risk of stroke.[5,6] As our relational connections become more barren, we are placing tremendous pressure on our marriage to provide a village's worth of support.

According to Dr. Andrew Huberman, a neuroscientist and professor at Stanford University School of Medicine, we have a brain circuit responsible for "social homeostasis."[7] Much like how our body sends cues for specific levels of food and water intake, we have a brain circuit that drives us to maintain specific levels of social connection.[8] Whereas introverts get a lot of dopamine from few interactions, extroverts get less dopamine from each interaction and therefore need more interactions to keep them satisfied.[9]

These social-desire differences can create friction in marriage. A partner who gets a full dose of homeostasis from their spouse alone might eventually influence the relationship to become more insular or codependent. On the other hand, a partner who wants an active social life outside of the marriage (a completely healthy desire) may risk deprioritizing their marriage in the process. Couples can benefit from openly discussing these differences and balancing their social needs in a way that ensures both partners feel connected, supported, and not overwhelmed or neglected.

### Cultivate Outside Interests

Pursuing passions outside of the relationship is another one of the best ways to deepen intimacy. The more you cultivate your personal interests, the more dynamic you become as a partner.

Early in a relationship, desire for one another often grows because both partners have their own separate interests. Maybe they traveled to distant places and returned with fascinating or hysterical stories, played in a quirky garage band, or became deeply invested in work or studies, making it hard to see them for days. One of marriage's unforeseen challenges is that it can reduce one of the most important ingredients for passion: separateness.

To love our partners fully, we must set them free to pursue the desires of their heart. If your partner loves athletics or writing, encouraging them to join an adult sports league or go on a creative retreat will enrich your relationship, because they will return with more desire. If a marriage can tolerate separation, it will be rewarded with deeper connection.

There will certainly be times when adding separateness to your marriage will not feel wise—such as during a major life transition or when raising young children. However, it's important to be mindful of the other reasons that might prompt you to restrict your partner's outside interests: fear of being alone, concerns about infidelity, or a personal struggle to expand your own identity beyond work or marriage. Although we don't typically do it intentionally, restricting our partner's freedom also reduces the quality of connection.

### Differentiation Is Required:
### The Story of Chuck and Libby

Chuck and Libby came to my office just before Labor Day weekend and asked me if I had plans. I mentioned a hiking trip that I do nearly every year with a few of my friends in the Alpine Lakes Wilderness in the Pacific Northwest. Chuck's eyes opened wide and he said, "Man, I would love to do something like that with my buddies!" Libby looked away. I engaged the dynamic I just witnessed: Chuck's desire for outside interests led to Libby's annoyance.

Libby responded, "I just don't understand why he wants to leave our family when he's not working." Chuck fired back, "You act like I am betraying you because I want to have a life outside of family and work." Libby replied, "Yes, I don't get it. Most husbands and fathers *want* to spend time with their family." Chuck looked away and then tried to reassure Libby. "I hear what you're saying, and I do want to be with our family. What do you want to do for Labor Day?"

As the session progressed, it became clear that Chuck's desire to develop interests outside his marriage was not getting a permission slip. And without a permission slip, he would not disappoint Libby. When I asked Libby what came up for her when she thought about Chuck hiking for the weekend, she again made it about Chuck: "A *good* husband *should* want to spend free time with their family." I took another pass and encouraged her to reveal her internal world. Eventually, she admitted that Chuck's desire for more outside their marriage made her feel empty inside—it scared her that she had so little life outside of her family. Keeping Chuck close was how she kept her anxiety at bay.

The question before Libby was: How could she learn to differentiate so that she could love Chuck more fully? For Chuck, differentiation meant no longer foreclosing his desires, because each time he did, he offered less of his energy and passion when they were together. To love one another better, both partners needed to expand.

Libby had previously put her graphic design career on hold while raising their young children, but now that they were older, she recognized how much unfulfilled potential she had been suppressing. When Chuck voiced his desires, Libby had to confront the unpleasant truth that she was also neglecting her own.

For their relationship to thrive, they both needed to develop outside interests. Just as financial investments may require short-term sacrifices for long-term growth, investing in separateness within a marriage may initially feel like it creates too much distance in the short term, but it strengthens the relationship over time. By cultivating friendships and personal passions, couples are making a valuable deposit into their future intimacy.

### Sustaining Love:
### Create Rituals and Routines of Love

The final skill we'll explore involves creating rituals and routines that nurture connection and keep the sense of adventure alive. While spontaneous moments of love are important, the marriage you want must be built intentionally, not just hoped for. So, let's get practical: Pull out your calendar and budget to bring this vision to reality.

Some of the recommendations may seem like conventional wisdom—like having a regular date night or celebrating your partner's birthday and accomplishments—but these rituals and routines go deeper than that, too. When you've spent time learning each other's stories, as we explored earlier in the chapter, you add significant layers of meaning to every ritual you create. All the scaffolding you've been building to prevent sabotage and build intimacy is about to pay off in a meaningful way.

### HOW TO CREATE RITUALS AND ROUTINES OF LOVE

I. **REGULAR DATES OF MEANING AND JOY:** Designate a time each month to build upon your partner's joys, past or present. For instance, if you learn that one of your partner's favorite childhood memories involved riding their bike to Dairy Queen, re-create that memory with a nostalgic bike ride to a local ice cream spot. If they love cooking or music, plan a few date nights around these activities, such as preparing a special meal together or attending a concert or workshop related to their passions. You could also explore significant places from their life, like visiting their childhood hometown or going on a road trip to one of their favorite childhood memories.

2. **REGULAR CONVERSATIONS ABOUT HEARTACHE AND GRIEF:** Set aside time for intentional conversations about your partner's heartaches or grief. This could be a regular check-in, such as a dedicated evening each month to talk about current emotional challenges, or it might involve delving into stories from their past. For instance, if your partner is dealing with the loss of a loved one or a strained relationship, create space to process how these experiences are affecting their well-being and how you can support them.

   An illustrative example of this approach occurred during a family road trip to the Chicago area. Knowing that my wife grew up in rural Illinois, we decided to take a detour to visit her hometown. This unplanned stop allowed us to explore her past—seeing her childhood home, the community pool where she learned to swim, and the cornfields that brought her experiences of comfort and mystery. As we walked through these places, she also shared vulnerable stories of harm she experienced with her best friend. Although this detour extended our trip by six hours, it resulted in a powerful connection and a deeper understanding of the land that shaped who my wife would become.

3. **CELEBRATIONS:** If you're honoring an anniversary or recent milestone in your partner's life, think about what that event means in the context of their story—where they've come from or who you see them becoming. Is there a way for you to create a meaningful celebration around that moment?

   Years ago, one of my friends played a role in the opening of a New York City park. Her husband invited several couples to tour the park, allowing my friend to share stories about the project's various stages and setbacks. The evening concluded with celebratory drinks back at their apartment. What made this celebration most meaningful was an insight her husband shared: As a child, she had always wanted to spend more time playing outside, but her parents were consistently gone and forbade her for fear of her getting abducted. She longed to be with her friends in the local park. Now, as an adult, she was helping create space for herself and the children to experience what she was never able to enjoy.

This celebration not only allowed her friends to appreciate her work but also provided a heartfelt way to honor her story more deeply. Be curious about the hidden layers of meaning behind any achievement or celebration, and reflect on those when planning any ritual or event.

4. SENDING: Arrange for your partner to have a restorative getaway to a place of natural beauty or personal significance. As you plan it, consider their current needs and state of mind over the last six months. Are they feeling stressed, overworked, or overwhelmed by daily demands, such as young children needing and touching them every waking moment? If so, a solo weekend retreat might be in order, to help them reconnect with themselves and find some much-needed relaxation. Alternatively, if they've been feeling lonely or disconnected, a trip with friends could offer an opportunity for play and laughter. To enhance their time away, include thoughtful gifts such as a new journal, a novel, a guidebook for their destination, or some of their favorite snacks.

5. JOINT PROJECT: Working on a shared project is another powerful way to build intimacy. Many couples I've worked with have found renewed closeness through a joint venture. One couple started hosting weekly summer barbecues for neighbors and continued with soup-and-bread nights in the colder months. Other examples include building garden boxes, restoring antique furniture, volunteering at a community kitchen, or starting a marriage book club to explore intimacy challenges with friends.

182 • DESIRE

The key is that this project becomes a "third entity"—a separate, unifying focus that both partners invest in. Like building a family, a business, or a shared legacy, the mutual effort strengthens the bond by giving you both a common purpose.

To implement this, start by discussing what you both want more of in your life together. Do you crave quality time with friends? Want to give back to your community? Or maybe you're looking for a more creative outlet. Once you've identified a shared desire, brainstorm a project that aligns with it. The most important part is committing to it together and putting in the effort as a team.

AS YOU PLAN AND implement these rituals and routines, you will face resistance. Doubts about time, money, or the project's success are normal. The temptation to revert to old habits and patterns will be strong. But by confronting these challenges together, you'll grow more resilient as a couple, learning to navigate struggles and celebrations with kindness and conviction.

The goal of these experiences is not just the outcome of the date or project, but what you learn about each other through the experiences. The *Desire Workbook* offers further guidance on turning these desires into actionable plans. For now, focus on setting up a system to accomplish them together.

## WHAT HALF OF THE RELATIONSHIP DO YOU FIGHT FOR?

In most marriages, each partner will fight for a vital, and often opposite, half of the relationship. Some will find it easier to cultivate outside interests, while others will lean into creating routines of love. One partner gravitates toward safety and stability, while the other seeks adventure and novelty. One may crave emotional connection, while the other needs more time apart. One partner may fight for intimate date nights, while the other fights for socializing with friends. These relational dialectics—opposing yet equally important—exist in every marriage.

To deepen intimacy, we will need to learn to embrace these differences rather than creating a monoculture of desires. More importantly, we need to grow in gratitude, recognizing that our partner is fighting for an essential aspect of the relationship that we might naturally overlook. When we recognize *and* respect these differences, we can approach marriage not as a competition but as a shared challenge to strengthen the whole.

The marriage we want will cost us the one we have. Let it happen.

### Conclusion to Part Three: Marital Intimacy Redeems Our Stories

In the early stages of emotional intimacy, we often find ourselves focusing on what our partner can do for us, or feeling disappointed when they don't meet our expectations. We cast them as saviors or scapegoats, setting up cycles of unfulfilled desire. But love is not built on transactional dynamics or cycles of idealizing and devaluing one another. Instead, love transforms us into allies.

In a loving marriage, we come to recognize that our spouse is the protagonist in a unique and compelling story, and we are privileged enough to be a lead character alongside them. This gratitude for our role empowers us to bear witness to the ways evil has worked against them and motivates us to actively support their flourishing.

Neuroscience shows that positive relational experiences can rewire our brain for the better. When we commit to developing our skills as a lover, we enhance our ability to offer consistent support, empathy, and delight—all of which reshape our partner's internal working model of attachment. As you might recall, trauma and heartache are often less about the events themselves and more about what occurs within us in the absence of an empathetic witness. In this light, marriage offers an unparalleled opportunity for relational redemption—a sacred space where we can know and be known, restore what was broken, and reclaim what was lost.

In the next part of the book, we will explore our fourth core longing: a desire for sexual pleasure. You've likely been waiting, perhaps with anticipation or even anxiety, to address the topic of sex. I recognize that, and I appreciate your patience. We live in an age where people freely reveal the nakedness of their bodies yet often conceal the most vulnerable parts of their hearts. Before diving into the topic of sexual pleasure, it was essential to address the areas where we may still be personally and relationally underdeveloped, and how these aspects all shape our relationship to sexual desire. Now that we've built a foundation of healing, growth, and intimacy, we are ready to explore our longing for sexual pleasure and how it can become a profoundly meaningful, provocative, and healing experience.

# PART FOUR

# A Desire for
# *Pleasure*

---

**SATISFYING
OUR LONGING
FOR SEXUAL
CONNECTION**

CHAPTER 11

# Sex Worth Having

*The day you were born, the world had a choice about what to teach you about your body. It could have taught you to live with confidence and joy inside your body. It could have taught you that your body and your sexuality are beautiful gifts. But instead, the world taught you to feel critical of and dissatisfied with your sexuality and your body.*

—EMILY NAGOSKI

## Lauren

As Lauren, my client from Chapter Two, gained awareness of how her mother governed her childhood desires, she felt increasingly motivated to change her future. She was giving herself permission to want—something that felt so simple in concept yet foreign, if not indulgent, in practice.

One afternoon, during a solo trip to the grocery store, Lauren noticed how tense her body had become. She was rushing through the aisles, feeling pressure to finish shopping quickly and return home to her family. In this moment, she paused and reflected, *Why do I always feel so pressured?* Then another thought followed. *What do I want to feel instead?*

A simple longing arose: a desire to sit outside of a local café and enjoy a latte. Though it initially felt wrong to spend the money and take the time on something that didn't seem necessary, she recognized the guilt was a result of her old programming, not a signal of any inherent wrongdoing. She honored the desire, taking fifteen minutes to herself, and returned home feeling grounded and empowered.

Despite progress in honoring her desires, Lauren's sex life remained a source of dread. At the start of one session, she sank into the couch and said, "We should probably talk about sex and why I don't like it." She explained the ongoing conflict in her marriage where her husband was often frustrated by her lack of sexual desire. Despite their years together, Lauren had never orgasmed with him, which left her feeling both sad and, in a strange way, satisfied. Sad, because she longed to be free in her body, to experience a kind of pleasure and eroticism that felt uninhibited and real. But satisfied, too, because something in her felt healthy knowing she'd never fully surrendered to a man she didn't truly respect.

This internal conflict lay at the heart of Lauren's struggle: She craved the passion and tenderness of sexual intimacy, just not with her husband. It wasn't that she wanted an affair. She just wanted to experience sex with someone who respected, even enjoyed her. Much to her surprise, her body was expressing a wisdom and protest that she had been unable to voice about their marital dynamics.

As we processed this dynamic, Lauren had a powerful realization: Her low sexual desire wasn't evidence that she was broken. Instead, it was doing exactly what it was meant to do: revealing the unhealthy dynamics she had been living under. This insight, though liberating, also brought with it a familiar doubt. For so long, she had viewed herself as the problem. She wondered if her new interpretation might be wrong and felt anxiety about how her husband might react if she shared it.

This is what sexual difficulties do best: They create friction and bring to the surface the deeper themes in our lives and relationships that need to be examined. The discoveries we make about sex not only set the stage for transformation in intimacy but also challenge us to live a more honest and fulfilling life.

## *Sex as Revelation, Provocation, and Healing*

I want to offer a paradigm shift in how we think about sex—one that challenges the common narratives about sexual compatibility. Instead of seeing sexual difficulties as obstacles to overcome or a sign that you shouldn't be with your partner, the invitation is to view them as a custom road map to better, more fulfilling sex. Great sex isn't achieved through better communication or learning new techniques. The best sex emerges when we embrace it as a source of revelation, provocation, and healing:

1. REVELATION: Sexual difficulties help us peer into our inner world, illuminating past experiences and showing how those stories now shape our capacity for intimacy and pleasure.
2. PROVOCATION: Sex is the great provocateur of desire. It stirs us to name and to move toward what we most want.
3. HEALING: Sex can be one of the most restorative experiences our body and mind will ever know—if we stop avoiding it or using it as a source of numbing or validation.

There's no living with sex until we accept its contradictions. Sex moves us closer to encountering both our shame and our glory. In sex, we feel our inadequacies so acutely, but when we're connected to ourselves and our partner, we also feel power and the blessed ache of our longings. Sex teaches us to integrate our humanity and experience how holy and vulnerable it is to be intimately known.

For many of us, sex doesn't live up to the hype. For others, it's something we can never get enough of. The reason for this is that we're all avoiding the revelation, provocation, and opportunities for healing that good sex requires. Not only that, but we will even use sex to sidestep encountering the most intimate aspects of ourselves. It's unnerving to allow ourselves to be seen in our vulnerability, especially when we're fully alive: craving touch, opening our eyes to our partner during an orgasm, and basking in gratitude for one another in the moments that follow mutual surrender. No wonder many couples have sex with their eyes closed or hide behind private fantasies. These dynamics are common, because they feel much safer than truly being seen and known by the person naked right in front of us.

Secondly, we tend to resist when sex asks us to grow beyond our current window of tolerance. When our partners point out issues like insufficient foreplay, limited emotional engagement, or how clandestine we can be with revealing our sexual desires, it can leave us feeling agitated. We might even blame them for wanting more from us. This choreographed dance is common for couples: One partner seeks deeper connection or intimacy, while the other feels badgered or misunderstood. As a result, both may withdraw, experiencing a mix of hurt and anger.

Couples who resist these provocations often end up reducing sex to a simple matter of frequency—meeting a quota of encounters that must be reached each week or month to avoid feelings of rejection or entitled tension. I frequently work with couples where one partner feels sexually neglected and the other feels emotionally overlooked. Rather than exploring what their sexual desires—or lack of them— might be revealing about their patterns of intimacy or differentiation, they use sex to ease tension and quell the provocation. The strategy works to avoid the intensity of conflict, but it always compromises intimacy and pleasure in the long run.

Finally, while the idea of allowing the erotic to heal us sounds appealing, we know the journey can be unpredictable and, at times, emotionally painful. For Lauren, the notion of using sex as a pathway to healing felt impossible. To her, sex was a microcosm of everything she loathed about her life—the places where her desires were muted, her preferences ignored, and her "no" used against her as a sign of selfishness. As Lauren began to differentiate herself from the governors in her life, however, she saw the erotic was not trying to reduce her but to expand her. Eroticism was beckoning her to a fuller, more embodied existence.

The dilemma of letting sex become a source of revelation, provocation, and healing is that our bodies know the cost. We wonder: Do we really need to take a path that will lead us to engage indelible wounds, insecurities, and sexual difficulties? Isn't sex supposed to be fun? Yet, there are so few places that exist where we can integrate the pain, meaning, and hope we bring to our sexual lives. I hope this part of the book can serve as one such space for you—and through the process, guide you to experience the rich meaning and abundant playfulness sex can bring to your life.

When we allow sex to reveal, provoke, and heal, its true power begins to emerge. Sex is certainly about pleasure, procreation, and relational bonding. But it's larger than that. It's one of the primary ways we push back against the heartache and despair in our trauma-filled world. Every time we enjoy sex, we resist the forces that seek to convince us that darkness will win. Maybe it's time we recognize that sex is an embodied act of defiance, a declaration that life and beauty will prevail.

## Sex in the Modern World

Many of my clients gravitate toward either an out-of-control or sexually avoidant existence. We will cover these dynamics in more detail in the next chapter, but it's worth addressing each of them briefly. With out-of-control sexual desire, the person often feels an insatiable craving for sex, which can manifest as porn consumption, casual hookups, or infidelity. In my experience, these individuals feel ashamed of what their sexual desires reveal. They believe they can't manage the provocative desires inside of them so they turn to sex as an opiate, convincing themselves that their desires need to be healed.

The truth is, these individuals have seldom, if ever, been invited to become curious about the meaning behind their desires. They've not been encouraged to bless and integrate the fullness of their sexual longings and to allow sex to heal them in ways that nourish their deepest needs. The irony of those with out-of-control sexual behavior is that, in many cases, the problem is that they have not yet become sexual *enough*.

Conversely, hyposexuality is characterized by a diminished interest in sexual activity and a lack of erotic energy. This often stems from unresolved trauma, rigid cultural attitudes toward pleasure, or a limited imagination for how erotic energy can enrich one's life. Hyposexual individuals tend to avoid situations where emotional vulnerability will be revealed, suppress any form of provocation, and avoid sex altogether to reduce the potential risk of harm or being overwhelmed with desire.

Ultimately, both polarities reinforce the belief that passionate and satisfying intimacy is unattainable, leaving partners disconnected from one another. Dr. Peggy Kleinplatz, a clinical psychologist, sex therapist, and professor at the University of Ottawa, notes, "Perhaps this is the ultimate human desire, that is, to be known and understood and fully accepted. This is the gift that is offered in the erotic encounter."[1] Yet, for many, this compelling vision of sex as a deep, connected experience remains elusive, even unimaginable.

Statistics reveal this growing divide, with a noticeable shift toward less sexual behavior. Between 2009 and 2018, the percentage of adolescents reporting no sexual activity, either alone or with partners, rose from 28.2 to 44.2 percent among young men and from 49.5 to 74 percent among young women.[2] When adolescents and young adults do engage in sex today, they often aim to avoid emotional connection. In *Girls & Sex,* author Peggy Orenstein notes that today's youth refer to emotional intimacy with a partner as "catching feelings": something to guard against, as undesirable as catching herpes or chlamydia.[3]

Do you see the conundrum? Sex is meant to be a window into our ultimate human desire, but it has become the very context we use to resist it. The modern world has stifled our erotic imagination, and it's time to reclaim it. We need a compelling vision of sexuality, one that rises above the tired sound bites of "We need more sex education!" or "You do you!" and superficial articles about G-spot stimulation or how to improve communication. The good news is that sex can be so much more beautiful, embodied, and powerful than anything you've experienced before.

## Lauren's Sexual Story

I asked Lauren to share a bit more about her sexual relationship with her husband. She immediately went to frequency. "We have sex every five to seven days," she said, "and before one of us goes out of town." I asked what happens on day eight if there's no sex. With blunted affect, she answered, "Emotional coldness and then a snap into intense conflict."

When I asked her to describe their sex, she, like many lower-sexual-desire partners, talked about orbiting around her partner's desire. They take off their clothes separately, and she begins stroking him until he goes from semi-erect to hard. Then he gets on top of her and finishes four to five minutes later. He grabs a towel, tosses it to her to clean up, and a few minutes later he's asleep. Then she scrolls through TikTok until she is upset at herself for wasting so much time.

I offered a simple reflection: "You've pathologized your supposed low desire, but how could you have a high desire for what you just described? I don't know anyone who would want that kind of sex." In placating her husband, Lauren was not merely deprioritizing her pleasure but conspiring with him to banish it. At this juncture, I knew any conversation about orgasm or "helping" her develop sexual desire would only reenact the pushy pressure she'd felt her entire life. Her mother and her husband were entirely different people, but the emotional pressure to conform was felt the *same* in her body. I asked instead about the last time she experienced sexual pleasure.

She shared a story of being in her college boyfriend's car. They had just gotten back from a hike, and they were eating peanut butter and jelly sandwiches at sunset while they listened to a Goo Goo Dolls CD. At dusk, they started making out, and he began rubbing her vulva above her pants. Lauren told me this was the last time she remembered vividly "wanting" to want a sexual experience. She not only enjoyed their emotional connection; she wanted everything in the scene intensified: the cool fall weather, the simple nourishment of PB&J, his touch, and the delicious pleasure she felt pulsing through her vulva. The contrast between the two scenes—the college hookup and the experiences in her marriage—could not have been more different.

Lauren's sexual story was leading her to ask one of life's most important questions: What type of sex is *worth* having?

Sexuality is more than what we do when we take off our clothes.

It's the integration of our whole self—body, mind, soul, and story. When sex is reduced to mere frequency, rote and obligatory sex follows. But when we allow sexual problems to reveal, provoke, and heal, the stage is set for a profound series of awakenings. If Lauren could pursue and ask for what she wanted in the vulnerability of sex, she could gain a tremendous skill to use outside of the bedroom, too. The simple but profound act of prioritizing her own desires was exactly what her childhood self needed but never received.

Through sex, we learn to strengthen our voice for what we want the most, engage our bodies with tenderness, and experience gratitude for the ability to give and receive love. And when we ask ourselves what type of sex is worth having, it naturally raises an even more important question: What type of *life* is worth living? If ordering a latte could feel so challenging and invigorating for Lauren, good sex would be as empowering as any experience she'd known.

## SEXUAL PROBLEMS ARE NORMAL

One of the greatest gifts you can give to yourself and your partner is the willingness to suspend the belief that sexual difficulties are a life sentence to sexual shame or a death knell to romance. With kindness, patience, and a bit of imagination, what once felt like a wasteland can transform into our most fertile ground for connection.

Sexual difficulties are far more common than we often realize. Below is a list of some of the most frequently reported sexual issues. While the tally may seem long, my hope is that you'll recognize that if you're facing a sexual desire issue, you are overwhelmingly normal.[4]

- Forty-three percent of women and 31 percent of men report a sexual dysfunction.
- Among sexually active men and women, 38.2 percent of men and 22.8 percent of women experience one or more sexual problems.
- Twenty-nine percent of women had orgasm problems, and 40 percent felt anxious or inhibited.[5]

- Thirty-five percent of men had moderate to severe erection problems.[6]
- Thirty percent of women and 15 percent of men report hypoactive sexual desire.
- Thirty percent of men report premature ejaculation.
- Ten to fifteen percent of women report sexual pain.[7]
- One-third of all marriages will be impacted by extramarital affairs.
- Forty percent of relationships end in divorce when infidelity takes place.
- Twenty-one million women suffer from betrayal trauma linked to infidelity.
- Porn use nearly doubles the probability of a couple getting divorced.[8]
- Fifteen to twenty percent of couples are in a "sexless" marriage, which equates to having sex less than ten times per year.[9]
- Women were twice as likely as men to describe their sex life as "boring" (12 percent vs. 5 percent). They were also much less likely than men to describe their sex life as erotic (18 percent vs. 33 percent).

While these numbers don't make the experience easier, they do show that we are neither alone nor abnormal. A growth mindset invites us to view sexual problems as human-making machines. Every struggle, every moment of confusion, and every sexual limitation we experience is an opportunity for us to lay claim to a part of ourselves we may have lost, or to dismantle the limiting beliefs that are holding us back from a more embodied and passionate life.

Initially, sex might lead us to confront and heal emotional numbness or unresolved pain, but over time, it pushes us to encounter the erotic energy within—that mysterious, life-giving force that lies at the heart of vitality, longing, and possibility. Sex is never fully about sex; it's about the life we surrender to and the life we hope to discover.

## ALLOWING SEX TO BE A SOURCE OF REVELATION, PROVOCATION, AND HEALING

If you're ready to embrace this paradigm shift in your sex life, the next two chapters will guide you deeper through some transformative questions:

1. Will I allow sex to be a source of revelation?
2. How can I outgrow unhealthy sexual patterns and cultivate healthier ones?

The first of those chapters will help you see sex as a space of revelation—where you'll uncover the personal, familial, and cultural forces that have kept you disconnected from your eroticism. We'll also explore the deeper and fascinating meanings behind your sexual fantasies. In the second chapter, we'll explore what it looks like to lean into the provocative and healing power of sex. My hope is that you begin to view this core desire not merely as a pleasurable activity but as a ritual that invites you to profound discovery, risk, and healing.

## CHAPTER 12

# Will I Allow Sex to Be a Source of Revelation?

*So skin is the greatest organ of
learning, even in a spiritual sense.
In touch we experience the world
and one another.*

—ELIZABETH
MOLTMANN-WENDEL

## Sex as Revelation

Jack and Tracy were in their mid-fifties when they decided their sexual difficulties needed professional intervention. Although Jack had no trouble maintaining an erection when he was alone, it was a different story with Tracy. He could sometimes manage to get erect, but at some point during intercourse, he would lose it. When Jack's penis was soft, his anxiety swelled. He feared he was sexually inadequate, and that Tracy was starting to think of him more as an old friend than a lover. Tracy, too, was experiencing lubrication issues, which increased her vaginal pain and reduced her sexual desire.

One Sunday evening they were having scheduled sex when Tracy asked to stop so she could get more lube. When she climbed back on top of Jack, however, his penis was flaccid. The entire scene imploded from there. Tracy's awareness of her cellulite intensified, and she made up a story about Jack not desiring her, which cascaded into the memory of her college boyfriend cheating on her with a cheerleader. When Jack couldn't maintain hardness, her sense of adequacy sagged.

In couples therapy, Jack and Tracy learned that they both struggled with a reflected sense of self. They relied heavily on one another to take away feelings of inadequacy, deficiency, or failure. They were so focused on using one another to confirm their desirability that they didn't have an imagination for how sex could offer kindness within the vulnerabilities of aging.

Near the end of a session, I asked each of them to gather two index cards for an exercise. On the first index card, I asked them to write "hard" on one side and "soft" on the other. On the second card, I wanted them to label one side as "wet" and the other side as "dry." They would take the cards home, spend the next week writing down the meaning they'd attached to each of the four words, and then bring the cards back to our next session.

Here were Jack's two cards:

- Soft: Failure, average, I'm a disappointment.
- Hard: Desirable, strong, success, accomplished.
- Wet: She wants me!
- Dry: I'm inadequate, not measuring up.

Here were Tracy's two cards:

- Soft: Is he having an affair? Am I not attractive to him anymore? I'm chunky.
- Hard: He wants me. I'm attractive.
- Dry: What's wrong with me? This isn't feeling good, but I can't let Jack know. I'll switch to a hand job.
- Wet: Phew. We're okay.

Jack and Tracy were relying on physical aspects of sex—erection and lubrication—as substitutes for addressing underlying insecurities. These enmeshed, and therefore undifferentiated, dynamics had always been present in their relationship, but they were becoming more pronounced with age. It takes great courage and curiosity to look at a significant sexual difficulty in a relationship and ask, "What is this revealing about us, and how might it eventually serve us?"

## *Connecting the Dots: Finding the Underlying Patterns in Our Sex Lives*

In their next session, I checked in with Jack and Tracy about how they were processing their recent revelations. Both acknowledged that they were placing enormous pressure on sex to confirm their desirability. Then Tracy asked, "Why do we do that?" I invited them to reflect on a time in their lives when they first felt inadequate or undesirable. By linking present difficulties to unresolved themes from the past, we can significantly increase the chances of finding resolution. In failing to connect the dots, couples risk getting trapped in maddening cycles, fighting each other or the sexual difficulty itself.

Jack shared first. He recalled that his older brother mocked his body relentlessly while they were growing up, and routinely degraded him in front of others. One particularly painful memory took place at a sleepover. His brother found Jack's underwear from the previous day and waved it in front of his friends, saying, "Jack, what the heck. Look at this streak—do you not know how to wipe?" Jack was humiliated but tried to ignore the situation by focusing on the movie and avoiding eye contact with his friends.

Tracy grew up with a father who abandoned the family when she was eleven. He showed back up periodically, but it was often when he was lonely around the holidays. After Tracy got her driver's license, he sometimes paged her when he was drunk or at a party, asking if she could pick him up. For Tracy, the pattern she learned was that a man would only desire her when she was useful or available. She felt stable and wanted when her partner's attention was on her, but her sense of self crumbled when that attention shifted elsewhere.

After Jack and Tracy shared their stories, I asked if they could see any connections between their past experiences and their struggles in the bedroom. Tracy spoke first. "I'm connecting a lot of dots. In Jack's story, I'm seeing how his brother's shaming at the sleepover and his family's constant demand for perfection is showing up in our sex life.

He feels humiliated and imperfect there, too! For my part, it's like I expect to be abandoned. So when Jack emotionally checks out, I probably take it a bit too personally, like I am going to be left all over again."

Tracy had summarized it beautifully, and I was curious what Jack would add. He looked at Tracy and me and said, "Yes, I agree. But what keeps coming to my mind—and it's so odd to say—is that the dynamics with our families feel like they're in bed with us. I'm troubled by that."

Dr. Suzanne Iasenza, author of *Transforming Sexual Narratives*, aptly points out that when you're with your partner in bed, "you are with your/his/hers/their family dynamics, intergenerational trauma, body image, religious upbringing, gender/sexual identity/race/class experiences, on and on. It's crowded in bed!"[1] The implication here is that our sexuality is shaped by experiences that on the surface may have little to do with sex.

In Jack and Tracy's case, sexual problems were doing exactly what their relationship needed. They hoped sex would allow them to escape their insecurities, but instead it was revealing them, offering a chance for greater growth and intimacy. Their difficulties raise an important question: What if we reframed sexual problems not merely as a consequence of bad things but as a summons to something better? Sexual problems reveal where we come from and open the door to the life we aspire to live.

## Four Revelations Sex Can Offer

Sex is far more than just a physical act or a way to connect intimately. It's a tapestry of meaning-making, fantasies, insecurities, unspoken truths, and great mysteries. Yet, we often reduce it to mechanics, frequency, or pleasure, setting the stage for the very problems and boredom we try to avoid. To enhance our sexual life, we must first be willing to explore and reveal our inner world with ourselves and our partners.

The aim of this chapter is to help you learn to *desire* the revelations that sex offers, rather than pushing them aside or ignoring them. Here are four key revelations sex can bring:

1. Sex reveals the messages we've inherited about our bodies and ourselves.
2. Sex reveals important power dynamics in our relationship.
3. Sexual difficulties reveal a path to growth.
4. Sex reveals the evolution of our bodies and desires.

## REVELATION 1:
## THE MESSAGES WE INHERITED ARE LARGELY INSUFFICIENT AND HARMFUL

We all inherit messages about sex from our families, communities, and cultures—some of them explicit and others unspoken. As adults, it's our task to sift through these inherited messages, discerning which are useful and affirming, and which need to be expunged.

In the Holistic Desire Survey, I asked participants to share some of the most unhelpful messages they received about sex. Unfortunately there was no shortage of responses, and the patterns were strikingly consistent. Below are a few of the most common themes shared by respondents, in their own words.

### Demeaning Messages About Gender and Sexuality

- "Boys are always thinking about sex."
- "All men are animalistic and it is my job to keep them from being tempted."
- "Boys can't control themselves. Girls need to be the gate-keepers."

Takeaway: These messages demean children and frame their sexuality as something that needs to be controlled or suppressed, offering little opportunity for healthy understanding or expression of sexual desire.

### Abstinence and Shame-Based Messages

- "My mom told us, 'Keep your dick in your pants, because if you ever get a girl pregnant you can pack your things and leave.'"
- "My mom said there was a monster inside me that I needed to keep from waking up."
- "My dad used to tell me, 'Just don't do it until you're married. You'll figure it out then.'"

Takeaway: Sex education often centers around fear and shame, with little to no guidance on healthy relationships, consent, or the emotional and physical aspects of intimacy.

### Misleading Advice

- "I had vaginismus, and after my first child was born, it hurt ten times worse (the pain felt like knives). We couldn't even accomplish intercourse, but I just kept being told that things would loosen up eventually and to use more lube."
- "My father told me that it was the woman's responsibility to take care of a man sexually and that if she didn't, it was her problem."
- "Church purity culture made sex seem bad, created unrealistic expectations, taught me my body is bad and dangerous."

Takeaway: Uninformed and harmful advice, whether from parents, religious teachers, or healthcare providers, is common. It can lead to confusion, poor self-esteem, and difficulties with intimacy later in life.

### Pornography and Misguided Expectations

- "Girls don't struggle with porn."
- "Don't use porn, it will rot your soul and ruin your sex life forever."

- "All the myths a lifetime of porn use has taught me, that now leave me with absolutely zero understanding of what normal sex is for a loving couple."

Takeaway: Pornography, while widely consumed, is not an effective education tool. It often perpetuates unrealistic expectations and unhealthy views about sex. Yet, it's often one of the first places people turn when they lack proper guidance.

### The Impact of Inadequate Sex Education

It's no secret that most of us lacked a proper sex education. In the United States, only twenty-two states require that sex education be comprehensive and scientifically accurate.[2] Thus, when sex ed is provided at school, it's often inadequate, mistimed, and unequal.[3] On average, adolescents receive just 6.2 hours of sex education over the course of high school, compared to spending over nine hours a day on social media. Most receive instruction after their first sexual experiences, and girls in nonmetropolitan areas are often the least likely to receive adequate education.

In the Holistic Desire Survey, we measured a respondent's knowledge of sex by whether participants could identify twelve terms by the completion of high school: vulva, gonorrhea, orgasm, clitoris, refractory period, condom, oral sex, scrotum, fellatio, cunnilingus, semen, and dental dam. Thirty-six percent of men and nearly 21 percent of women reported they could not have identified any of these terms by the end of high school. Furthermore, we found that 30 percent of men and 23 percent of women had been exposed to porn before age eleven. The most significant age of exposure was between eleven and twelve.

Most of us enter adulthood with a limited understanding of healthy sexuality, yet we are bombarded with unrealistic and harmful beliefs about sex from porn and media. Sadly, this doesn't need to be the case. A Harvard study found that 70 percent of young adults between the ages of eighteen and twenty-five desired more conversations with their parents about sex and intimacy than they received growing up.[4] Several participants in the Holistic Desire Survey shared that positive, open conversations with adults in their lives made a significant difference in how they approached their bodies, sex, and intimacy:

- "I appreciate how unashamed my mom was when she talked about sex."
- "I remember my dad described sex to me in a positive way; that it was beautiful, pleasurable, enjoyable."
- "A nurse in seventh grade took the girls into a room after 'the official talk.' She answered questions freely, e.g. about vaginal discharge, when you could get pregnant, etc. I asked no questions but she answered all the other questions without shame."

The benefits are unambiguous, but for many parents, this isn't easy. How can they provide guidance if they themselves were never given proper education?

## PORN EDUCATION

The absence of sex education sets the stage for pornography to become the primary educator for children. One study found that approximately 45 percent of teens who consumed porn did so in part to learn about sex.[5] Similarly, other research finds that one in four eighteen- to twenty-year-olds (24.5 percent) listed pornography as *the* most helpful source to learn how to have sex.[6] As one Holistic Desire Survey participant put it, "As much as it pains me to admit, I learned a lot about anatomy and sexuality from porn. It's where I came to understand the basics of genitalia, orgasm, sexual stimulation, etc." When families, schools, and faith communities abdicate their responsibility to educate a child, the porn industry is happy to step in.

### Trauma as Sex Education

Tragically, we live in a society where many people's earliest and most formative sex education comes through trauma. One of the most troubling findings from the Holistic Desire Survey was that individuals with the highest sex education scores were six times more likely to have experienced childhood abuse. Similarly, those who possessed the most sexual knowledge by the time they graduated high school were more likely to have been exposed to porn at a young age.[7] We can and must do better.

What these messages and statistics reveal is that harmful and insufficient teachings don't just begin in childhood; they persist into adulthood. This reality is disturbing, but it should also inspire us to action, both for ourselves and for future generations. When sex corners us with confusion or difficulty, we need to respond with a desire to learn, rather than succumb to the shame or anxiety of our formative years. By taking the initiative to better understand our sexuality, we can show our younger selves that silence and misinformation no longer have to define our sex education.

## REVELATION 2: THE POWER DYNAMICS OF SEX

Sex is never simply about sex. It's a dynamic dance of power, an arena in which couples navigate and concretize the underlying dynamics of their relationship. These dynamics manifest in who tends to initiate sex, whose desires are prioritized, who expresses longing, and who is more likely to withdraw. They also surface in how freely consent is communicated, how it is respected, and what each partner is willing to reveal about their erotic mind before, during, and after intimacy.

In sex, couples often rehearse or attempt to reverse the central themes of their relationship. Sometimes these power dynamics are overt—such as fantasies of dominance or submission, or experiences like BDSM. But more often, they show up in subtler ways—emotional power plays such as withholding affection and cajoling a partner for more frequent sex. They also appear in behaviors like secretive porn use, emotional affairs, or infidelity. These secretive behaviors serve a twofold purpose: escape from relational tension and getting back at a partner for the relational sins they have yet to atone for.

Here are a few examples of how these power dynamics have shown up in the sex lives of my clients:

- Kent struggles to verbally express himself or share his emotional world with his partner, which leaves him feeling inferior. Yet, in sex, he feels like a poet—bringing passion and creativity to his partner. It is one of the few areas of his life where he feels "good enough."
- Regina controls every aspect of her professional and personal life and can be emasculating toward her spouse when maintaining that control. In sex, though, she tells me she wants a reprieve from decision-making, so she gives her partner free rein to be assertive and aggressive with her. Her partner initially felt uncomfortable with his aggression, but the exchange of power gives him an immense high as he imagines punishing her.
- Lydia feels emotionally and sexually used in her marriage. When she does consent to sex, she always closes her eyes. Her mind often drifts between making lists of errands she needs to complete or fantasizing about colleagues and ex-lovers she finds more alluring. She suspects her partner is imagining having sex with someone else, too.

The ways that couples connect sexually powerfully reflect the core dynamics in their relationship. Yet, most couples rarely engage these dynamics with honesty. A key question to ask yourselves as a couple is: What do our sexual patterns reveal about the state of our relationship? The quality and nature of our sexual connection reveals what we need to know, even if it's not always what we want to know.

While the power dynamics connected to sex are vast and multifaceted, we'll focus on two common challenges: sexual desire discrepancies and porn use. My intention isn't to provide a simple resolution to these issues, but to offer a way of thinking that encourages couples to approach them more collaboratively. The sex life we want is often buried in the revelations we've been avoiding.

### *Desire Discrepancies: High and Low*

Sexual desire discrepancies rank among the most common issues that bring couples to therapy.[8] According to Dr. David Schnarch, the rule of committed relationships is that one partner will become the "high desire" partner and the other will become the "low desire" partner.[9] This doesn't mean one person wants sex too much and the other wants it too little. It simply reflects the reality that no two people will consistently desire sex at the same level over time. As a result, the lower-desire partner typically determines the frequency of sex in the relationship.

This dynamic is true in all areas of the relationship—whether emotional intimacy, time spent with friends, cleanliness of the home, financial responsibilities, or sexual desire. However, sexual desire discrepancies are unique because they affect us at such a deep level of vulnerability and intimacy. When couples face sexual desire conflicts, Schnarch explains, they often resort to methods like "begging, cajoling, criticizing, demanding, and withdrawal."

In the Holistic Desire Survey, participants frequently mentioned desire discrepancies as a major issue in their relationships. Here are a few responses:

- "She will say yes, but later that day or evening I'll ask again or wait for her to initiate, and she never does. So frustrating."
- "Her libido is much higher than mine. She would gladly engage in sex multiple times a week, but once a week is about all I feel I can handle. This creates conflict between us where she doesn't feel loved by me."
- "Most arguments are around one of us wanting sex and the other kind of wanting it but being too tired. In the first year or two of marriage, my wife had more libido than I did. Now I have more than she does, especially since she gave birth to our first child about nine months ago."

For too long, mental health professionals have emphasized that sexual desire conflicts can be resolved through better communication and deeper emotional focus. While these elements are important, they are not the panacea the psychology field has presented. Many couples communicate their needs effectively and foster emotional bonds, yet still struggle with sexual intimacy. In response, some marriage experts suggest couples "manage" the issue by staying friends and prioritizing sex. While these practices are valuable, what should couples do when basic rapport is lacking, or when one or both partners can't seem to want sex?

The real challenge in desire discrepancies is not communication or intimacy management; it's differentiation. If one partner struggles to maintain their sense of self when their sexual desires are rejected, or if they resist growth when their spouse encourages them to expand beyond their current erotic limitations, unhealthy power dynamics will emerge.

The high-desire partner, especially at low levels of differentiation, may pester or criticize their partner for not sharing the same level of desire. These individuals struggle to remain collaborative and emotionally grounded when their partner does not match their desire or meet their sexual needs. Frustration over these differences can lead to deceptive behaviors, such as infidelity. A desire for sex is a very good thing, but badgering a partner for it can undermine both sexual frequency and satisfaction. It may also cross into intrusive or abusive territory.

Low-desire partners exist on a spectrum. Some genuinely want and enjoy sex, just not *as* much as their partner. Others experience what is referred to as *responsive desire*, meaning they don't experience the spontaneous desire you typically see in the sex scenes of Hollywood or porn. These partners need more flirting, playfulness, or kissing to be open to the possibility of sex.

On the other end of the low-desire spectrum are individuals who feel as though they have lost all desire for sex. They might be content never to have sex again or lament feeling like their erotic pulse is gone. Instead of developing an imagination for what they *want* sex to look like, many low-desire partners simply refuse to want. This can leave the high-desire partner feeling angry or deflated, as sex becomes framed as their "need" rather than a shared longing.

The core issue with desire discrepancies is not the disparity itself, but how the couple goes about honoring it. When faced with uncomfortable truths about entitlement or avoidance, will partners use their power to confront what is unhealthy within themselves? Or will they dig in their heels, justifying their ingrained patterns? Unfortunately, these dynamics typically devolve into fights about unmet needs or old wounds. Yet, their deeper purpose is to invite couples to expand, not only in personal growth but in our gratitude for one another. The power of a strong relationship lies in accepting our partner's feedback because, on some level, we recognize it reveals how we are holding ourselves and our connection back from experiencing the full delight sex can offer.

### Porn and Power Dynamics

One of the more complex power dynamics many couples navigate is the issue of porn. For years, porn has been a lightning rod for controversy, existing at the intersection of important topics like gender, race, free speech, violence against women, and sex education. Because of this, porn elicits strong reactions and polarized viewpoints. On one side, progressives criticize conservatives for pathologizing and restricting sexual behaviors that fall outside of a monogamous, heterosexual marriage. Some also see the anti-porn rhetoric as manipulative, shaming, and based on cherry-picked research to advance specific agendas. On the other side, conservatives are often baffled at how progressives can view porn as "ethical" or sex-positive, given the objectification and degradation they see in its portrayal of sex.

In the ongoing cultural debate, what often gets overlooked is that porn isn't just about the content—it's also about the emotional attachments that drive people toward or away from it. I suspect this omission is partly by design. It's easier to engage in a moral debate than unpack the emotional bonds at play. For some, porn may be linked to past trauma, including childhood abuse, which can leave them using it to reenact these patterns. For others, porn was the most reliable source of pleasure, comfort, or distraction during a difficult or formative time in their lives. It may have also served as their primary source of sex education. If we look beyond the traditional arguments, porn can offer critical insights into a partner's personal history and the unresolved power dynamics in a couple's relationship.

What often happens, though, is that the person using porn will passionately defend their right to watch it while neglecting to engage the question of why they're watching it in the first place—often, an inability to self-soothe without relying on an orgasm, or to process anger with their partner without resorting to porn. This stubbornness can reflect a desire to maintain unyielding power or a need to assert control in the one area where they feel they have any say. Others vehemently reject porn but never confront the personal issues it raises for them: insecurity about their body when a partner uses it, suspicion about sexual arousal, or their tendency to binge on it only to later try to purge themselves through self-hatred or moral condemnation. Porn then becomes the scapegoat for all the dynamics that aren't being addressed—such as entitlement, hiding, and shame.

In a healthy relationship, porn does not need to remain a polarizing or secretive topic. When approached with curiosity, it can help couples uncover deeper insights about each other's origins, emotional needs, and the power dynamics shaping their relationship.

Through my clinical practice and research, I've found that porn appeals most to individuals who are at low levels of emotional differentiation. These people struggle with self-soothing, navigating conflict, and developing healthy, collaborative relationships. Furthermore, research from my book *Unwanted* revealed that men were seven times more likely to escalate their porn use if they lacked purpose in their lives.[10]

On the surface, the allure of porn might appear to stem from the fantasy world it offers: beauty, eroticism, or novelty. While partially true, this overlooks the quality that drives people to it more than any other: a desire for power. In the real world of a marriage, a person may feel powerless, rejected, or lonely. But in the realm of porn, they control the narrative, deciding what they want, who they want, and when they want it. What real-life relationship could possibly compete with that? However, the more someone uses porn to escape their life, the more their feelings of powerlessness, loneliness, and futility will intensify. Porn offers temporary relief, but it feeds the very dynamics that lead to its consumption.

### The Consequences of Porn
### Use in Relationships

While porn may offer a temporary sense of power and satisfaction to those who use it, its impact on relationships is much more complicated. Renowned marriage experts Dr. Julie Schwartz Gottman and Dr. John Gottman addressed the issue in an open letter, emphasizing that frequent porn consumption can reduce both the quality and quantity of sex in committed relationships. They argued that the negative consequences of porn use far outweigh any perceived benefits.

Here are some of the most common ways they found that porn affects relationships:

- *Sexual withdrawal:* Porn users are more likely to turn away from intimate connection with their partners.
- *Unrealistic expectations:* Regular porn use can condition men, in particular, to expect their partners to be immediately ready for sex.
- *Violence and aggression:* Studies have shown that 88 percent of popular porn videos contain violence.[11] Other studies, however, have shown that violence against women is depicted in 2–36 percent of videos.
- *Pressure to participate:* Over half of participants (51 percent) in a study reported being asked to watch porn together by a partner. Of those, 58 percent were not happy with the request.[12]
- *Increased divorce risk:* Porn use nearly doubles the probability of a couple getting divorced.[13]

The Holistic Desire Survey revealed that about 84 percent of men and 41 percent of women reported watching porn. Those who watched porn the most also had higher levels of depression, a greater likelihood of having experienced childhood trauma, and, as we are about to see, a higher incidence of infidelity.

For men who watched porn, we found that 25 percent reported being unfaithful, while men who did not watch it had an infidelity rate of 2 percent. For women, 22 percent of those who watched porn reported being unfaithful. When women did not watch porn, their infidelity rate went down to 8 percent. To put it another way: For every one hundred men who watched porn, twenty-five of them reported being unfaithful, but for every one hundred men who didn't watch it, only two were. For women, for every one hundred who watched porn, twenty-two were unfaithful, while for every one hundred who didn't, eight were. The more men and women watch porn, the more likely they are to be unfaithful.

To summarize: Porn users are more likely to turn away from intimate connection, develop unhelpful sexual expectations, face considerable mental health challenges, be exposed to more sexual violence, pressure their partner into activities they are uncomfortable with, and get divorced.

### The Need for Conversations and Understanding

Given these findings, it's essential that couples engage in open and honest conversations about how they view porn within their relationships. Some couples may see pornography use as a normal—even positive—part of their sex life, while many others experience it as a form of betrayal. Research shows that 87 percent of men and 31 percent of women use porn, and that 67 percent of men and 49 percent of women view it as acceptable. These differences highlight the importance of exploring what porn means to each partner and how it affects intimacy within the relationship.[14]

To start, rather than defending, hiding, or berating each other for porn use, partners can ask one another questions like: When were you first exposed to it? What has it taught you about sex? How has it shaped your sexual and emotional development? Does it align or conflict with your values? How has it affected the quality of our intimacy? Five years from now, what do you (and we) want your relationship to porn to be?

Until these conversations are addressed intentionally, they tend to lead to repetitive, unproductive conflict or become another demilitarized zone. A few responses from participants in the Holistic Desire Survey illustrate this:

- "We have argued so much about pornography usage and the effects it has on our sexual relationship. It never goes anywhere."
- "He likes to watch porn and he would rather watch porn than have sex with me. I don't even bring it up because nothing gets resolved."
- "After my pornography use came out, my wife keeps bringing it up, even though I have been in good recovery for six years. It continues to make her feel insecure."

Although much research shows the negative consequences of porn on individual and romantic health, data alone is not enough to redirect desires. In my clinical experience, individuals don't tend to fully address the impact of porn use in their relationship until they can acknowledge how it contributes to self-betrayal: low self-esteem, low levels of differentiation, unaddressed trauma, and, in some cases, erectile dysfunction.

Ultimately, the critical question about porn is whether it's leading us, individually and collectively, toward greater integration and embodiment. If our sexual desires don't promote wholeness for ourselves and others, they are likely driven by core negative beliefs, unresolved trauma, or low differentiation. Only by honestly examining which stories and dynamics drive us toward or away from certain sexual desires can we experience healthy erotic energy and a more embodied sexuality.

## REVELATION 3:
## SEXUAL PROBLEMS REVEAL
## ROAD MAPS TO GROWTH

The French psychoanalyst Jacques Lacan wrote that every person has a symptom—but in this, he was making a play on words. The French word for symptom (*symptome*) sounds similar to *saint homme,* the French meaning "holy man." For Lacan, our symptoms act like holy prophets, speaking what the patient has not yet been able to acknowledge. Imagine a nagging ache in your lower back. It could be a holy messenger urging you to address poor posture or an injury from a past event, like a car accident. In this way, our symptoms are communicating valuable messages to us, truths we have yet to engage with. Yet we don't typically welcome the message these prophets bring.

Sexuality brings its own set of symptoms. These might manifest as out-of-control desire, low desire, performance anxiety, sexual pain, unwanted fantasies, and many others. For maybe the first time in your life, I want to invite you to suspend your impulse to condemn, ignore, or excuse your sexual symptoms. Instead, become curious. Problems emerge not to condemn us but to show us the path of liberation. One empowering question to ask is: What might this sexual problem want to reveal to me?

In my clinical practice and research, two of the most common sexual symptoms are out-of-control sexual behavior and low sexual desire. These dynamics can cause significant dread in my clients. Some fear they will never be able to turn off their desire for sex, and some believe they would need a defibrillator to revive it. These difficulties rarely resolve on their own; they require that we listen to the prophetic messages they carry. Furthermore, these two challenges often occur together—one partner may struggle with compulsive behaviors, while the other deals with inhibited sexual desire. In the following sections, we'll explore how these difficulties arise and offer you valuable insights, whether you're grappling with them within yourself or in your relationship.

## Out-of-Control Behaviors

When someone is struggling with an out-of-control sexual behavior, they feel that their desire for sex, love, or porn has become compulsive or detrimental to their well-being. The core experience is one of ambivalence—feeling contradictory emotions at the same time. On one level, they feel a strong drive to pursue the behavior to satisfy a craving or avoid an unpleasant experience, like loneliness. On another level, however, these behaviors can erode their self-esteem, damage relationships, and consume valuable time. Ultimately, what once felt desirable becomes an unwanted dimension of their life.

Out-of-control sexual behaviors are labeled differently depending on the psychological or cultural lens. In conservative communities, terms like "sex addiction," "unwanted sexual behavior," or "compulsive sexual behavior" are commonly used. More progressive communities may refer to it as simply "out-of-control" sexual behavior, if it's acknowledged at all. Regardless of the terminology, the core issue remains: How do we address these behaviors in a way that promotes integration rather than shame or defensiveness?

In my clinical work, I've identified three common strategies embedded within unwanted sexual behaviors: reversal, repetition, and revenge. These strategies shed light on some of the maddening aspects of sexual desire, and they hint at how we might move toward growth instead of resigning to despair. While one strategy may be more prominent at a given time, it's not unusual for people to experience all three at different stages of their lives.

### Strategy #1: Reversal—Turning Trauma into Triumph

Many of us use sex as a way of turning trauma into triumph. For example, if we felt emotionally abandoned as a child, sex may become a way of feeling wanted. If we experienced humiliation by a parent or peer, sex might serve as a space where we can regain a sense of power and control. If our nervous system was terrorized through childhood trauma, we might use sex as a context where we can feel something we couldn't find when we were young: rest. Whereas trauma influences us to feel undesirable, powerless, and distressed, our sexual desires are brilliant at helping us to reverse them.

To discern whether our reversal strategies are genuinely serving us, we need to reflect on whether they lead us toward greater embodiment and relational connection, or if they push us into dissociation and disconnection. When we try to reverse our powerlessness by using another person or remedy our pain through behaviors that increase judgment or isolation, these are destructive reversals. But reversals can be restorative when we allow sex to heal our shame by being intimately loved. They occur when sex becomes a space where we express our voice, reveal our deepest longings, and find refuge and pleasure amid the relentless waves of stress.

Consider my client Tim, who has felt inadequate throughout his life. He felt ashamed of his father's farming profession; the large, noisy diesel trucks their family drove; and his lack of a college education. His dad was a man of few words and great, searing expectations. His mom kept busy during daylight hours, but in the evenings, she poured cheap wine from a jug and became belligerent when Tim or his siblings annoyed her. In high school, he got a smartphone and spent most nights in his room watching porn after supper.

Now in his early thirties, Tim lives in an apartment twenty minutes from where he grew up and works in middle management at a technology company. He's tried online dating several times, but his dates have never asked for a second meetup. He's resigned to being single for now and fears that he has an out-of-control relationship to porn. He uses it multiple times a day: at least once in his work bathroom and typically again at home before he falls asleep. He joined a community of guys on the Reddit website and sought me out after learning how his childhood might be influencing his unwanted sexual behaviors.

When I asked Tim to share a bit about the type of pornography he views and the fantasies that flow through his mind, he told me that it's mostly amateur porn of couples making love. He imagines having a partner who pursues him and wants him, and in this erotic exchange, he feels life in his body. As we explored Tim's behavior, it became clear that porn creates a safe world where his sense of inadequacy is temporarily suspended and his sense of passion can emerge. For fifteen to twenty minutes every day, he experiences a reprieve from the grim realities of his life. Why would he want to give it up?

Unfortunately, in the long run, his porn habit has only provided more evidence for how inadequate he perceives himself to be. To outgrow this unwanted desire would require him to return to the noisy, bucolic origins of his life. There, he would need to attend to the specific stories that solidified his core belief that he's undesirable: a father who preferred scorn to delight and a mother who wanted cheap wine over intimacy.

In the Holistic Desire Survey, we learned that individuals who had more stress than support in their childhoods were twice as likely to develop unwanted fantasies. Furthermore, men who reported childhood trauma were three times more likely to have unwanted fantasies, and women with high childhood trauma scores were 2.4 times more likely to have unwanted fantasies. This points to a clear connection between our sexual desires and the unresolved trauma and stress living inside of us.

If this reversal strategy resonates with you, the key questions to ask are: How might my unwanted sexual fantasies be trying to reverse a difficult experience from my past? And once I recognize this, how can I navigate this dynamic without sabotaging my sexual desires or overall well-being?

### Strategy #2: Repetition—Reenacting Trauma

In Part One, we discussed reenactment, an unconscious pattern of replaying formative dynamics from our family of origin or adverse childhood experiences. The purpose of reenactment is to give us an opportunity to confront and rewrite these old narratives. However, it becomes detrimental when we repeat these unhealthy patterns without understanding the themes and stories we're reenacting.

If feeling shameful, dysregulated, or used is "normal" for us, we may turn to sex to re-create these familiar experiences. The repetition itself is not something to be ashamed of, but it is something to be curious about. Our sexual dynamics offer countless opportunities to engage with our story and actively author our future. Let's look at a few case studies.

Phoebe had an emotionally enmeshed relationship with her father. They could talk for hours about anything. Eventually, her mother began to feel like a third wheel. As a teenager, Phoebe became keenly aware of what was missing in both her parents' lives: Her dad longed for a conversation partner, but her mom, driven by her type A personality, was too focused on order to engage with him meaningfully. Phoebe's mom had her own complaints. She wanted someone dependable, but her husband was often careless and forgetful. To keep the family from falling apart, Phoebe learned to shape-shift to fill those gaps. She became meticulous with details and incredibly talented at telling stories.

At thirty-six years old, Phoebe found herself in a familiar role when her best friend and that friend's husband confided in her about the struggles in their marriage. She soothed both of them with her presence, but several months later, she and the husband started an affair.

Carlos was a playful kid who lived in a neighborhood with several older boys. In fifth grade, a seventh grader named Patricio invited him over to play video games. Midway through the game, Patricio mentioned how boring video games were and asked Carlos if he wanted to watch something more interesting. Patricio introduced Carlos to porn and then asked him to act out what they watched together. Carlos felt torn about what he was being asked to do, but he longed to be enjoyed, and Patricio's delight meant so much to him. Later in life, Carlos would find himself drawn toward older men and mentors, craving their approval. While some of these men were honorable, many of them would end up exploiting Carlos, either sexually or financially.

Both Phoebe and Carlos were repeating the relational power dynamics and sexual patterns of their youth. While they would eventually need to confront the debris of their adult choices, the more important work lay in understanding how they were re-creating their formative patterns. The sexual problems they faced as adults were holy prophets, inviting them to address stories they had long dismissed as inconsequential.

If this pattern of repetition resonates with you, the key questions to ask are: How might my sexual desires be reenacting a formative trauma or heartache? And once I recognize this, how can I move toward the underlying pain instead of eroticizing it?

### Strategy #3: Revenge

At times our sexual desires are driven by anger, whether toward ourselves or someone else. In these cases, sex can become an outlet not for intimacy or self-medicating, but for revenge. Rather than confronting conflict in healthy ways or expressing our vulnerability in a way that leads to connection, we end up eroticizing our rage.

We see this in the case of Sally, who wants more relational intimacy, but her husband conditions her to expect less and less every year. It used to be that she acclimated to his low desire, but recently she's been having one-night stands on business trips. Or consider Craig. He is the high-desire partner, and when his partner doesn't want sex, he feels angry and questions his self-worth. He has a hard time calming himself down in these situations and uses his VR headset to have virtual hookups. Afterward, he leaves his semen-saturated towels in the basement for his partner to clean up.

While it's more common for us to inflict harm on others, we can also inflict harm on ourselves through our desires. My client Frank grew up in a fundamentalist community that led him to believe homosexuality was one of the worst sins someone could fall into. In his twenties he attempted to go through the harmful process of conversion therapy to change his sexual orientation. After three months of feeling like the process had worked, he began using porn again.

That night, he looked at himself in the mirror and saw a despicable man. In one of the lowest moments of his life, he instinctively began slapping himself. He didn't stop until he clobbered himself with a final violent strike. The next day, he woke up with a desire to visit a bathhouse in a nearby city. He wandered through the dimly lit corridors of the establishment until he found a man who looked unsafe. Minutes later, the man violated Frank's body and dignity.

The strategy of revenge, whether against another or ourselves, reveals that many of our sexual desires are not pursued for the purpose of flourishing or soothing, but for anger and humiliation. There is violence in all of us, and if we can't identify it, it will inevitably get infused into our erotic life.

If this pattern of revenge resonates with you, the key questions to ask are: How might my sexual desires be a form of revenge against someone I am angry with? And once I recognize this, how can I engage the conflict or pain directly, rather than channeling it through sex?

. . .

Because these three strategies are so common and complicated, reducing any of them to being simply "bad" or "normal" is an adventure in missing the point. Fantasies are a normal part of human sexuality, but as we've learned, they are often shaped by unresolved trauma and unaddressed relational challenges. Once you've identified your primary strategies, the next step is to reflect on how you can become the type of person who can outgrow the destructive patterns. Out-of-control behaviors are not a life sentence to sexual shame or compulsivity. Instead, they can serve as a road map for what needs to heal and grow.

## Key Drivers of Low Desire

While some individuals struggle to turn off their sexual desires, others experience the opposite. We saw this in Lauren's story, when her lack of desire eventually became distressing to her and her partner. Rather than pathologizing herself, she began to see that her low desire was a symptom of the larger problems she'd been avoiding in her life and marriage.

Research shows that 10–30 percent of people report inhibited sexual desire (ISD). Although women report it more frequently, it affects men, too. While ISD and being the low-desire partner are not synonymous, several key drivers can influence either experience. Below, I want to explore five key drivers of low sexual desire: protest, past harm, shame, a general medical condition, and self-care factors.

The drivers of low desire usually go unexamined, which leads to a predictable cycle of frustration for both partners. Each of these factors can contribute to low desire, but their real power lies in how they intertwine and reinforce one another. For example, a person might come from a religious background that taught them to feel bad about sexual arousal (Shame), feel shut down by the pressure to soothe their partner's ego through sexual availability (Protest), and begin to suffer the initial effects of perimenopause, such as vaginal dryness (General Medical Condition). Low desire must be addressed in a holistic and collaborative way if it is to be resolved.

## 1. A FORM OF PROTEST

In some relationships, the low-desire partner feels as though they're constantly orbiting around the high-desire partner's needs and expectations. This dynamic often extends beyond sex and into other areas where they are expected to comply, such as finances, parenting, or even how vulnerable they are with friends.

This dynamic becomes especially problematic when the lower-desire partner senses their sexual availability and passion are needed not just for intimacy, but to avoid conflict and soothe their partner's emotional needs. Many high-desire partners want sex not just for connection and pleasure but as evidence of their desirability. In my clinical practice, I've also observed that many men struggle to recognize or express any emotional needs beyond sex. This puts tremendous strain on their partners to offer physical intimacy in the absence of its emotional counterpart, which inevitably erodes desire.[15] When the low-desire partner can't say no without riling up entitlement or wounding their partner's ego, they are in something of a hostage situation. In this context, low desire becomes a form of protest.

Each of us needs the freedom to say no before we can offer an enthusiastic yes to our partner. In relationships marked by entitlement, a lack of sexual desire may be the only "no" the low-desire partner feels like they have left. Orgasm, by its very nature, involves surrender. Therefore, an absence of desire might reveal an inner integrity, a way of resisting someone who has become a tyrant.

## 2. A SIGN OF PAST HARM

A lack of sexual desire can be a sign of past harm, including sexual abuse, emotional abuse, and betrayal trauma. When we've experienced hurt, our bodies may instinctively shut down sexual desire as a protective response. Until these memories are processed and we regain a belief in the safety and goodness of our bodies, low desire may work to prevent us from experiencing further vulnerability and pain.

In cases of sexual abuse, many perpetrators initially offer the connection and kindness that our bodies long for, especially if we grew up in emotionally distant or harmful family systems. The more pleasure, connection, or harm we experienced with our abuser, the more ambivalence we may feel about sexual desire later in life. Many survivors find themselves grappling with self-contempt for the pleasure they experienced, which often leads them to shut down their sexual longings in the future.

Betrayal trauma, as we saw in Chapter Eight with Michelle and Chris (the dentist who had an affair), has a similar effect on low desire. Research suggests that about 30 percent of marriages will be impacted by infidelity. Betrayed partners who underwent these humiliating marriage events were six times more likely to be diagnosed with a major depressive disorder.[16] Betrayal does more than shatter a relationship; it dims the lights in our soul.

One key brain region involved in processing all forms of harm is Broca's area, a speech center in the left frontal lobe. When we experience trauma, we struggle to put our thoughts and feelings into words. When Dr. Bessel van der Kolk's research team did brain scans on people who were having flashbacks or being triggered, they found that Broca's area went offline. You may have experienced this yourself when heartbreak renders you speechless, or when the only thing you can say is, "I have no words." While the left brain shuts down, the right brain lights up, flooding our bodies with anxiety and negative memories, often tied to touch, sound, or smell.

If you have experienced past harm from abuse or betrayal, the *Desire Workbook* will guide you through four restorative practices: learning to bless desire, grieving the harm, expressing anger at what was stolen, and taking authority over your sexual future. As discussed in Part One of this book, healing from trauma often requires an empathetic witnessing of our wounds. When past harm is engaged with empathy, it becomes a bridge to deeper connection with our partner.

### 3. SEXUAL SHAME

Sexual shame is the internalized and painful belief that our sexual desires, bodies, and expressions are inherently flawed or unworthy of love. It's a powerful force that can erode personal dignity and relational connection, and when left unchecked, it can deeply corrupt our relationship with the erotic. Sexual shame may arise from a variety of experiences, such as feeling used, causing harm to others, or being taught that sexuality itself is dangerous, sinful, or shameful.

For some of us, looking back on our sexual histories brings up memories of encounters when we didn't truly desire or consent to what we did with the other person. Being used for someone else's sexual gain can leave us feeling ashamed, gradually disconnecting us from our bodies and desires. Alternatively, if we've engaged in sexual behavior that harmed others, or acted with entitlement toward a partner, it can lead us to believe that our sexuality is untrustworthy, fundamentally flawed, or beyond redemption.

One of the most significant cultural influences on sexual shame, especially for those from evangelical faith communities, was purity culture. Emerging in the 1990s, the movement gained extensive momentum when Lifeway Christian Resources launched the True Love Waits campaign, which encouraged young people to commit to abstinence from lust and sex until marriage. While abstaining from sex before marriage has been a traditional Christian belief, the movement went further, attempting to wage war against sexual desire itself.

Purity culture, though framed as sex education, failed to provide crucial information about the human body, sexual development, consent, emotional intimacy, or boundaries. Instead, it fixated solely on abstinence. What the movement lacked in education, it more than made up for in merchandise and media. Purity rings were given to teenage girls by their fathers as a symbol of their virginity. "Purity balls" were created for parents to dance with their children and encourage them to remain celibate before marriage. These ceremonies would end with girls pledging to refrain from sex, while their fathers pledged to be examples of integrity.

The consequences of this movement were far-reaching. Adolescents and young adults began to see their self-worth rise and fall based not only on their commitment to abstinence, but on their ability to eliminate even the slightest hint of lust or sexual fantasy from their lives. Men were groomed to see themselves as slaves to lust, in need of constant and invasive accountability, monitoring, and confession. Women were asked to take on double duty: not only remaining pure from sex and fantasy, but also bearing responsibility for preventing their peers and adult men from "stumbling" into sexual desire for them.

One of the gravest effects of this trend was its distortion of women's sexuality. The movement erroneously taught that women were less sexual than men and if they did have desire, they should learn to shut it down. For millions of young men and women, their lives became a twisted version of the famous experiment in which Pavlov's dogs salivated at the sound of a bell. As a clinician, I've seen how purity culture conditions women to experience their bodies and desires through the lens of shame. Desire—whether felt internally or directed at them— becomes something to fear or manage, rather than something to explore with curiosity and agency. As adults, their bodies carry this sexual shame, even after they've gotten married or their beliefs begin to shift.

Whether sexual shame comes from being used, from harming others, or from the damaging communities we were part of, its consequences severely distort our relationship to sexual desire. Shame is a merciless narrator of our sexual lives, telling us that our desires are selfish or foul. We would do well to question its narration in our lives and share these stories in the presence of empathetic witnesses. By challenging shame and opening up to vulnerability, we can open the door to a healthier, more integrated sexual identity.

## 4. A GENERAL MEDICAL CONDITION

When experiencing low sexual desire, it's crucial to consider whether any underlying medical conditions or medications, especially as you age, could be contributing. This should be the first "rule out" before addressing the relational or psychological factors that might be influencing your sexual challenges.

For men, conditions such as increased weight, diabetes, hypertension, low testosterone, high cholesterol, and struggles with infertility are all potential causes of reduced libido. For women, hormonal changes related to menopause are often a major factor, leading to vaginal dryness and a decrease in sensitivity, which can dampen sexual interest. Additionally, conditions like vaginismus, a painful experience where the muscles in the vaginal wall contract, can make penetration painful or impossible. Interestingly, women in certain religious or cultural communities (such as evangelical Christian groups) experience vaginismus at twice the rate of the general population. The condition is exacerbated when the woman feels pressured to engage in sex despite a lack of desire.[17]

Despite being one of the most common sexual difficulties, vaginismus remains widely underdiscussed, with much less public awareness compared to common male sexual issues. This is largely because male sexual challenges both dominate the public conversation and receive a disproportionate amount of research funding.[18] If you're struggling with vaginismus or any other sexual difficulty, seeking specialized care is crucially important. As one participant in the Holistic Desire Survey shared, "Seeing a pelvic floor physiotherapist for vaginismus saved my sex life." It's a reminder that, with the right support from certified sex therapists and knowledgeable healthcare providers, these issues can be addressed, and sexual health can flourish.

Equally important is to have open conversations with your partner about any changes you are experiencing in your libido due to general medical conditions. When sexual desire decreases, it can be especially challenging for couples, particularly if one partner's sense of self-worth is closely tied to being either desirable or available. This dynamic can create tension in the relationship, but it also presents an opportunity for growth. General medical conditions can function as a crucible, asking couples to separate their self-worth from sex and foster more compassionate, patient interactions with one another.

### 5. SELF-CARE FACTORS

When I ask men and women to describe the moments when they feel most erotic or sexual, they often don't reference their partner at all. Instead, they say things like:

- "I feel sexually desirable when I've slept for eight hours."
- "I feel sexier when I've been taking care of my body—eating good food, exercising, and listening to music that I love."
- "When I am putting my best foot forward at work, that builds a lot of self-confidence, which impacts the way I show up in the bedroom. When I am struggling at work, I honestly feel more pathetic sexually, too."
- "I am a parent of young kids, and one of the most loving things I do once a week is to get a babysitter to come in so I can have five hours where no one can touch me, spit up on me, need something from me. When I prioritize this for myself, I am so much more available to sex that evening with my partner."

In the Holistic Desire Survey, those who reported fewer psychological stressors were 1.7 times more likely to have high sexual satisfaction. Good sex often hinges on self-care. The paradox is that the more we care for ourselves, the more we can experience greater intimacy with the one we love.

The connection between self-care and sexual desire is undeniable, and for many of my clients, three factors play a key role: sleep, body image, and stress.

The way we feel when we're awake depends in part on what happens while we are sleeping. One study found that women who get more than seven hours of sleep per night see a 14 percent increase in libido.[19] Prioritizing consistent bedtimes, avoiding screens and alcohol, and lowering your resting heart rate through a wind-down routine are all strong predictors of sleep quality.

The quality of our connection with our partners often reflects the strength of our connection to ourselves. When we feel ashamed or disconnected from our bodies, sexual satisfaction naturally suffers. Research shows that men with higher body mass indexes (BMIs) are at a 30 percent higher risk of erectile dysfunction than those with a healthy BMI, and more than 40 percent of obese men report both sexual performance issues and low desire.[20] Similarly, 40 percent of obese women report a lack of sexual enjoyment.[21] These findings reveal that sexual challenges aren't always about relational problems, but rather signs that we've lost touch with our bodies.

Effective stress management is not only a cornerstone of overall health; it also has a direct impact on sleep and body health. In a qualitative study examining the factors that inhibit and enhance sexual desire, stress emerged as the most frequently cited reason for a lack of sexual desire for both men and women.[22] Stress reduces sexual interest in 80–90 percent of people and reduces sexual pleasure in everyone—even the 10–20 percent for whom stress temporarily increases desire.[23, 24] Here are some best practices to manage and reduce stress:

1. **IDENTIFY YOUR STRESSORS.** What's weighing most heavily on your mind? Researchers typically find stress is most connected to work or feeling overly busy.

2. **RECOGNIZE HOW STRESS MANIFESTS IN YOUR BODY.** Stress doesn't just stay confined in your mind; it shows up in your body. Do you find yourself getting angry, distracted, reactive, or physically tense (e.g., clenched teeth or tight muscles)? If

so, don't let it just sit there; engage it. Shake it out, breathe into it, or move your body in a way that disrupts the tension.

3. FIND STRESS-RELIEF STRATEGIES. Experiment with different strategies to relax and feel centered. It could be exercise, meditation, journaling, or a long conversation with a friend.

4. SCHEDULE A STRESS-REDUCTION ACTIVITY. To ensure you complete your stress-response cycles, be sure to schedule one or two activities each day to help lower your stress levels. This is especially important if you're working on a big project or have just concluded a particularly stressful season. Whether it's a long walk, a hobby, a celebratory meal, or a yoga class, put it in your calendar and make it a nonnegotiable.

Low sexual desire, regardless of its underlying causes, has the potential to guide us toward a deeper reconnection to ourselves and a stronger sense of differentiation. Let your inhibitions serve as a compass, pointing you toward the next steps, conversations, and practices necessary to transform your erotic life.

### *What's Next? Don't Try to Stop Sexual Problems; Outgrow Them*

When my clients first attempt to change their sexual life, they feel overwhelmed or ashamed by persistent problems. This leads them to try strategies for managing their sexual difficulties, like New Year's resolutions, internet monitoring (for unwanted porn use), and any number of quick-fix tactics. These attempts inevitably fail because they neglect the underlying meanings behind their behaviors and low desire.

A more effective approach is to ask: How can I become the type of person who will outgrow these challenges? The focus should shift from simply stopping our sexual problem to evolving into a person who moves toward a healthier, more embodied sexual life. Perhaps you need to learn how to self-soothe without relying on an orgasm or external substances. For others, allowing an orgasm to teach you how to soothe or co-regulate with your partner may be a profound source of healing.

In some cases, sexual wholeness requires confronting the stories of hatred or shame that have taken root in us—stories that can be processed and reframed through psychotherapy. Or maybe it's time to expand your emotional window of tolerance so you can regulate your emotions during conflict and outgrow the urge to withdraw from intimacy or engage in a compulsive behavior. Instead of fighting to stop sexual problems, seek to outgrow them.

## REVELATION 4:
### THE EVOLUTION OF OUR BODIES AND DESIRES

Jane, a fifty-year-old woman from Texas, was struggling with sleeplessness and unpredictable mood shifts. Some months she felt like a live wire, easily enraged at her partner and adult children for seemingly small offenses. Other months, she experienced overwhelming anxiety. On top of these mental health challenges, she was experiencing vaginal dryness. She assumed it was mostly due to increased emotional disconnection from her spouse.

Jane eventually confided in her general practitioner about her sexual difficulties during her annual physical. The doctor encouraged her to see a mental health therapist and implied that her physical symptoms were all a normal part of aging. The therapy sessions helped her excavate her story, which was helpful but only added to the physical and mental disruption she was already facing. What no one told Jane was that she was going through perimenopause.

A woman reaches menopause when she hasn't had a menstrual period in over one year, typically around the age of fifty-one. Years before this milestone, however, perimenopause arrives, characterized by irregular menstrual periods and dramatic fluctuations in the reproductive hormones estrogen and progesterone. Unfortunately, most physicians receive little to no training on menopause care, with most medical residents reporting that they only had one lecture or less on the subject.[25] A Johns Hopkins survey even found that only one in five American obstetrics and gynecology residents had received formal training—that's 20 percent of *gynecologists.*[26]

Here's the point: For many of us, puberty may be the first major bodily shift our bodies are unprepared for, but it's far from the last. As adults, when we finally find the courage to talk about something difficult our body is undergoing, we tend to receive inadequate information, even from medical professionals. But much like the 70 percent of young adults who *wanted* more conversations around sex and intimacy, adults, too, need better sex education and resources.

Our bodies and sexuality naturally evolve as we move through different stages of life. In this final section of the chapter, we'll examine how our sexual desires shift over time, debunk myths that diminish our capacity for pleasure, and offer insights that can lead to fulfilling sex as we age.

While many believe we can't change the past, I am less convinced. We change the past each time we care for the child and adult within us by seeking the education and resources we need to navigate the various physical and sexual shifts that occur throughout our lives. Confusion, misinformation, and harmful messages may have described our past, but they do not have to define our future.

### The Myth of the Sexual Prime

Let's start with some good news: Your sexual life can improve dramatically as you age.[27,28] You may have been told in high school sex ed or read somewhere that you'll reach your sexual prime during adolescence or early adulthood. This narrative suggests that once we reach middle age, it's all downhill from there—just graying hair and becoming targets for Viagra ads. However, this outdated view overlooks a growing body of research that shows the opposite: Those who expect great sex and those who develop self-acceptance, assertiveness, and confidence with age tend to report high sexual satisfaction in their later years.

Great sex as we age starts with the belief that it's possible. The most reliable path to fulfilling sex as we get older is to remain optimistic about our sexual future. A 2023 study of partnered adults ages forty-five and up asked them to rate how they expected their sexual satisfaction to be ten years in the future. A decade later, researchers found that those who were optimistic about their sexual future reported greater satisfaction and more frequent sex.[29] Women who had high sexual expectations were significantly more likely to engage in sex weekly, compared to those with low expectations. Additionally, a study of more than seven thousand British couples over the age of fifty found that they were more sexually satisfied as time passed, with women in their eighties often finding it easier to become aroused than women decades younger.[30]

While sexual satisfaction tends to increase with age, there are some changes to expect along the way. Genital responsiveness—the speed at which our body responds to sexual fantasy and stimulation—does peak in young adulthood. So, while our genital prime may arrive early as an adult, our sexual prime in terms of emotional connection, intimacy, and pleasure often becomes more refined with age.

Another change is a decline in the frequency of sex. A typical American twenty-year-old has sex an average of eighty times a year, compared to twenty times per year for those in their sixties. Women are also less likely to be sexually active than men at all ages.[31] According to other research, 73 percent of people ages fifty-seven to sixty-four are sexually active, but that number drops to 53 percent for those ages sixty-five to seventy-four, and to 26 percent for individuals ages seventy-five to eighty-five.[32]

The key takeaway? Stay optimistic about your sexual future while recognizing that your body will change. Preparing for these challenges, along with an ongoing expectation of good sex, will contribute to maintaining a fulfilling sexual connection as you age. Now, let's look at some best practices that can help you do just that.

### A Brief Guide to Pleasurable Sex
### as You Age

1. **TAKE YOUR TIME.** As you enter your forties and fifties, hormonal changes become more pronounced, and you may notice that your sexual response cycle slows. Don't be dis-

## CHAPTER 13

# *How Can I Outgrow Unhealthy Sexual Patterns and Cultivate Healthier Ones?*

*Sexual healing involves a great deal of unlearning. Along the way, we learn a new way to think, feel, and behave sexually. We need to create goals that respect the time it might take us to integrate smaller changes.*

—WENDY MALTZ

## *Jamal*

Jamal shared with me that every time he has sex, he feels like he needs to prove his worth by impressing his partner. "I've never said this out loud, but I'm essentially yelling and ridiculing myself to stop from coming too soon." The only time he feels able to fully connect is after it's over. "But only if it goes well," he adds. For him, "going well" means that his partner orgasms first or the two of them do so at the same time. If he is the first, then the sexual experience is a failure. For Jamal, sex is not about pleasure or connection, but a stage that amplifies his anxiety and demands a good performance.

The first question we needed to address was what this sexual dynamic was revealing about Jamal. Once we gained clarity on that, we could consider how it was serving as both a provocation and a pathway to healing.

Jamal's father, a former college baseball player, had always tried to push his son in the same direction. When Jamal was in high school, his father constantly yelled at him from the sidelines—to get himself in ready position on defense or protect the plate more aggressively as a batter. When he didn't do well, his father was distant and cold. But if

Jamal performed well, his father would find him after the game to put his arm around him and tap Jamal's chest with pride.

Unbeknownst to Jamal, sex had become like another athletic event. But instead of his father yelling from the sidelines, it was his own voice echoing in his head. Mistakes, whether on the field or in the bedroom, meant emotional disconnection. But a good performance would offer a moment of emotional connection afterward.

In this chapter, we will explore how sex, if we allow it, can provoke and heal us in ways uniquely tailored to our needs. In our sessions, I worked with Jamal to share parts of his story with his partner, vulnerably *revealing* how his father's performance expectations were playing out in their sexual relationship. We also explored how sex was *provoking* him to learn how to soothe his anxiety before and during intimacy. If he could not be hospitable to his own body, he would drift away from his partner and continue hounding himself to perform.

Next, we discussed what it might look like for Jamal to risk orgasming first, allowing himself to receive kindness from both his partner and from himself. Like many of us, Jamal believed that he needed to overcome his vulnerabilities and inadequacies to be loved. In reality, it works the opposite way: Love empowers us to overcome. Sex could be a *healing* experience, but only if he allowed himself to make a "mistake" and trust that he and his partner were strong and compassionate enough to handle it.

A few weeks later, Jamal had an experience where he was about to orgasm sooner than he wanted and noticed that he was chiding himself. Instead of letting his anxiety run wild, he looked his partner confidently in the eyes and said, "This is feeling incredible, and I'm going to come." Instead of berating himself, he allowed himself to experience the pleasure and take in his partner's delight. Sex was now provoking him to heal his story, not reenact it.

The antidote to our culture's anxiety-filled, disconnected, and disembodied relationship with sex is to allow the erotic to provoke and heal us. When we do, we begin to experience what we never dared imagine: that we can be known and deeply enjoyed, full stop, in all our beautiful, imperfect glory.

## *The Provocation of Sex*

To say that sex is provocative is hardly surprising. On a purely physical level, it can evoke intense arousal and intrigue, disgust, profound pleasure, or a combination of all three. But the true provocation of sex goes beyond our senses. It pushes us to take personal risks to reveal our desires and show up with our strongest sense of self.

Yet, most of us prefer to either avoid the provocative nature of sex or chase after a fantasy of it—romanticizing the idea that sex should be a spontaneous, combustible experience like the version that we see on screens. In reality, the most powerful sex happens when we allow our desires, fantasies, and vulnerabilities to provoke us—initiating profound personal changes and helping us live more fully embodied, erotic lives. This is what we will explore in this chapter.

## *Good Sex Does Not Come Naturally*

One of the most persistent myths about having sex is that it should come naturally to us. This belief sets relationships up for disappointment and eventually contempt. The loudest voices in progressivism and conservatism have sold us the lie that good sex will happen if we follow their prescribed paths. Maybe you've tried to liberate yourself from antiquated Puritan views of sex, or practiced abstinence before marriage and monogamy within it, only to find that your approach led to plateaus and dead ends. Disappointed, with no other vision to turn to, we feel contempt rise: "What's wrong with me?" or "What is wrong with you?"

No one starts out being "good" at sex. While the basic elements of physical arousal and genital pleasure might be present at first, they don't automatically transform into the rich, meaningful experiences that weave together erotic intimacy: knowing what brings both comfort and ecstasy to one another; the confidence to express "I love this" or "This isn't working"; the ability to stay grounded in ourselves while being in close proximity to the one we love. More often than not, it's through bad sex that we are provoked to find better sex. And through good sex, we begin to dream: How can we have *that* again? Can it be even better? The ability to have good sex is acquired.

In this section, we will explore three specific ways sex is designed to provoke us toward greater erotic connection with ourselves and our partner.[1] We will start by learning what it means to know our own minds.

## PROVOCATION 1:
### WILL WE KNOW AND REVEAL OUR SEXUAL MIND?

Each of us has a unique fantasy template—an intricate collection of images, relational archetypes, fetishes, facial expressions, body types, and longings that ignite sexual arousal. We don't always know what to do with these fantasies. Some of us impulsively chase after every fantasy, while others—especially those of us raised in families or subcultures that trained us to be silent about sex—can feel disturbed or guilty about what we imagine. To develop as lovers, we need to understand the erotic meanings we're bringing to the experience and learn how to reveal our sexual minds, to ourselves and to our partners.

The most generative approach is to view your sexual fantasies as valuable data. For example, if you're having sex with your partner and a colleague, ex, or friend enters your mind, try not to judge yourself or indulge the fantasy in an attempt to reach climax. Instead, gently bring yourself back to the present moment, reconnecting with your body or your partner. Later, reflect on why this particular fantasy surfaced or what led to the disconnection. Ask yourself: *Does the person in my fantasy make me feel alive, powerful, playful, or desired? Or am I drawn to a dynamic that might leave me or someone else used or degraded? What do these fantasies want to communicate to me?*

Once you've reflected on the possible meanings behind your fantasies, let the insights provoke you toward greater differentiation or healing. For example, if your romantic relationship has become apathetic, the fantasy of an old or new lover might bring you a sense of aliveness. But you also sense that this fantasy is a shortcut, an escape from the more challenging work required in your relationship.

Alternatively, you might notice that in your fantasies you feel playful, adventurous, or emboldened, but in your real sexual life you feel restricted or inhibited. In this case, your fantasy might be provoking you toward greater differentiation: to take the risk of becoming the person you've only allowed yourself to be in your fantasies.

Similarly, if you notice recurring themes of dominance or humiliation in your fantasies, it's worth exploring where you've experienced those dynamics before, whether in your family of origin, porn, previous relationships, or even workplace dynamics. These intricacies of your sexual desires could be alerting you to important themes in your story that are unresolved.

To get to know your sexual mind more intimately and decipher its deeper meanings, consider the following questions:

### FANTASY MEANING QUESTIONNAIRE

- Who are the primary characters in your ideal sexual fantasy? Are they from the past or present, or are they strangers?
- What archetypes or traits are you most drawn toward (e.g., a specific body type, height, race, or gender)?
- What thought, image, or dynamic brings you to orgasm?
- What sexual fantasies are you ashamed of?
- What sexual fantasies are you curious about?

See the *Desire Workbook* for more fantasy questions.

### REFLECTION TIME

- What surprised you as you were completing the questionnaire?
- What do you think your fantasies might be saying to you?
- If you're in a partnership, what might your fantasies say about your relationship?
- How might your fantasies be inviting you to heal?
- What is one way your fantasies might be inviting you to grow?

Fantasies contain incredible clues that are meant to provoke us toward the fullest experience that sex can offer. The fantasies we find most perplexing or shameful often hold the greatest lessons. By acknowledging and reflecting on them, we open the door to greater erotic connection—and with it, a fuller, more integrated relationship with desire.

**PROVOCATION 2:**

**WILL WE KNOW OUR BODIES AND SHARE**

**WHAT TURNS US ON WITH OUR PARTNERS?**

One of the most effective ways to deepen sexual intimacy is by gaining a deeper understanding of our own bodies. Once we have this knowledge, the next provocative step is sharing it openly with our partner.

In 1994, Erick Janssen and John Bancroft at the Kinsey Institute developed what they called the Dual Control Model. They found that our sexual response is impacted by two systems: the sexual excitation system (SES) and the sexual inhibition system (SIS). The SES is responsible for what excites or stimulates us, while the SIS involves the factors that inhibit or slow us down. In other words, these are the two systems that work in tandem to either turn us on or off.[2]

In her bestselling book *Come As You Are,* Dr. Emily Nagoski suggests that the SES is like the accelerator (gas pedal) on a car, while the SIS is the brake that stops or slows us down. In the *Desire Workbook* you will be able to write down your own SES and SIS examples, but here are a few common ones:

**SES (ACCELERATOR)**

- Something visually erotic
- Spending time with your partner
- A date night
- A specific time of day
- Skin-to-skin embrace

### SIS (BRAKE)

- Relationship problems
- Entitlement
- Stress or exhaustion
- Children or job responsibilities
- Negative body image

According to the Dual Control Model, sexual arousal builds as the accelerator is activated and the brakes are deactivated. As Nagoski summarizes, "So your level of sexual arousal at any given moment is the product of how much stimulation the accelerator is getting and how little stimulation the brakes are giving."[3]

When working with clients who want to improve their sex life, I see a common pattern: People focus almost all their attention on pressing their gas pedal harder. They believe going on a date, buying a new sex toy, or trying a new technique will lead to sexual excitation, and they think their gas pedal is to blame when it doesn't work well enough. By focusing on the accelerator, however, they may not realize that their other foot is firmly pressing the brake.

For example, if you have a critical view of your body, if you're in a relationship where you feel obligated to have sex, or if you are exhausted from stress or a lack of sleep, stepping on the gas pedal will not fix much. Just like a car, if the brakes are on, you won't be able to move forward effectively.

As you reflect on your own SES and SIS, you may notice a variety of dynamics at play. Perhaps your brakes are very powerful, but your accelerator feels weak. Or maybe you feel the opposite. You find yourself aroused in situations where you feel like you should be hitting the brakes—like hooking up with someone you know could sabotage your life, or being attracted to someone with a significant age or power difference. While most of us experience a moderate balance of sensitivity in both our accelerator and brake, this isn't always the case. Some people have a highly sensitive brake pedal, while others experience very little inhibition.

There is still such mystery around how these brakes and accelerators form, but we do know early sexual imprints and cultural attitudes toward sex play a significant role. For example, patriarchal and many religious cultures have historically conditioned women to suppress their sexual desires, viewing them as temptations or something to be ashamed of. This can result in an overdeveloped SIS, making it difficult for women to embrace arousal, even in contexts where it's sanctioned. On the other hand, many men have been socialized to believe they cannot help but have an overactive SES, leading to underdeveloped brakes when it comes to ensuring that all forms of touch and sex are pleasurable and consensual for their partner.

In *The Great Sex Rescue*, researchers surveyed the sex lives of tens of thousands of Christian women. They found that women who adhered to the tenants of purity culture were 79 percent more likely to have sex out of obligation and 59 percent less likely to experience arousal.[4] Peggy Orenstein, in her book *Boys & Sex*, highlights a comparable dynamic in mainstream culture when men feel the right to sexual pleasure and "how dejected and even potentially angry they become when denied it."[5] These patterns show that both our personal histories and the cultural narratives we are immersed in will influence how we respond to sexual arousal.

### The Provocative Next Step: Communicating Your Erotic Preferences

One of the most empowering ways to invite provocation and excitement into your marriage is to communicate openly about your sexual preferences. If a couple can discuss what they want for dinner, they should, over time, feel just as comfortable sharing their erotic desires. Communicating what turns you on—and what turns you off—is vital for enriching intimacy. Yet, many couples never have these conversations, or they feel embarrassed about revealing even a small portion of their sexual minds.

A powerful step toward a more provocative and playful sex life is to create a menu of sexual preferences. This exercise helps you learn what excites your partner and encourages the exploration of a wider range of pleasures, experiences, and erotic longings. Your menu might include:

- *Foreplay:* What types of touch or intimacy bring you alive?
- *Sensory experiences:* Massages, baths, or dancing—what sensations appeal to you?
- *Times of day:* When are you most receptive to sexual intimacy? Morning, evening, spontaneous moments?
- *Turn-ons:* What sights, sounds, smells, gestures, locations, etc., excite you?
- *Turn-offs:* What kills the mood instantly? Rushing through sex, moving directly to genital stimulation, poor hygiene, not locking the door to your bedroom, feeling distracted, etc.?

Once you've each created your menus, share them with one another. This process provokes vulnerability and opens the door to new levels of erotic discovery. It shifts the mindset from a goal-oriented approach ("Let's have sex") to a more exploratory, pleasure-centered approach.

When we've pursued the deeper meanings of our sexual desires with integrity and are working to outgrow underdeveloped behaviors, we can begin trusting that it's safe to share our sexual longings. This doesn't mean acting on every thought or impulse, but rather becoming more willing to reveal our minds and engage in conversations about the meanings and erotic possibilities within them. This willingness to vulnerably communicate is an essential building block for navigating the next provocation: the problems in monogamy.

### PROVOCATION 3:
#### WILL WE RESPOND TO THE PROBLEMS OF MONOGAMY?

How can two people maintain sexual desire for one another over the course of decades? In an interview with *The Atlantic,* Dr. Marta Meana of the University of Nevada at Las Vegas noted that monogamy is tough on desire, particularly on female desire.[6] She pointed to three key reasons why monogamy can diminish passion: over-familiarity with a partner, the institutionalization of the relationship, and the de-sexualization of roles within it. It's all too easy for couples to keep each other in rigid roles, insisting that they fit each others' vision of who they should become or remain. Companionate love is a gift, but to keep desire alive, we need the excitement of witnessing ourselves and our partners transform.

Several studies referenced in the article highlight concerns specifically related to female desire within monogamy:

- A 2017 study of more than 11,500 individuals between the ages of sixteen and seventy-four found that for "women only, lack of interest in sex was higher among those in a relationship of over one year in duration."
- Two German longitudinal studies (2002 and 2006) showed that female desire dropped dramatically over the seven years they were studied, while men's held relatively steady. Women who didn't live with their partners did not experience this drop.
- A seven-year study on more than 2,100 Finnish women (2016) showed that those in long-term relationships reported less desire, arousal, and satisfaction. Annika Gunst, one of the co-authors of the study, initially suspected this might be related to having kids. But when the researchers controlled for that variable, it had no impact.

Historically, women have been believed to have a lower baseline libido, but psychiatrist and sexual-heath practitioner Elisabeth Gordon notes, "That explanation conveniently ignores that women regularly start relationships equally as excited for sex."[7]

In a study of over 38,000 people cited in *The Journal of Sex*, the majority of men and women were both satisfied during the first six months of their relationship. After that window, 27 percent of women and 41 percent of men grew dissatisfied.[8] However, the decline in satisfaction wasn't inevitable; 38 percent of women and 32 percent of men claimed their sex lives were still as passionate as when they first got together. What fueled this sustained satisfaction? Couples who beat the odds had regular sex, more oral sex, intentionally set the mood before sex, communicated about their sexual connection, and incorporated a variety of sexual acts into their repertoire.

## *The Orgasm Gap*

One of the most indicting critiques of heterosexual love is something researchers have coined the "orgasm gap." Multiple studies have shown that around 95 percent of heterosexual men report experiencing an orgasm always or most always during sex, compared to only 48 percent of women. That 47 percent difference is known as the orgasm gap.[9]

Lisa Wade, author of *American Hookup*, points out, "The orgasm gap is not a biological fact; it's a social one."[10] It has far more to do with gender norms, expectations, and power dynamics within relationships than it does with how our bodies work. For example, the gap does not exist nearly to the same degree for men or women in same-sex relationships: 86 percent of lesbian women say they usually or always orgasm when they are sexually intimate.[11] If sexual satisfaction is influenced more by social factors and power dynamics than biology, how might this be inviting heterosexual couples to create a more balanced and mutually fulfilling sexual dynamic?

In the Holistic Desire Survey, we found three consistent predictors of orgasm difficulties in women:

1. The quality of the relationship with a partner
2. How her desires were engaged as a child
3. The age at which she learned she could orgasm

When women haven't been taught about their bodies, when their desires are ignored throughout their lives, and when they feel obligated to have sex, orgasm difficulties skyrocket. In my survey, the strongest predictor of orgasm challenges was the ratio of positive to negative experiences they had with their partner outside of the bedroom. This might seem so obvious that it's easy to overlook its importance: When the overall quality of the relationship improves, orgasm difficulties tend to take care of themselves. Yet, even when couples understand this, they don't always practice it. Why is that?

It's not that heterosexual women are incapable of orgasming as often as men, but rather that our social environments haven't typically centered on mutuality. Too often, men are conditioned to have their world—including sex—orbit around their desires. Women, on the other hand, are more often taught to deprioritize their desire in favor of someone else's. To close this gap (which I believe we can), men will need to be taught how to be better lovers, and women will need to be encouraged to embrace and express their desires. Dynamic sexual intimacy can only occur when there is a mutual giving and receiving of pleasure and honor.

Often, a significant orgasm gap in a marriage reveals deeper relational issues that aren't being addressed. Some men want their wives to have intense, passionate desires in sex, but outside of the bedroom they either block their partner's desires or show indifference toward them. It's a mind game of sorts: "Show up in bed ready to want me, but I'll be indifferent or frustrated with your wants and needs if they disrupt the rest of my life." Erotic energy isn't meant to be confined to sex; it's a vital force within us intended to permeate our entire lives.

Orgasm difficulties can be agonizing, but embedded within them are provocations—calls for us to learn how each other's bodies work *and* to become comfortable mutually prioritizing our desires. If the partner who isn't experiencing orgasm difficulties can avoid creating an atmosphere of sexual obligation, and if the other partner can cultivate a desire to learn their own body (especially in proximity to their partner), they will greatly increase the likelihood of a breakthrough.

### Connection and Adventure

So, how can couples who aren't experiencing sexual passion cultivate it? And for those who feel they have a solid foundation, how can they deepen their sexual connection? The Jungian analyst and author James

Hollis suggests that the purpose of a committed relationship is not to take care of each other or to reinforce a parent-child dynamic, but to grow through and with each other. "Relationship," he writes, is meant to be full of "soulful encounters that temper and enlarge." Hollis continues, "One of the best bridges between the sexes, to be sure, is sex. But men, too often feeling deficient in discourse, place too much emphasis on intercourse."[12] The point here is not to shame men, or anyone, for desiring sex but to invite them to a wider purview for what is required to enlarge intimacy.

Renowned therapist, bestselling author, and TEDx speaker Esther Perel highlights well the contradiction of modern love: We crave the comfort of the familiar, yet we also yearn for passion, adventure, and novelty. According to her, the problem for many of us might not be a lack of connection, but an absence of distance. Sexual desire, she argues, is often cultivated when we see our partner in their element outside the relationship, in settings where they excel in what they do.[13]

In a different, compelling perspective, Dr. John Gottman argues the problem isn't separateness, but the inability to deepen intimacy. In a study of one hundred couples over forty-five years old, half with high sexual satisfaction and half with low, Gottman found those with great sex lives reported two things: They maintained a close, connected friendship; and they made sex a priority.[14]

So, which one is it? Do long-term relationships need more distance or connection? Dr. Emily Nagoski sums up both schools of thought well with a food metaphor: "Perel's style is about hunger as the secret sauce that makes a meal delicious. Gottman's is about arriving home from work and cooking dinner with your partner, having a glass of wine while you cook, feeding each other all the strawberries you meant to keep, then sitting down together and savoring every mouthful. In the Perel style, you come to your partner with your fire already stoked. In the Gottman style, you stoke each other's fire."[15] Both models highlight one of the central premises we've explored in this book: Individual authenticity and meaningful connection are both needed.

To cultivate sexual desire in a monogamous relationship, each couple needs to mindfully ask themselves: "Do we need to introduce more emotional space for differentiation to grow, or do we need to deepen the quality of our connection?" If you're someone who frequently desires more space, it might be time to lean into more connection. If you're someone who consistently needs connection to thrive, it might be time to challenge yourself to tolerate more separateness. The dynamic that makes you most anxious is often the one that holds the greatest opportunity for growth.

Although maintaining sexual desire for a partner can be difficult—particularly for women in monogamous relationships—intimacy problems push partners to make significant and necessary shifts in their relationship. If your relationship has become stale, stagnant, or ingrown, let these challenges provoke you to create more emotional space and separateness. On the other hand, if you feel disconnected, overworked, or emotionally distant, these issues may be provoking you to establish inroads to deeper connection.

So far, we've explored how the erotic can be a source of revelation and provoke us to greater desire. Now we're ready to discover how sex can provide a powerful space for healing.

### AM I WILLING TO ALLOW SEX TO HEAL ME?

#### Leslie and Ryan's Sexual Healing

Leslie and Ryan have not had sex in two years. They came to me because they felt uniquely screwed up—even though, as we saw earlier, around 15 percent of married couples have not had sex in the last year.[16]

Leslie struggled with anorexia throughout high school, but she stabilized significantly in college, thanks to effective counseling and group therapy. When her mother died two months into their marriage, however, Leslie's condition deteriorated. She made the difficult decision to leave a job she loved and focus on treatment. Ryan, empathetic and patient, stood by Leslie's side, hopeful that the issues would resolve within a few months. For him, masturbating and going without intercourse felt like a necessary, even virtuous, sacrifice under the circumstances. But months turned into years, and the emotional and physical distance between them continued to grow.

Then Ryan had a poignant dream. In the dream, he and a small boy were running through a field. The boy then looked up at him and said, "Dad, let's climb trees!" Ryan looked around, but there were no trees to be found. He found himself crying, and as his tears fell to the earth below, his body suddenly transfigured into a towering oak tree. His arms became branches that stretched high and powerfully into the air, offering the boy a place to play and find shelter from the oppressive sun.

The dream stirred something unexpected in Ryan: a yearning to be a father. But he knew all too well that there was a high cost to following that dream. His desire for sex and parenthood would disrupt Leslie beyond what she could potentially handle.

Ryan and Leslie had entered into an unspoken agreement to forgo sexual desire. What they didn't realize was how deeply this decision would affect other aspects of their relationship. Anytime Ryan expressed a desire for something, Leslie's anxiety would interfere. Their vacations were restricted to nearby locations, because she had regular appointments that couldn't be missed. Ryan's time with friends was also limited, as Leslie couldn't sleep unless he was home by nine P.M. Even Ryan's favorite restaurants became off-limits due to her food triggers. What started as a simple agreement to focus on stability now felt like a series of compromises that slowly confined their love.

Their relationship was doing what marriage does: revealing the major themes each partner has been sidestepping and provoking them, both individually and together, to move into a life of desire. They had once believed avoiding sex was the most loving thing they could do—and perhaps it really had been, for a season. But in doing so, they had closed themselves off to the possibility that sex could be a source of profound healing.

### Healing Sex

I worked with Ryan to claim and hold on to his desires for intimacy and fatherhood, while encouraging Leslie to expand her tolerance for distress. The goal wasn't for one partner to triumph over the other, but for both to grow in their shared need for integrity. Ryan lacked integrity with his desires, and Leslie lacked integrity in her willingness to tolerate anxiety.

I asked Leslie and Ryan to describe their current physical connection. Leslie shared that they cuddled most nights, with Ryan comforting her after challenging therapy sessions or difficult days dealing with her relationship to food. These moments, though small, provided me with an initial understanding of their emotional and physical foundation, one I believed they could build upon. Sensing where I was headed, Leslie suddenly interjected, "I know where this is going, and I really can't deal with the thought of having his penis inside me." Ryan laughed and said he felt quite intimidated by that prospect, too.

Together, we explored how they could honor their bodies while also working to increase their receptivity to the erotic within them. I introduced the concept of sexual brakes and accelerators and asked them to recall specific moments, either in the past or in their fantasies, where they felt sexual desire for one other. At first, they were uncomfortable revealing their minds, but they began to open up. Ryan shared that he felt a strong desire when he saw Leslie come out of the shower, wrapping herself in a towel before brushing her teeth. He fantasized about coming up behind her and kissing her neck. But he often hesitated, worried that initiating this might influence her to feel overly self-conscious about her body. Leslie, in turn, shared that she felt most drawn to Ryan when he was reading in bed at night or playing his guitar. It was his artistic side that had initially attracted her, and as she spoke, tears fell as she realized how much she had held herself back from pursuing him fully.

From a treatment perspective, I was thrilled. Their integrity in addressing their sexless marriage was revealing their longings for one another, provoking them to experience sexual pleasure together, and moving them closer to the healing power of sex. As we explored how to increase their tolerance for sexual intimacy, Leslie came up with an idea to lie in bed facing one another naked. She was quick to clarify, "I'm not saying I'm crawling into bed naked! I'll take my clothes off *under* the covers and then Ryan can join me." As they left the session that day, I was hopeful but uncertain as to what would transpire between them. Would desire flow back into their life, or would their story continue to be authored by anxiety and shame?

### Increasing Tolerance for Erotic Intimacy

When most couples have sex, they move quickly to genital stimulation, oral sex, or intercourse, and end up bypassing an important experience of embodiment and connection. The reality is that having intense sex with your eyes closed is a lot easier than revealing your erotic mind to your partner. Playfully entering intimacy, sharing what turns you on, revealing what you're enjoying, and allowing your eyes to be open and connected to your partner during an orgasm can all feel like too much. Yet each time we avoid this more powerful and vulnerable form of intimacy, we defer our experience of sexual healing.

At our next session, Ryan gave me a powerful update. For the first time in two years, he and Leslie had lain in bed together naked. It wasn't without awkward moments, but through laughter and kissing, they were able to move through the discomfort. I was delighted for them and so curious as to how they were processing this seismic change in their intimacy threshold.

Ryan shared that his heart was racing, feeling almost overwhelmed by the intensity of his desire. A familiar feeling emerged to rein in his longings in order to protect Leslie from himself. He noticed this impulse and, instead of shutting himself down as he had so many times before, he gave himself permission to allow all of himself to be present in the relationship.

Leslie, too, noticed familiar feelings arise, including self-consciousness about her body and anxiety when she noticed Ryan's erection. We had prepared for these experiences in our previous therapy session, and she focused on calming her body by breathing through the discomfort. In doing so, her mood lightened and she playfully said "hi" to the "stranger" attached to Ryan's body. The most encouraging part of the experience for Leslie was realizing that her body was giving comfort and even pleasure. As she put it, "That night, I felt like my body was *good*. Even when nothing overtly sexual was happening—just lying there with him—I could feel the connection. My body was giving and receiving pleasure, and that felt so powerful."

Their physical intimacy developed over the coming months, but that first evening lying naked beneath the covers became the inflection point of their erotic journey. To some, it might seem vanilla, hardly a PG-13 moment. Yet for them, it represented a significant milestone that very few couples experience: They confronted their emotional and erotic limitations, choosing to show their longings with vulnerability. In doing so, they ventured into unknown territory, where they could either be overwhelmed by anxiety or begin to liberate their relationship to desire.

### Is Sex Healing, Hurting, or Stunting Us?

Good sex is meant to heal us. Through it, we find ourselves nourished, our relationships deepened, and our sense of vitality restored. Yet despite our longing for sex to be transformative, for many, it becomes a place where our core wounds are exacerbated or we experience immense futility in our patterns. According to participants in the Holistic Desire Survey, when their sexual relationship wasn't satisfying, men tended to feel unwanted, while women often felt used by the sex they were having. While these experiences are not universal—many women feel neglected, and many men feel obligated—the sentiments reflect how much room for growth couples have in their sexual lives.

#### FEELING UNWANTED

- "I desire to have sex more often than my partner. Sometimes this leads to an argument because I feel unwanted."
- "I feel rejected when she says no to sex. She recently shared that sex can be a burden for her, and that also made me feel insecure."
- "The biggest problem I have is that I want to feel desired."

### FEELING USED

- "I am used as a pressure release for him."
- "He used Bible verses and his sin to guilt me into sex. I didn't enjoy sex at all then and never orgasmed. It was something I did just for him. My first orgasm was thirteen years into our marriage."
- "Until very recently, my wife couldn't see how she was burdening me with constant sexual disappointment. It was either about me not initiating enough, not being passionate enough, or not lingering long enough after sex."

In these accounts, sex often reenacts our core experiences rather than healing them.

### Are We Asking Too Much of Sex?

As we've been exploring, the erotic holds immense power to heal our stories of shame, mend heartache, and move us into a more embodied and passionate existence. But is it foolish to expect sex to carry all this weight? Can the erotic truly thrive if we place such high, seemingly impossible demands on it? My belief is that the erotic is more than capable of withstanding all the desires, disappointments, and unresolved dynamics we throw at it. In return, though, it asks something of us.

It calls us to grow in both hope and greater honesty. Through the erotic, we are invited to embrace a kind of innocence in our desire, to believe that sex can be a place of intimate love and transcendent joy. Yet it also challenges us to outgrow our naiveté, urging us to be honest about those moments we prefer to use sex as a shortcut or escape instead of confronting the deeper dilemmas we're facing. If we are desiring the fullness of sex, it should be making us both younger and wiser.

One area where we may be asking too much of sex is in the pursuit of orgasm. Over time, the orgasm has been elevated as the central goal of the sexual experience. This focus leads us to become preoccupied with frequency, techniques, and measuring our experiences through the lens of success or failure. Instead of embracing the healing potential of sex, we turn it into a scoreboard, adding more wounds to heal and more expectations to detox from. While this insight has been acknowledged in some academic and therapeutic circles, it's still not the cultural norm. For many, the expectation of orgasm is so deeply ingrained that anything less feels like failure or deprivation, compounding our sexual wounds.

Orgasm may contribute to sexual satisfaction, but it is not necessary for it. If orgasm occurs, that's wonderful. It even has health benefits. In one Harvard study, men with higher ejaculation frequency also had a 31 percent lower risk of prostate cancer.[17] But the goal should not be to measure the sexual experience by who orgasmed, how many orgasms were had, or how quickly someone climaxed. Instead, the aim should be to feel known, loved, and reconnected to what is good, true, and beautiful within and around us.

There are forces in our world that work against us achieving this vision of sexual flourishing. Television and film, social media, clickbait articles, and porn all shape how we understand sex and judge the quality of our sexual experiences. These influences prime us to expect sex in a specific way: spontaneous arousal, instant connection, and the orgasm (maybe two of them) as the inevitable apex of the experience. If we don't deconstruct these ideas, they will not only limit our sexual potential but also undermine the potential of sex itself.

### Moving Into and Through
### Sexual Insecurities

However, simply resisting these unhealthy influences is not enough. We need a counter-formation. This involves a deliberate shaping of our sexual experiences through reflections and rituals that will help us cultivate a life of sexual healing. To begin this process, here are some questions to help you reflect on your relationship with sexuality. As you process your answers, pay attention to any themes that bring up grief or surprise you.

### AREAS OF INSECURITY AND GROWTH

- What parts of my body do I feel insecure about?
- What aspects of my sexuality feel underdeveloped, neglected, or unexpressed?
- What aspects of my sexuality am I ashamed of (e.g., premature ejaculation, low desire, or size of breasts or penis)?
- In what ways do I feel my sexual mind or instincts are untrustworthy or misaligned with my values?
- What aspects of my sexual mind, fantasies, or desires are difficult to reveal to myself or my partner?
- If I could heal or repair one dimension of my sexual life, what would it be, and why?

### AREAS OF SEXUAL FLOURISHING

- What aspects of my sexual fantasies bring me into deeper passion?
- What parts of my body feel powerful?
- What aspects of my sexuality do I enjoy?
- What aspects of my partner's sexuality or body do I enjoy?
- When did my heart, mind, and body last feel fully integrated during sex (or another experience)? If they haven't, can I imagine ever feeling this?

Acknowledging our vulnerabilities is just the beginning. To move through them, we need to discover rituals and practices that will promote sexual healing. Here are a few practices to explore:

- *Offer Hospitality.* Identify areas of your body or sexuality that feel insecure, or that hinder your ability to experience pleasure. How can you move toward these parts with kindness and creativity? For example, if you feel ashamed of your stomach, start your day with a ritual of massaging it with coconut oil while affirming, "My belly is good and deserving of care." Too often, we speak to ourselves in ways we'd find abusive if they were directed at another person. Shifting from contempt or willpower to kindness is the key to healing.

- *Observe Your Breath.* Pay attention to your breath during sexual experiences. Are you holding it? Is it rapid or shallow? Deep, relaxed breathing enhances sexual energy and pleasure. Practice five to ten minutes of abdominal breathing each day, using the muscles in your stomach to pull air into your lungs. This simple practice will improve not just your sex life but also your overall physical and emotional well-being.

- *Engage Your Anxiety.* If you experience anxiety before, during, or after sex, especially around issues like premature ejaculation, use the power of your breath to ground yourself. Slowing and deepening your breath reduces anxiety and centers you in the goodness of your body.

- *Build Connection Outside the Bedroom.* To enhance sexual connection, it's important to practice synchronization in our everyday interactions with our partners. Couples often struggle to align during sex because their connection outside of the bedroom is either weak or absent. Strengthen your bond by hugging until both of your bodies fully relax, holding hands while listening to music, or dancing playfully (or passionately) while maintaining eye contact. When you practice connection in daily life, you'll see a significant difference in your sexual relationship.

- *Use tools to Enhance Arousal.* Remember that tools like lubrication, toys, and even medications can support a more fulfilling experience. These are not shortcuts, but ways to enhance your body's natural arousal and make sex more mutually enjoyable.

### Habits for Strengthening Sexual Connection

In addition to overcoming our insecurities, it's important to nurture both the strong parts of our sexuality and the areas with great potential for growth. Here are several habits that will help you continue to experience deeper healing through sex.

- *Build Mindful Imagination.* Use your imagination to set the mood for sex. Experiment with lighting, music, and scents to create an environment that enhances your connection and pleasure. This is your time to practice being an artist, crafting a beautiful space for intimacy.
- *Set Intentions.* Before engaging in sex, set a clear intention. Is this time for a deep, luxurious, and slow connection? A quick burst of passion? A moment for one partner to relax and receive? Or perhaps it's a time when greater mutuality is especially important, such as after a conflict. Setting an intention helps guide your sexual energy and focus.
- *Deep Breathing Together.* Practice synchronized breathing with your partner. Slowly inhale and exhale together, noticing how your bodies and sensations shift as you form a rhythm together.
- *Practice Pelvic Floor Awareness.* Outside the bedroom, strengthening your pelvic floor muscles through regular exercises can significantly enhance both sexual function and pleasure. Try performing Kegel exercises (the muscles you use to hold your urine) by squeezing your pelvic floor muscles for three seconds, then releasing. Repeat this ten to fifteen times per session, two to three times a day. These exercises are beneficial to both men and women. For example, men may experience improved erections and more intense orgasm through this practice.
- *Continue to Love Your Body Outside the Bedroom, Too.* Activities like yoga, dance, or exercise all help us maintain what is thriving in our body. These practices increase our awareness of our body and enhance confidence.

Each of these habits helps us move into greater vulnerability and build upon what is already strong within us. These practices also center us, helping us resist unhealthy cultural influences and foster mindfulness in how we approach sex. By engaging in these healthy practices, we are forming ourselves into wholehearted and embodied lovers.

## Conclusion: The Healing Power of Sex in Society

The healing potential of sex extends far beyond the individual; it has the capacity to foster healing in society as a whole. Healthy, mutual, and pleasure-centered sex helps all of us become better humans.

For some, sex can be an entry point to experiencing desire for the first time. For them, the question becomes, "How do I live more fully into a life of desire—not out of obligation, but to experience something beautiful and empowering?" Sex teaches those whose desires have been suppressed or denied that it is okay to *want* to want.

For others, sex teaches them how to ensure that their presence brings goodness and honor to others. The question becomes: "How can I create a space where others feel known, enjoyed, and honored?" Many people, especially those without models for healthy intimacy, have required others to orbit around their desires, neglecting the needs of others. Sex teaches those who've indulged their desires the beautiful art of learning to serve.

Imagine if we allowed good sex to inform how we showed up in the world. This wouldn't be about sexualizing our interactions with others, but about bringing the core themes of greater desire, deeper honor, and mutual delight into all our interactions with our neighbors and even our enemies. When we experience good sex and take what we've learned into the world, we can help transform the small slice of life that we inhabit.

Through our sexual desire, we awaken to the powerful force at work within and around us. This erotic energy opens us to a sense of abundance and possibility—a flow that moves through me, through you, through all of us together. It's so potent that it can overcome even the forces of decay and trauma that shape our world. Sexual desire is a profound gift, and we can receive that gift each time we allow it to be a source of revelation, provocation, and healing.

This brings us to the final phase of this book: the desire for a meaningful, purposeful life. It's here that the previous four core longings—sexual pleasure, intimacy, personal growth, and wholeness—converge. Collectively, they have been forming us into the kind of people who don't merely desire meaning, but who embody it. What does this meaningful and purposeful existence look like? It's a life we are about to discover, beginning with the next chapter.

# PART FIVE

# A Desire for
# *Meaning*

—

SATISFYING

YOUR NEED

FOR A

PURPOSE-FILLED

LIFE

## CHAPTER 14

# What Inner Traits Do I Need to Live a Meaningful Life?

*May you have the courage to listen to the voice of Desire*
*That disturbs you when you have settled for something safe.*

—JOHN O'DONOHUE

### Kenji

Kenji grew up in New York City, where his parents enrolled him in all the leading music classes, museums, and arts experiences the city had to offer. He attended an elite preschool (thanks to his parents placing him on a waitlist before he was even born), and throughout his childhood, he was given the latest fashion, gaming systems, and academic training.

His family traveled internationally for most vacations, but one spring break when Kenji was ten, his parents decided to rent a car and road-trip to Hilton Head, South Carolina. As they were driving down I-95, they hit three hours of traffic. Kenji's dad, incensed by the inconvenience, called his assistant to arrange airfare back to New York at the end of the trip.

After Kenji shared the Hilton Head story in therapy, numerous others followed. One winter break, he wanted to learn how to make cinnamon rolls. His dad chuckled dismissively and said it would take too long. Instead, they ordered a driver to pick up the treats from a bakery and deliver them to their apartment. Kenji did the math and noted that his parents would rather pay $60 than spend a few hours to nurture his curiosity. The message he metabolized was that his desires were inconvenient, and life would be smoother if he stopped expecting them to be cultivated. Kenji's family sacrificed meaning and connection on the altar of efficiency.

There's an old saying: "Prepare the child for the road, not the road for the child." Kenji's road was prepared for him before he could walk. Although one interpretation of his story could be that his parents schemed to give him the best life possible, the reality is that they were attuned far more to their expectations than to honoring Kenji's unique desires. He wanted to learn board games like Settlers of Catan, but his mom was always heading out to a social engagement or fundraising gala. He wanted to bring a friend on a family vacation, but his dad disclosed to him that his friend was "on a scholarship" and didn't come from the best family. Over time, Kenji learned to mold his desires to fit his parents' agenda: academic success, athletic achievement, and exposure to the arts.

Kenji excelled. He lettered in two sports in high school and was recruited out of his Ivy League undergraduate program to work in an up-and-coming financial sector. By his late twenties, he had an enviable physique and career. To anyone looking from the outside, Kenji's life seemed perfect. But beneath the surface, he suffered from a gnawing sense of meaninglessness. He felt disconnected from his hopes and emotions, lacked relationships where he was deeply known, and had no clear direction for where his life was headed.

During this season of therapy, Kenji brought in an excerpt from Harvard professor Arthur Brooks that deeply resonated with him: "When people see themselves as little more than their attractive bodies, jobs, or bank accounts, it brings great suffering. You become a heartless taskmaster to yourself, seeing yourself as nothing more than *Homo economicus.* Love and fun are sacrificed to the question *Am I successful yet?* We become cardboard cutouts of real people."[1] Without being conscious of it, Kenji realized, he had become little more than the person his family and culture had shaped him to be. He looked at me and defiantly said, "I want to be real."

The following Saturday morning, Kenji woke up hungover, and a subtle rage grew within him. He texted a few friends about meeting up for brunch because he couldn't stand the thought of working or being alone. As he was waiting on his friends' response, he felt a familiar agitation driving him to go for a run around Central Park. Then, seemingly out of nowhere, a thought came to him: *Make cinnamon rolls.*

He left his apartment to gather the ingredients, but much to his disappointment, he realized they would take over two hours to prepare. He could feel his dad's presence inside him, prompting him to use a delivery service, but he persisted. He spent the night prepping the dough, and the next morning he put the rolls in the oven. Twenty-one minutes later, the rolls were golden brown and slightly underbaked. He was so happy that he cried.

In therapy the following week, more grief surfaced. Kenji realized that he wanted to fall in love with the process of learning, to embrace the feeling of struggle, and to resist the ever-present temptation of convenience and external success. He wasn't going to be a professional baker, but he vowed to bring the mindset of a baker to everything he desired. A cinnamon roll had become the inflection point in his relationship to desire.

## *The Paradox of a Meaningful Life*

When we initially desire more from life, we often focus on freeing ourselves *from* something that has held us back: an unhealthy relationship, self-hatred, or a reliance on a destructive behavior. While wanting freedom *from* something is important, the more pressing question is, What do we want to be free *for*?

In the early stages of maturity, we often fixate on wanting less difficulty and more of what we believe will bring us "the good life." We think our problems will be solved if we acquire a life partner (or a different one), advance to a higher income bracket, or finally outgrow a problematic behavior. Yet, problems are not mere thorns in our side. They emerge to show us where we've been—and eventually make us whole. Life's challenges shape our identities, expand our capacity for intimacy, and, as we'll see, remake us into people of greater purpose and love.

So, what is it that you want to do with this wild, odd, and remarkable life you've been given?[2] There is no formula or guru or training program that can make this choice for you. We don't experience a meaningful life because we wake up one day and declare, "I am going to live a meaningful life!"

A meaningful life is a paradox. On one hand, we don't "pursue" a meaningful life. We already *have* a meaningful life, in the sense that our lives are suffused with meaning. What we're learning is how to wake up to that meaning and begin honoring who we truly are. In this sense, meaning really can be cultivated, though not typically through ambition or striving. It's something we see most clearly in hindsight, through remembrance, rather than something we actively set out to find.

Questions of meaning become most salient when we find ourselves in a place of powerlessness or we enter an unexpected situation and have no idea how to proceed. In these moments, we feel pulled back toward the familiar—the dissociated life, the life of optimization, or the pursuit of a bigger paycheck. If we have not awakened to the meaning of our existence and are not intentionally pursuing a life of purpose, we are in danger. There is no shortage of forces—culture, corporations, family systems—that would like nothing more than to become squatters in our unlived life. Over time, they will also steal our desires and ambitions to serve their interests. The saddest, most disturbing part is that you will not even recognize the con job has happened. What we think is our ambition to receive recognition, more success, and a favored seat at the table may have been quietly grafted into us by others.

We need to prepare now for the resistance we'll face when we pursue a more meaningful life. Take Michael Phelps, the most decorated Olympian of all time. During the 2008 Beijing Olympics, his goggles filled with water in the middle of a race. While this would have derailed many swimmers, Phelps swam blind for 175 meters of the 200-meter butterfly and set a world record. When asked afterward how he managed this, he said, "I was relaxed because I reverted back to my training." His coach, Bob Bowman, had deliberately conditioned him to swim without goggles and with poorly fitted goggles, preparing him for any scenario.[3]

As you picture the type of life you want to live, consider a few key questions: What desires burn within you? What would you give up everything to experience? Who do you want to walk alongside you on this journey? We may not be setting world records, but we will inevitably face obstacles in our respective lanes. The answer to these questions will determine how far we're willing to go and what we're willing to endure to make it possible.

This is where ambition becomes essential. While it often carries a bad reputation, ambition is the steady and necessary determination to bring our imagined future to life. It's the ability to tend to the flame of desire that is burning inside you. It's the call to something deeper and the force that disturbs you when you've settled for something safe, shallow, or false. When your ambition is healthy, it will fuel a meaningful endurance, dislodge you from complacency, and free you to outgrow the superficial cravings of the ego.

The final part of this book is designed to guide you toward cultivating a life of meaning and purpose. We'll explore the core traits necessary to develop it, how to lay claim to your heart, and the pillars that make it all possible. This final desire we'll be exploring together has the power to define the course of your entire lifetime.

## Three Traits That Define a Meaningful Life

As I underwent my own midlife chrysalis—a phrase that, for me, better captured the experience than the typical "crisis"—I became powerfully drawn to stories like never before. I immersed myself in classic novels like Homer's *The Odyssey*, sought out biographies and memoirs of historical icons who navigated significant inflection points, and reflected on the stories of several clients who had made bold decisions to alter the course of their lives for the better. In doing so, I began to notice three core traits that connected their journeys. I share these with you now in the hope that they can guide you as you awaken to and cultivate a meaningful life.

1. Embrace both grief and play.
2. Confront resignation and avoid self-sabotage.
3. Choose anxiety over depression.

### TRAIT 1: EMBRACE BOTH GRIEF AND PLAY

One of the most fundamental truths, and one that almost no one tells us about living a meaningful life, is that we will experience pain along the way. We see this truth reflected in the great journey of Odysseus. He weeps so consistently throughout his journey—for the home he cannot reach, the futility he can't escape, the lives lost around him, and the deep ache of separation from his family. In the same way, a meaningful life will intensify confusion, highlight our inadequacy, and might even evoke a sense of guilt as we shed the roles that others expect from us.

We might know, intellectually, that the cost of growth is pain. But there's a distinct kind of pain that comes from living with integrity. If you're experiencing pain as you move toward a more authentic existence, welcome it.

Carl Jung said, "Real liberation comes not from glossing over or repressing painful states of feeling, but only from experiencing them to the full."[4] Many of us were raised in environments where pain was either dismissed or inflicted, leaving us ill-equipped to know how to navigate it. To move through our pain, it's essential to create both safe and challenging spaces where we can process our feelings in our pursuit of greater purpose. This might mean carving out time to talk to a friend, journal, or engage in creative pursuits that allow us to know and express our feelings more authentically. One helpful practice is to look at a childhood photo from a time when we felt stuck or alone. Holding that image in mind, we can move forward not just for our adult selves, but for that child as well. Remembrance of pain, paired with creative action, is a powerful combination.

### Grieve Deeply

Grief has the power to reshape our desires. In the absence of grief, our desires lack substance. We end up trapped in a cul-de-sac of superficial pursuits—striving for a better body, accumulating more possessions, or pining for social recognition. Before committing significant time or resources to a desire, consider how grief might liberate you from a potentially fruitless search. Here are two examples of questions you can ask:

- *What is motivating my desire?* For example, a client of mine spent much of his thirties chasing a financial milestone to support his family. This good desire for financial security masked the deeper reality that his childhood vulnerability was not caused by a lack of money, but by a poverty of love. This insight freed him from feeling the pressure to earn enough for his family and to focus on how he could engage his spouse and kids more playfully and intentionally. They didn't need him to work himself into the ground; they needed his presence.

- *How are my good desires distracting me from my best desires?* One of my clients told me that she wanted to prioritize personal fitness in the year ahead and enrolled in a fancy gym with infrared saunas. All good desires. But in her pursuit of self-care, she noticed her desire for a gym membership was distracting her from something more core and indeed more difficult: a desire to feel at home in her body. Her tears fell softly with the realization that she hadn't felt free in her body since she was eight years old. She still got the gym membership, but her grief helped her understand that the better priority in the year ahead was to see a nutritionist to help her engage the intense longing and dread she had around food.

Grief doesn't always mean relinquishing the pursuit of something. Rather, it asks us to confront whether we're using external desires to sidestep an internal reality. As the Gospel of Matthew reminds us, "Blessed are those who mourn, for they will be comforted" (NIV). In the fertile soil of grief, yesterday's stories soften, allowing us to plant new desires for tomorrow, desires not dominated by shame.

Finally, grief prepares us for a more playful existence. Depth psychologist Dr. Bill Plotkin describes a "loyal soldier" within us—parts of our psyche that are fighting against threats that no longer exist. This concept derives from Japanese soldiers who remained loyal to their mission long after World War II had ended, unaware the war was over. When these men were discovered, they continued to exhibit extreme loyalty to their military mission, even firing at unsuspecting visitors. Although technically free, they remained trapped in a war that was over.[5]

We all have these loyal soldiers within us. We need to do what Japan ultimately did for their loyal soldiers: thank them for their service, reassure them that the war is over, and help them find more constructive roles for their talents. We can honor our soldier but also grieve how it kept us locked in unnecessary battles, robbing us of years of joy. Sorrow is what ultimately sets us free to play.

### Pursuing Play

One of the greatest gifts children offer us is that they remind us how to play. When my son was four and my daughter was two, their imaginations were alive with adventure. My son loved to transform into a jaguar, silently stalking his family and friends at the park, while my daughter would become a rattlesnake, pleading to be lifted up by her ankle so she could attempt to bite me before an amused audience. These playful afternoons were meaningful because I could let go of adult roles and find myself on a safari or in the middle of a sketchy snake-handling act.

Somewhere along the way, adults have learned to age too quickly. We need to become young again. Desire is the playground of adulthood.

Play doesn't just cultivate creativity or help us move through grief. On a physical level, it can *make* us younger. In 1981, eight men in their seventies entered a converted monastery in New Hampshire designed to be a time warp. Everything inside—the books on the shelves, the magazines, and the black-and-white televisions—were designed to remind them of 1959, the year when they were twenty-two. Led by Harvard professor Dr. Ellen Langer, they were encouraged to psychologically embody their younger selves, to pretend to *be* the person they were.

Before arriving, the men were assessed on physical and mental measures. After five days, the men were retested and outperformed a control group, showing increased dexterity, better posture, and even improved vision.[6] This experiment demonstrates the mind-body connection: When we engage in play, we can transform our physical and mental health.

Play doesn't have to look like reenacting your college years or putting on a field day with your friends (though that might be a good idea, too). It's about infusing the spirit of play into every dimension of life.

Is your work playful? Do you banter with your colleagues and customers, or feel safe enough to take creative risks? How about your sex life? The Sanskrit word for sexual intercourse is *kridaratnam*, which translates as "the jewel of games."[7] When was the last time your bedroom felt playful—when sex was full of laughter, lighthearted teasing, or something completely unexpected? Consider, too, the major conflicts in your life—are you free enough to approach them with a sense of humor? Play is all around us, inviting us to join.

When we talk about great composers like Mozart and Beethoven, we don't say they "worked" or "labored" at the piano. We say they *played* the piano.[8] While not all of us can be world-renowned musicians, we can all embrace our own artistry and allow play to infuse our endeavors.

We don't just need play as individuals; we need it as a society. When play and rest are absent, we cease to be fully human. In the Hebrew Bible, the people of Israel are encouraged to keep a Sabbath, a day of rest from labor. The rationale for this was to remind them they had once been slaves in Egypt but their God had delivered them. American minister, scholar, and poet Eugene Peterson notes, "The reason for Sabbath-keeping is that our ancestors in Egypt went four hundred years without a vacation."[9] The implication is clear: When play and rest are absent, we cease to be fully human and become like slaves, captive to the pharaohs of work, technology, and obligations.

In our society, one of the clearest impacts of this lack of play can be seen in education. When academic performance becomes the sole or primary focus, students suffer. Research shows that students at high-achieving high schools were three to seven times more anxious and depressed than the national average. Similarly, in China, despite their high academic rankings worldwide, over 75 percent of students reported feeling sadness and misery most or all of the time.[10] The health of our society should be determined not by its performance but by its capacity for joy.

### PRACTICAL WAYS TO PURSUE PLAY

- *Reflect on your life.* Where do you create—or where did you once create—as an act of play? How do you embody the essence of Mozart? Does your hospitality leave guests feeling cherished or wowed? Do you lose track of time while landscaping or baking? Do you compete in sports with passion and fire? Do you sing or play an instrument that brings awe or comfort to others?

- *Get outside for twenty minutes per day.* Research shows that spending as little as twenty minutes outside in nature or a green space can lead to a significant reduction in cortisol.[11] Take a walk, play Frisbee, or go birding. Invite a colleague or family member to come with you.

- *Revisit childhood joys.* Think about what you loved playing with as a child and find a way to pursue it next month. Whether it was riding a bike, hosting a board game or capture the flag, playing the guitar, or diving into a video game with friends, reconnecting with these activities can reignite your playful spirit.

- *Plan shorter, more frequent vacations.* Instead of placing immense pressure on one long vacation, prioritize shorter, more frequent getaways. One two-week vacation is a setup to come in exhausted and leave disappointed.
- *Introduce scarcity.* Consider abstaining from media or refraining from purchases one weekend per month. Then see what happens with that space you've created. Invent a game with items in your home; make a meal from the neglected items in the back of your pantry or freezer; allow yourself to get bored and see where your imagination takes you.

To live a meaningful life, lighten up. Allow your desires to become a playground where joy and meaning can flourish together.

### TRAIT 2:
### CONFRONT RESIGNATION AND AVOID SELF-SABOTAGE

Living a meaningful life demands active engagement with life's obstacles. Our brains are naturally designed to burn as few calories as possible, and living a meaningful life tends to expend considerable energy. On our journey with desire, we will be tempted to settle into resignation or seek self-sabotage. We will need to learn to confront both of these tendencies, or our lives will be defined not by meaning, but by regret.

Resignation is when we fall into the belief that "this is as good as it gets." In our choice to settle, we may conserve energy, but we will also reinforce the patterns we want to change. Overcoming resignation requires two traits: defiance and imagination.

### *Defiance: A Bold Stand Against Defeat*

Defiance is the bold refusal to believe that our lives don't matter. It's an act of rebellion against the evidence that convinces us hope is futile. When we commit to live purposefully, we might wonder: *Is it too late for me? Do I have what it takes? Am I worth the effort? What makes me think* this *time is going to be different?* These voices of doubt grow louder as we approach a tipping point, but we must meet these messages with defiance.

Defiance is more than willpower. It's a muscle that requires practice. One critical brain region that plays a significant role in our ability to persevere through adversity is the anterior midcingulate cortex (aMCC). The aMCC is activated when we make decisions that require effort, such as overcoming obstacles or enduring discomfort. Athletes typically have a larger aMCC, while individuals with more sedentary lifestyles often have a smaller one.

Recent neuroscience suggests that the aMCC is not just linked to willpower, but also to something more profound: the will to live.[12] While willpower helps us to push through immediate challenges and achieve short-term goals, strengthening our aMCC allows us to push through pain, maintain hope in the face of despair, and choose vitality despite overwhelming odds.

We can strengthen this part of our brain through both physical and soulful work. Practically, this might involve pushing past physical limits—carrying a heavy rock up a hill or running a longer distance than we thought possible. But don't miss the metaphor. Engaging our soul's hunger for meaning and purpose can push us past any limits we've set for ourselves. Sharing our hopes for change with a trusted friend, addressing self-sabotage with a therapist, or confronting our manipulation in a relationship are all decisions we often avoid. Yet each time we commit to this difficult work, our aMCC grows and we cast another vote for a meaningful life.

### Imagination: Creating a Compelling Vision

Imagination is more than just daydreaming about a better future; it's a cognitive tool that helps us overcome the limits we and others place on us. There will always be data that seduces us to despair and realities that seem to bind us. But our imagination can never be fully caged. Through it, we begin to consider a future we long for that does not yet exist.

In one study, the first group of participants was given flight suits and told to imagine themselves as skilled Air Force pilots. The second group stayed in their normal clothes and were told that the flight simulator was broken, but to still imagine they were flying a plane. After that exercise, both groups were given a vision test, in which the first group performed 40 percent better than the second group. Dr. Ellen Langer, who designed the study, noted that "mind-set manipulation can counteract presumed psychological limits."[13]

Many of us perceive our lives as broken-down simulators, unable to recognize our full potential. But what if we could reframe that narrative? What if we saw ourselves piloting an immensely valuable asset: our own lives?

Is it wild to you that imagination can improve vision? Imagination isn't about escaping reality, but about reshaping it to serve our potential. Many of us think we're simply going to therapy—but what if we see ourselves as the protagonist in a novel about healing generational trauma? We think we're just going to a job—but what if our work is contributing to the flourishing and reconciliation of all things? These aren't fairy tales; this is your life. If a little imagination and a flight suit can improve eyesight, we simply have no idea what could be achieved by honoring our hope within.

### Avoiding Sabotage:
### Breaking the Cycle of Destruction

While defiance and imagination are nonnegotiables for overcoming resignation, we also need to confront one of the most insidious obstacles to living meaningfully: self-sabotage. These often unconscious thought patterns and behaviors inhibit us from experiencing the life we want, mocking us each time we try to change. One of the reasons my clients struggle to want more from their lives is they have not taken self-sabotage seriously enough. Too often, we frame overindulgence, procrastination, or destructive decisions as mere ways to cope with the difficulties of life. But if we're honest, we know that these choices consistently lead to judgment, isolation, and the death of creativity. These are the markers of self-sabotage.

Why would we intentionally choose behaviors that will make us feel bad about ourselves? The answer lies in the negative beliefs and agreements we form in childhood, which then become ingrained in adulthood through destructive behaviors. Our behaviors mirror how highly or poorly we think about ourselves. Negative core beliefs like "I am too needy," "I am too impulsive," or "I'll never have the life I want" are more than perceptions—they are architects of our future.

Research shows that adverse childhood experiences often contribute to destructive adult behaviors. For instance, individuals who experienced childhood trauma are more likely to develop problematic drinking habits as adults.[14] The leading cause of alcoholism in men is household mental illness, while for women, it's emotional abuse.[15] Similarly, one in four gastric bypass recipients will develop alcohol addiction because the underlying drivers are not addressed.[16] Self-sabotage is complex. If we don't get to the root causes, there will always be another weed to deal with.

Psychologist and author Dr. Dan Allender told my graduate school that "all addictions are an effort to kill hope."[17] Allender is moving us toward our deeper war with freedom. Each time we sabotage ourselves, we are killing our hope that our life, our marriage, our career could be any different than what it is today. The endgame of sabotage is to convince us that we are broken beyond repair and incapable of meaningful transformation.

### The External Forces of Sabotage:
### Substances and Technology

Beyond the internal forces of sabotage, we live in a culture that promotes overindulgence—whether it's in food, substances, or technology. In the West, for example, sugar now contributes to more loss of life through diabetes than does human violence through war, crime, and suicide.[18] This excess has fueled the rise of diet culture and drastic interventions like gastric bypass surgery. Dr. Anna Lembke, author of *Dopamine Nation*, says it well: "The fact that we must resort to removing and reshaping internal organs to accommodate our food supply marks a turning point in the history of human consumption."[19] The madness of excess is that we crave more and more, yet our desires pull us in opposing directions, leaving us stretched and eventually torn between indulgence and wisdom's call for restraint.

Substance abuse, including alcohol, cannabis, and prescription drug misuse, plays a significant role in self-sabotage as well. In one study involving opioid addicts, participants were asked to complete a story beginning with the line, "After awakening, Bill began to think about his future. In general, he expected to . . ."[20] The average response for the addicts reflected a future spanning nine days, while a control group envisioned a future of nearly five years.

Our digital consumption is another major source of sabotage we need to address. Johann Hari's *Stolen Focus* reveals alarming statistics:[21] The average American spends over three hours on their phone daily, the average college student switches tasks every sixty-five seconds, and the average worker in an office only stays on task for three minutes. Another study found that workers lose around twenty-three minutes of concentration each time they are interrupted.[22] Professor Earl Miller, a neuroscientist at MIT, describes our current environment as "a perfect storm of cognitive degradation"[23] that erodes our capacity for deep, meaningful work.

While it's easy to blame unhealthy habits and predatory industry practices, the deeper issue is that we allow these external forces—technology, social media, consumerism—to become squatters in our lives. It takes a lot less work to let them occupy our mental and emotional real estate than to invest the effort in the renovation work required to make our life into a place we love enough to protect.

### Breaking Free:
### Practices for Confronting Resignation
### and Avoiding Sabotage

To overcome resignation and sabotage, we need to develop intentional focus and deliberate restraint. Here are some practices that can help:

- *Prioritize Time Management.* Start your day off with clear, prioritized goals. Break tasks into manageable chunks to prevent overwhelm and procrastination.

- *Focus on One Thing at a Time.* Practice single-tasking. Use apps that block distractions, or physically remove saboteurs, like turning off notifications, entering focus mode on your phone, turning off Wi-Fi, or putting your phone in another room.
- *Batch Tasks.* Group similar tasks together to build momentum and efficiency. Whether it's making calls, paying bills, writing emails, or doing creative work, batching helps reduce cognitive overload.
- *Create Rituals.* Develop simple rituals to signal to your brain when it's time to focus or rest—like lighting a candle before starting work or ending your day with a favorite beverage.
- *Reflect on Past Creativity.* Recall times when you were fully engaged and creative without relying on external sources. For example, a time you made up a game or completed a DIY project instead of hiring a contractor. What did that feel like?
- *Carve Out Creative Hours.* Dedicate three to five hours each week to activities that require deep creative engagement—writing, cooking, music, carpentry, etc.

By combining defiance, imagination, intentional restraint, and focus, we create the mental framework necessary to confront resignation and avoid sabotage. Each small act of resistance against these forces strengthens our brain's capacity for change and brings us closer to a life of meaning.

### TRAIT 3: CHOOSE ANXIETY OVER DEPRESSION

In John Steinbeck's novel *Cannery Row*, the character Henri is a master shipbuilder, but he has never finished a boat, despite working on them for years. His friends notice this pattern, and some are beginning to wonder if he's nuts. "You don't understand," his friend Doc says. "Henri loves boats but he's afraid of the ocean." Another friend asks the obvious question: Why does he want a boat, then? Doc replies,

"He likes boats. . . . But suppose he finishes his boat . . . he'll have to go out in it, and he hates the water. So, you see, he never finishes the boat—so he doesn't ever have to launch it."[24]

Desire launches us into the unknown sea, a place filled with anxiety but also the possibility of expanding who we are. Taking risks threatens the security of our lives, but remaining stagnant will prevent us from realizing the life we desire. Just like Henri, we must be willing to risk launching the boat, even if the waters are uncertain.

Anxiety can be a signal that we are stepping outside of our comfort zones, venturing into the unknown. Depression, on the other hand, stems from the belief that we are powerless to change or move forward. The Jungian analyst and author James Hollis wisely advises that we must choose anxiety over depression:

> If we move forward, as our soul insists, we may be flooded by anxiety. If we do not move forward, we will suffer depression, the pressing down of the soul's purpose. In such a difficult choice one must choose anxiety, for anxiety at least is a path of potential growth; depression is a stagnation and defeat of life.[25]

Hollis's words underscore a crucial truth that anxiety is a natural companion on the road to a meaningful life. Therefore, anxiety is not an enemy, but a sign that we are on the verge of something new.

As we navigate this tension, the task is to learn how to work *with* our anxiety. As the eighteenth-century philosopher Søren Kierkegaard wisely advised, we must learn to be anxious "the right way."[26] By this he meant increasing our tolerance for anxiety without needing to escape it. Modern neuroscience supports this idea, showing that one person's anxiety is another's excitement. The difference often comes down to how the individual interprets and works with the energy within their body.

In my research, we noticed that some individuals had very high anxiety scores—those who felt overwhelmed by life, overcome by challenges, and viewed themselves as generally anxious or fearful. For these individuals, anxiety wasn't something they were able to work with—it had become a debilitating force, leading to low confidence, heightened feelings of futility, and diminished sexual satisfaction.

Do you see the conundrum we face? Anxiety will visit all of us on the path toward a meaningful life. For some, it pushes them forward, confirming they are moving toward their desires. But for others, it becomes a crippling force, paralyzing them in fear. This shows us that the goal should not be to try to eliminate anxiety or let it control us, but to strengthen our ability to tolerate it and transform it into something that ultimately serves us. If we don't learn to work with anxiety, we increase the likelihood that we will fall into depression.

### The Trap of Depression and
### the Joy of Finding Your Heart

Early in my clinical practice, I saw depression as a signal that something painful or unbearable had occurred within or around a person. But, over time, I noticed more clients were experiencing depression symptoms not because of their innate personalities or life circumstances, but because they were comparing themselves to others. They'd scroll through social media and see friends, influencers, or colleagues who seemed confident and purposeful. In comparison, they felt stuck, unsure of themselves, or lost. This dissonance, the gap between what they thought others had and where they actually were, pressed down on their life force and undermined their self-worth.

But there's a shift some of them were able to make: Rather than fixating on a singular, predefined sense of self-worth shaped by the expectations or examples of others, they learned to define meaning on their own terms. Together, we explored questions like: *When do I feel like my life matters? What experiences or relationships have brought me joy, or even heartache?* These questions helped them connect with their authentic desires—not those shaped by unrealistic success metrics or the endless quest to keep up with others.

The key to overcoming stagnation and comparison-based depression lies in reconnecting with your heart. When you're disconnected from it, you will feel adrift, easily influenced, and eventually imperiled.

But your heart will always be a safe house. We can reconnect to it through finding our "yes"—those experiences that bring us laughter, joy, and hope. Conversely, we can also reconnect to it through our "no"—the trauma, heartache, and injustices that we've encountered.

Take the example of aspiring to become a Michelin-starred chef or be interviewed by Oprah or Joe Rogan. These are fine aspirations; but the pursuit of purpose requires a deeper dive into one's heart. It's about cultivating a profound love for your craft—finding joy in the work itself, regardless of whether those external outcomes materialize. And in doing so, you might increase the odds of Oprah and Rogan finding you.

Many Michelin-starred chefs became who they are because they connected to their "yes." Take the Italian chef Massimo Bottura, who recalls beautiful moments of hiding under a table in his grandmother's kitchen and stealing pieces of tortellini that fell to the floor. Reconnecting to this childhood story was instrumental in guiding him to create one of the world's best restaurants.[27] Similarly, many who have been invited onto Oprah's stage have allowed their "no" to be shaped by a deep commitment to justice or overcoming trauma. These individuals didn't spend their days preoccupied with what others had; they looked inside to discover where their heart came alive.

On the other side of the anxiety, you may feel—whether now or as you move forward—the deep satisfaction of knowing you've honored your longings, endured discomfort, and ventured deep into discovering your heart. Let anxiety push you forward, toward the person you desire to become.

### Personal Risks

What I hope has become clear throughout this book is that each of us has imposed significant limits on ourselves as a result of our upbringing and the difficulties we've encountered. We might want an expansive life, as massive and soaring as a cathedral, yet feel confined to a small shack of existence. Self-limiting beliefs reveal themselves through our negative self-talk. For example, you might find yourself thinking, *I want to fly-fish, but I have no idea how to use all the gear,* or *I want to learn how to cook, but I can barely make oatmeal,* or *I want to have better sex, but my body has never been my own.*

Behind every self-criticism lies a deeper wish. Perhaps you long to spend more time in nature, express your creativity through cooking, or foster deeper connection and differentiation with your partner. By identifying the desires beneath your criticisms, you can better understand where your life is summoning you to take a risk.

One great place to practice taking risks is in your creative life, outside of your job. The stakes are often lower here, but the lessons are immensely valuable. You might want to push yourself to learn a technique that intimidates you. This could mean journaling with your nondominant hand, attempting a complex DIY project, or embracing a physical challenge with a low risk of injury but a high chance of failure. Once you've identified a risk, write down two or three actionable steps that will bring you closer to your goal, and schedule them soon.

### Professional Risks

Ron Carucci, in his book *To Be Honest,* highlights the serious consequences of a lack of purpose in our work. He writes, "Disengagement is the resignation syndrome of organizations. And meaninglessness is the virus that causes disengagement."[28] When our work lacks meaning, we disengage, and because our professions are such a core dimension of our lives, this meaninglessness will inevitably spill over into our mental and physical health. Here are just a few studies that underscore this connection between our work and our well-being:

- Unemployed people had higher markers of inflammation in their bodies and were therefore at higher risk of illness.[29]
- Australian researchers found that a bad job is worse for mental health than being out of work.[30]
- In a famous study on British civil servants, a lower ranking on the ladder of authority was a greater predictor of death from heart disease than commonly listed risk factors such as smoking, cholesterol, or hypertension.[31]

- Only 39 percent of respondents in a 2019 Pricewaterhouse-Coopers survey reported they could see the value they created. A mere 22 percent agreed their jobs allowed them to fully leverage their strengths, and more than half weren't even "somewhat" motivated, passionate, or excited about their jobs.[32]

While our job may not always be the deepest source of our purpose, the research is clear: We need to feel like we are contributing to something meaningful at work, no matter how small. To shift this dynamic, we can find ways to bring more risk, whether playful or creative, into our professional lives.

One way to begin is by embracing small experiments. Challenge yourself to break the cycle of disengagement by intentionally stretching your skills or adjusting the energy you bring to your work. When you're feeling uninspired or uncomfortable, take fifteen to twenty minutes to step away from your desk, go for a walk, and consider how to engage more deeply with the work in front of you. This could be as simple as making a playful connection with a customer, brewing a pot of coffee and bringing it around the office to spread kindness and energy, or inviting a colleague to lunch to brainstorm how to reimagine a project or process you're both working on. Small, intentional acts compound into greater professional satisfaction.

When we feel inspired by our work and the ideas we generate, others are likely to feel inspired, too, contributing to a collective sense of purpose and vitality. Ultimately, it's crucial to our well-being that we spend a good portion of our days engaged in endeavors that hold significance, those that provide tangible evidence that *we matter*.

### Conclusion

Throughout this chapter, we've explored how to confront the obstacles that arise in our desire for meaning and purpose. We've learned that embracing pain, engaging in play, confronting resignation, avoiding sabotage, and choosing anxiety over depression are all essential steps on this path. These actions challenge us to move beyond superficial achievements and discover our hearts that yearn for authenticity and purpose.

Joseph Campbell, the renowned writer and mythologist, once said, "People say that what we're all seeking is the meaning for life. I don't think that's what we're really seeking. I think that what we're seeking is an experience of being alive."[33] I appreciate this nuance but don't believe the dichotomy between meaning and aliveness needs to persist. They are not separate, but interdependent. The more meaning we cultivate, the more it will prompt us to take greater risks, which will infuse vitality into our spirits. And the more alive we feel, the more meaningful our existence becomes.

In the next chapter, we will dive deeper into the skills and practices needed to cultivate meaning and purpose. We'll uncover the power of solitude, the role of meaningful relationships, and the importance of personal agency in creating a legacy that truly matters. The commitments you make to each of these elements will shape the quality of your life and ripple outward, influencing the lives of many generations. You have within you the power to design the life you most desire.

## CHAPTER 15

# How Do I Cultivate a Meaningful Life for Myself and Others?

*If you do not express your own original ideas, if you do not listen to your own being, you will have betrayed yourself. Also you will have betrayed our community in failing to make your contribution to the whole . . . apathy adds up, in the long run, to cowardice.*

—ROLLO MAY,
*Courage to Create*[1]

## Defining Meaning on Our Own Terms

In 1962, President John F. Kennedy was touring a NASA facility when he stopped to speak with a janitor. The president asked the man what he did for NASA. In a now-famous reply, the janitor said, "I'm helping put a man on the moon."[2]

I often think about this story when I work with clients like Kenji, who we met in the previous chapter. How is it that some people could find deep meaning in janitorial work, or something as simple as baking a cinnamon roll, while others—even those in professions dedicated to helping others—languish in their careers and feel stymied by a sense of purposelessness?

In today's world, we are driven by a powerful zeitgeist that ties meaning to grand achievements: building companies, changing the world, accumulating wealth.[3] But this narrow definition of success often leaves us feeling an acute sense of futility.[4] We keep seeking more money, a higher social status, and greater social impact than our neighbors. Yet no matter how much we accomplish, we're still left wondering: *Have I done enough? Am I successful yet?*

One of the greatest gifts we can give ourselves is to untangle our sense of meaning from our wealth, social status, and career achievements. Some of us will find our deepest meaning through our careers, but not everyone gets that opportunity. Not every job will turn itself into a passion project. So how can we define meaning in a way that feels authentic to who we are?

Instead of chasing external markers of success, we need to ask ourselves more personal questions:

- *Where do I feel joy?*
- *When do I feel truly alive?*
- *Who or what makes me feel like I matter?*
- *What unique abilities allow me to feel a sense of agency?*

In this chapter, we'll explore three pillars that are essential for cultivating lasting meaning and purpose in our lives. Much like the United States Constitution distributes power across three branches—legislative, executive, and judicial—to prevent any of the three from becoming too powerful, our pursuit of meaning thrives best when all three elements function in harmony. These three pillars are:

1. SOLITUDE: making space to listen to our soul and cultivate passion
2. RELATIONSHIPS: finding people who mirror and sustain our meaningfulness
3. PERSONAL AGENCY: understanding our calling and making a lasting mark on the world

Solitude helps us to define and develop a meaningful life. Relationships sustain that meaning. Personal agency empowers us to take actions that transform our lives—and the lives of future generations.

It's easy to devote too much focus to one pillar and neglect the others. For example, those who spend too much time alone can fall into a pattern of deprioritizing friendships, becoming disconnected from the heartbeat of their community and the places where they might receive and contribute. Those who focus heavily on relationships may do so at the expense of solitude, which limits their personal growth and, therefore, the depth of their connections. Others, obsessed with leaving a legacy, can become so fixated on managing their image or controlling their environment that they neglect their own hearts, turning their relationships into mere transactions.

### Solitude: The Practice of Listening to Our Soul and Cultivating Our Passion

Solitude is the slow, intentional practice of learning to be alone. It's a practice that allows us to listen to our souls, uncover what is truly meaningful in our lives, and devote time to nurturing it. In a world where loneliness is at epidemic levels, the idea of intentionally choosing to be alone might seem counterintuitive. However, while we are spending more time alone than ever before, much of it is spent in the company of distractions—digital screens, substances, or numbing behaviors. Therefore, the first step in cultivating solitude is learning how to be alone without an escape hatch.

Many believe, as experts suggest, that the antidote to loneliness is to establish meaningful connection with others. While this is partially true, Jungian analyst James Hollis offers a different perspective. "The antidote for loneliness is to embrace loneliness. As in homeopathy, the wound is healed by swallowing a bit of the toxin itself."[5] This suggests that rather than running from our feelings of loneliness, we should take small sips of it, allowing us to reflect, understand, and ultimately befriend these emotions. The cure for loneliness is in its embrace, and this can only happen when we have a practice of getting quiet and focused.

As we mature, we learn that we no longer need to flee from life's dismal places. Solitude shows us that we can trust in the strength of our bodies and the kindness of our minds to tend to the discomfort. As the noise of loneliness, anxiety, and the ego's need to perform lessens, we become more attuned to the longings of our hearts and where they wish to lead us. Without solitude, we risk using people as buffets and objects as opiates, grazing or numbing our way through life. We are indeed hungry people, but if we can see the metaphor in our desire for more, our hunger can become an ally in our quest for a meaningful life.

In this way, solitude is not about isolation but about creating a boundary that allows us to develop and refine our inner life. When we return to the world after time spent in solitude, we do so with greater clarity, differentiation, and purpose. If we don't learn to enjoy our own company or establish rhythms to develop our passions, we increase the odds of feeling aimless and meaningless. These negative symptoms serve as our soul's way of inviting us to enter solitude.

As you will see in the graph below, around the age of forty, there is a marked decrease in time spent with others. Regardless of our current age, it's essential to prepare for this inevitable shift and learn how to use this time for self-reflection and greater creativity.

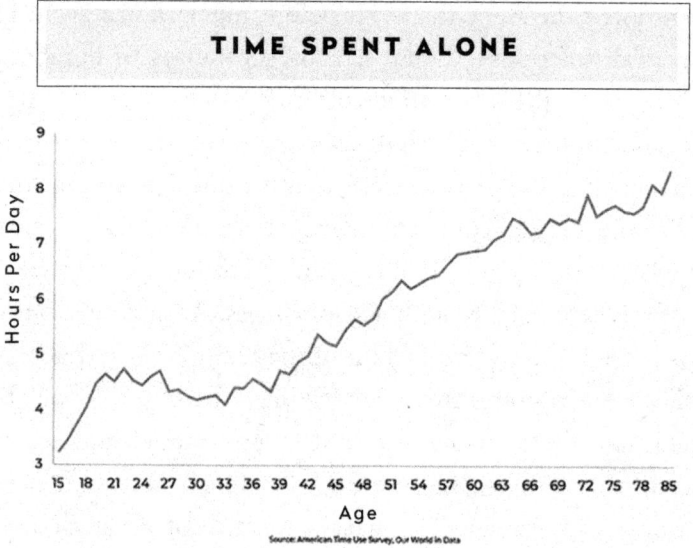

**TIME SPENT ALONE**

Source: American Time Use Survey, Our World in Data

Through solitude, we carve out intentional time to cultivate our passions. Many people lament not having enough time to engage in meaningful or creative activities. While work and family obligations certainly limit our time, the deeper issue often lies in how we choose to spend the time we do have. We must confront how much of it we spend on screens—endless reeling, scrolling, and numbing ourselves with digital content—and choose to instead transform that time into something meaningful.

For those who feel overwhelmed by the demands of their careers, stepping into solitude may feel impossible, even selfish. Yet, even carving out just twenty minutes a day to connect with yourself can be incredibly powerful. Solitude is a declaration that who we are becoming and what we love truly matters. Whether it's starting a carpentry project, pursuing an artistic endeavor, or contributing to a community initiative, solitude provides a fertile space where we can connect with our innermost longings and transform them into tangible creations. It's the space we've been waiting for to design the life we want.

While there is no exact prescription for practicing solitude, all of us need to develop practices to help us attune to our hearts and create space to create a life that is meaningful. In the *Desire Workbook,* I've included a list of daily and seasonal practices that have proven beneficial in my own process, along with prompts for reflection, if you're looking to get started.

## Relationships: The Mirrors and Sustainers of Our Meaningfulness

Relationships have always been, and always will be, complicated. Our family of origin can inflict indelible wounds, romantic partners bring us experiences of heaven and hell, and the absence of meaningful friendships can leave us feeling bereft. Yet, when we look back at the best moments of our lives, we often remember the faces of those who loved us and the people we gathered with around a table to plumb the depths of our existence. Relationships make life difficult, but they also make life worth living.

In this section, we'll explore two kinds of relationships that are essential to our journey to a meaningful life: guides and friends. Guides offer invaluable insight that can profoundly shape the direction and quality of our journey, while friendships act as mirrors, reflecting who we're becoming and bearing witness to the sorrow and achievements we encounter along the way. Both types of relationships are essential for discovering and awakening to a life of greater meaning.

## Finding a Guide

Several years ago, my friend Andy invited a group of friends to summit Mount Rainier (Tahoma) in Washington State. The terrain is filled with glaciers and permanent snowfields, and most of us had never encountered such a challenging climb. Around four A.M. on the day we were to summit, Andy decided to take a different route than the other mountaineering teams. My anxiety began to build, and my mind recalled a news story about a climber who lost their life on the mountain days before. I questioned Andy, asking why we were deviating from the path everyone else was following. His calm response, without the slightest hint of pretension, was, "I've taken this route on my previous three summits."

Every hero's journey includes moments when guidance is needed beyond what a friend, lover, or community can provide. Whether you're growing a business, facing a mental health challenge, or searching for answers to profound spiritual questions, turning to an expert for guidance is a wise investment. Guides know the way to the destinations we seek, and their confidence is a secure base to which we can bring the anxiety and doubts that swirl within us. To live a great story, we need to find a guide.

Despite the obvious benefits, we often resist seeking guidance. Our previous programming may tell us that no one can truly help, that we don't have the resources, or that we're not worthy of investment. One of the heartbreaking findings from the Holistic Desire Survey was that men with high rates of childhood stress and very little support for their desires tended to fare poorly as adults. The odds of them having good psychological health as an adult were reduced by 73 percent. For women in similar circumstances, the odds dropped by 64 percent.

Here's the important point: Those of us who need guides the most are also the least likely to seek them. When we lack guidance as children, it sets a template for what we come to expect from guides and other authorities as adults. Learning to desire a guide is, therefore, an act of defiance against this conditioning.

The guides we choose will serve as mirrors of where we are in our journey. For instance, if you're in a confusing existential season, be cautious about seeking a guide who promises to remove your uncertainty by telling you exactly what to do. On the other hand, if you're facing a health crisis, finding a knowledgeable healthcare provider who can guide you with confidence and specificity is not just wise, but essential.

Here are a few questions to help you establish a healthy interrogation for the guides you seek:

- Do I respect this person? Do I want to become like them?
- What kind of person will this guide help me become?
- Why am I drawn to this person? (Do they appeal to a confused, wounded, or angry part of me?)

Many guides attract followers through charisma, social media presence, or a glittering public image. But deep down, we may sense that if we follow them too closely, they will mold us into someone we don't want to be. Listen to that voice. It's important to recognize that some of the most influential voices offer a path that helps us avoid the hard, iterative work of truly building one's life.

### Diversify Your Guidance

Rather than seeking one guide on our journey, we should pursue multiple sources of wisdom. A therapist helps us move from the life we have to the life we want. Spiritual teachers help us integrate the horizontal aspects of life to vertical, eternal perspectives. A dietician or personal trainer can help us reconcile our competing desires for health and ease. Guidance, like our desires, must be diversified. The common denominator among all the guides we will find is that they will help us integrate the disparate parts of ourselves, calling our attention to ways we live and think that we haven't been able to articulate for ourselves.

It's also crucial to diversify our guides not just according to expertise, but by demographics. Do your guides share the same gender, ethnicity, religion, or age? Holistic growth requires perspectives that span philosophy, culture, and life experience. The tension and ambiguity between these differing viewpoints can help us cultivate our own inner knowing, grounded in the wisdom found in tradition. Choose wisely. The guidance you will one day offer to others will be shaped by the guides you let into your life today.

Finally, remember that while a guide can offer invaluable support, they cannot and should not make your choices for you. In Homer's *The Odyssey*, Circe is a complex character, but one of her key roles is as a guide. She tells Odysseus of the underworld he must visit and advises him of the dangers he will face as he sails near the Sirens, Scylla, and Charybdis. Yet no matter how much preparation Circe offers, it's Odysseus who must face the temptations and chaos ahead. A guide can show us the route, but only we can choose to sail through the anxiety and anguish that lie in our path.

## Cultivating Friendships

The novelist and philosopher C. S. Lewis makes a helpful distinction between companions and friends. A companion shares an interest with us, such as a common religion, profession, or hobby. A friend, Lewis suggests, is someone who shares a common question—a person with whom we explore life's deeper mysteries and purposes. According to Lewis, these two people need not agree on the answer, but they agree that the questions inside of them are of great importance.[6]

Consider the five core desires we've been exploring: Wholeness, Growth, Intimacy, Pleasure, and Meaning. If we are to live lives of purpose, our hope should be to build friendships with people who are themselves growing in these areas and questioning how to do so most authentically. For example, I have friends who are passionate about optimizing their personal growth—we share inspiring podcasts, tackle physical challenges together, and grab a beverage to hold one another accountable. Because of them, I now do yardwork while wearing a GORUCK rucksack. Other friendships are built on the foundation of shared vulnerability. I know these people's most sacred memories, and they know mine. I have other friends who are on their own journeys of meaning and influence. Together, we celebrate each other's milestones, but just as importantly, we share in the struggles that accompany such journeys.

It's rare to find one friend who embodies all five of these desires in the same season of life. Instead, our goal should be to diversify our friendships, increasing the likelihood that each desire is being cultivated.

### Loneliness: The Barrier and Bridge to Friendship

For many of us, the challenge isn't just a lack of diversity in our friendships. It's the absence of friendships altogether.

Loneliness is growing in our world, and the consequences are lethal. A meta-analysis of 148 studies concluded that a deficiency in interpersonal relationships increases the risk for mortality to levels comparable to smoking, alcohol, and heart disease.[7] And for men, building relationships can be even more challenging, as they are often conditioned to suppress their vulnerabilities. One study found that 15 percent of men report having no close friends, a fivefold increase since 1990. Additionally, only 21 percent receive emotional support from friends on a weekly basis.[8]

Loneliness is an epidemic, but it can also become a bridge to connection. The paradox is that disconnection, while painful, is often the precise thing that drives us to make more meaningful bonds with others. This doesn't happen by accident, however. It requires us to develop two essential qualities: vulnerability and mutuality. Together, they create what Dr. Dan Siegel describes as "feeling felt," the sense of being truly understood and connected to another person.[9] Whether we're grappling with loneliness or seeking to deepen an existing friendship, vulnerability and mutuality are key to unlocking greater meaning and purpose in our lives.

## *Vulnerability: The Gateway to Meaningful Connection*

In today's world, vulnerability can be a mind-bender. We're encouraged to embrace our imperfections and prioritize connection, yet society continues to glorify heroism, personal triumph, and relentless hustle. When was the last time you saw someone recognized for their extraordinary ability to be vulnerable against all odds? Instead, we're taught to view our limitations as flaws to work on rather than pathways to intimacy. Society may preach the gospel of connection, but it immortalizes rugged individualism.

The cost of avoiding vulnerability is immeasurable: isolation, a life spent chasing success metrics set by unhealthy systems, and, ultimately, meaninglessness. When our sense of self becomes tethered to the roles we perform rather than the authenticity we embody, we grow disconnected from others and our true sense of purpose.

Yet vulnerability comes at a cost, too. It exposes us to two agonizing but essential experiences: being seen in our shame and enjoyed in our glory. Both can feel unbearable. But without embracing them, real intimacy remains out of reach. Vulnerability isn't just part of connection; it is the price of admission.

Shame is one of the harshest forces on earth, distorting our self-perception and convincing us to believe we are unworthy of belonging. But shame is more than just a painful emotional state; it is a diabolical vortex that hurls us far away from living a meaningful and purposeful life. It meticulously documents our flaws, bringing them into sharp focus anytime we attempt to grow or change. Left unprocessed, it can annihilate the very life force inside us.

In my research, I've found that vulnerability plays the essential role in overcoming shame and the self-destructive behaviors that accompany it. Participants who had someone to confide in reported feeling far less shame and engaging in fewer self-destructive behaviors. The paradox is this: *When I need vulnerability the most, shame will make me desire it the least.*

Shame tells us it is better to improve ourselves before we allow ourselves to be known. We mistake this self-protection for wisdom, but in reality, we are being servants of shame. Dismantling shame requires an uprising of vulnerability. Shame cannot survive in an environment rich in kindness. This is its ultimate defeat: The shame that once isolated us becomes the very foundation for our strongest relational bonds.

Even more challenging than being known in our shame is being enjoyed in our glory. In my work as a psychotherapist, I've come to believe people find it easier to endure criticism than to suffer praise. While having our flaws exposed is painful, if you really want to see people run for the hills, try delighting in them. They will downplay their achievements, deflect praise onto others, and make self-deprecating remarks to soil the beauty and dignity you recognize in them.

One reason we struggle being enjoyed is that we're taught from an early age that it is more blessed to give than to receive. Receiving can feel like weakness, a public confession of our emotional hunger. Therefore, it's psychologically easier to see ourselves as generous than as people who need and want the generous presence of others. While the world certainly needs more generosity, the greater task of our time may be to recognize how essential it is to be receivers.

When we choose to cultivate our relationship to desire, our progress will eventually become evident. It's important to consider how we will respond when others celebrate our growth. A voice within may insist that praise is premature or receiving delight is a trait of neediness. As friends, it's part of our job to playfully call out these deflecting strategies so that we can bask in giving and receiving kindness for one another.

Friendship gives us a front row seat to one another's glory. We have the privilege of bearing witness to who our friends are becoming and the antagonists they've needed to overcome. In many ways, becoming a better friend is simple, but it requires intentionality. We might grab a meal with them after a significant stretch where a lot was required of them—caring for an aging family member, completing a major work project, navigating considerable conflict in their marriage. Rather than offering general platitudes, we ask them to tell stories. We listen not only to the events they recount but to the meaning they've made of them. A good friend creates space for reflection, asking questions that deepen understanding. But above all, we take the vulnerable risk of expressing delight—celebrating how beautiful we find their compassion, brilliance, or integrity to be. Good friends hold up mirrors for one another and refuse to take them down until they remember all over again how beautiful they are.

## Questions to Deepen Connection

If you're ready to practice more vulnerability in your relationships, or if you feel like your conversations with your closest friends are falling short, consider asking a few of the questions below to someone you trust. These questions have increased my vulnerability with friends in recent years. Feel free to adapt them to inspire your own vulnerable conversations.

- What's one challenge I'm facing right now that my shame is telling me to keep quiet or hide?
- How can I experience greater freedom in my professional work rather than feeling bound to an old identity? (For example, sometimes being a licensed mental health therapist can feel like an extension of the "helpful" and "good" provisional self I learned in my family.)
- What has been the most difficult aspect of being in a friendship with me? And how has that affected you? (For example, I've been told I will often prioritize work or new opportunities at the expense of relationships.)
- Here's a specific fight my wife and I keep having: _____. I recognize my contempt is a major factor, but I'm so frus-

trated by her actions. Given what you know about me (or us), what do you hear?

- Here are a few aspects of being a dad, therapist, or human being that I'm loving and experiencing success in: _____. What have you observed in those areas? Are there any other areas of my life where you see me alive and living in alignment with my passion or talents?

Vulnerability paves the way to the life less traveled. Through intentional acts of vulnerability, we increase both the quality of our friendships and the meaning of our lives.

Now let's turn to the second core dimension of friendship: mutuality.

### Mutuality: How Friendships Help Us Sustain Health and Stay Accountable

Many of our friendships form around shared circumstances, such as living in the same neighborhood, having children in the same school, or working together. While these situational bonds have value, they don't typically form us into the best versions of ourselves. To do that, we need to move beyond proximity and shared routines and into full participation in one another's lives.

At its core, mutuality is the commitment to becoming empathetic witnesses to one another's lives. As adults, our potential for joy and heartache increases with each passing year. We get the promotion, welcome a child into the world, or reach a milestone in marriage or our twelve-step program. Yet too few of us have friendships where we feel truly seen and celebrated in these moments.

At the same time, heartache is an ever-present reality: a chronic health condition, job dissatisfaction, a divorce or family conflict, or something we never could have anticipated. As we've discussed, trauma isn't just about the harmful event itself, but about enduring it in isolation.

When friendships lack mutuality, we're more likely to turn to unhealthy behaviors instead of relationships in times of pain. This leads to isolation, numbing, and a sense of powerlessness. Each of these is kryptonite to our desire to be known by others and live a meaningful life. Mutuality, however, helps prevent trauma from taking root and significantly reduces the chances of self-sabotage taking over.

Another crucial aspect of mutuality is accountability. For many, this word carries negative associations, and for good reason. It's often been tied to a culture of surveillance, where people feel judged for not measuring up. Healthy accountability is something entirely different. It's not about catching someone doing something "bad"; it's about catching them as they wake up to the deeper desires of their heart. Friendships offer a space to learn from setbacks, receive encouragement, and support one another in creating a life we long to experience.

There are several ways to make sure accountability remains healthy and effective. The first is for good friends to take time to understand each other's stories before offering accountability. Instead of just hearing one another's goals—whether for fitness, career, or spiritual growth—we need to understand the deeper motivations behind them. This ensures that we're not imposing rigid expectations or supporting underdeveloped desires but reminding each other how these goals connect to the larger story of who we're becoming. Friends who understand each other's "why" are best able to help one another calibrate their desires for the road ahead.

The second aspect of effective accountability is the courage to be honest. In our modern world, our progress may be hindered not by too much accountability but by too little. We sometimes avoid being honest out of a fear of conflict or of hurting the other person, or simply because we've never seen intentional support modeled. While avoiding discomfort may reduce tension in the moment, abdicating our power will ultimately diminish the quality of our friendships. Love is not about being nice. It must be strong enough to risk disruption for the sake of flourishing. Think of it like this: I may not like my dentist giving me feedback that I have a cavity, but it's better than him telling me two years later that I'm going to need a root canal.

The motto of mutuality in friendship could be summed up like this: *We are for one another, we are with one another, and occasionally, we are against one another—all in the service of love.* True friends stand with us, but they also challenge us to be more when we lack authenticity or when we're headed down a path of ruin. Sometimes, our love for one another is most clearly displayed in our willingness to be against each other. Challenge, when given with great kindness, helps us remember what we want and who we are meant to be.

See the *Desire Workbook* for the five best practices for offering feedback.

## One of the Primary Barriers to Mutuality: Envy

Envy is not only a primary barrier to mutuality and a meaningful life, but it also has the power to destroy both. According to psychologist Dr. Dan Allender, envy resides at the intersection of lust and anger. It's when an intense desire for something we don't have converges with resentment or contempt for those who do. There will be times in life when we will envy others, and times when others will envy us. Recognizing and preparing for this dynamic is essential for maintaining healthy relationships—and, as we will see, calibrating our sense of purpose.

A poignant portrayal of how envy can destroy a life is seen in 1984's Academy Award winner for Best Picture, *Amadeus,* where the composer Antonio Salieri becomes consumed by envy of Mozart's extraordinary talent. Salieri cannot accept that God gave Mozart a gift that he has not been able to achieve despite decades of rigorous effort. His unchecked envy becomes the defining force of his existence, leading him to bitterness and eventual self-destruction.[10]

Take a moment to consider what you envy in others. This feeling can be triggered by virtually any realm of someone else's life—their wealth, beauty, marriage, singleness, children, body, or career. When envy is unexamined, it distorts our perspective, narrowing our field of view to the point where we can only see what we lack and what others have in abundance. This can lead us to jockey for social position, compete for validation, or turn toward gossip or vitriol to make others suffer for what they have.

On the flip side, when others envy us, it can feel deeply uncomfortable. We may notice our achievements being undermined or our talents critiqued in the worst possible light. It's common to feel like we need to diminish or hide our successes or inherent beauty to avoid making others feel "less than." While being the envy of others might seem like a more favorable position than the alternative, it comes with the heavy burden of having a target placed on our backs.

One of the tricky things about envy is that it's often misidentified. We might label a friend as *needy* or say they have a "high-conflict personality." While these descriptors may contain some truth, they fail to address the root cause of envy. A friend who seems needy may be immensely envious of the life we have (lust), and when they don't receive the attention or validation they crave, their frustration escalates to anger or passive-aggressiveness. In an instant, a friend or family member, once a source of deep connection, can shift into someone carrying decades of unprocessed bitterness, resentment, and a long, detailed list of grievances in their armory.

Envy is not typically something that can be quickly fixed, but the first steps toward growth are recognizing it and developing curiosity about why it is manifesting. At times, envy is an invitation to realign with our authentic identity. At other times, it's a window into our deepest desires. When we acknowledge our envy and respond to it maturely, we can spare ourselves from days, or even a lifetime, of emotional turmoil.

The most effective antidotes to envy are gratitude and curiosity. When we see glory in one another, we are meant to celebrate it and honor the backstories that forged the beauty or strength we now behold. Envy can also show us what we most deeply want. Learning to be curious about why we envy someone can prevent its dark energy from consuming us. Maturity lies in allowing envy to be a signpost to the life we most desire and calibrating our next steps accordingly.

## Breaking Barriers: The Golden 13 and the Power of Vulnerability and Mutuality

A powerful real-life example of mutuality and vulnerability in action is the story of the Golden 13, the first African American officers in the U.S. Navy. In 1944, despite the navy having one hundred thousand Black men enlisted, none of them held the rank of officer. Under pressure from President Roosevelt's administration, the navy was charged with creating a pathway for African American men to rise to officer status. The stakes were extraordinarily high. These men faced racism on the job and were under immense pressure to prove that they had the right temperament and talent for leadership.

To sabotage their success, some of their leaders cut their training from sixteen weeks down to just eight, essentially setting them up to fail. But instead of succumbing to injustice, these men chose to lean into mutual support. They understood their success would impact not only their own futures but also the future of Black men in the navy. They leaned on one another, vulnerably and creatively offering support through the immense challenges before them.

The men were supposed to be in bed with lights out by 10:30 P.M., but each night they draped sheets over their windows to conceal their light, studying together by flashlight in the bathroom. Their effort paid off. They scored so well on their exams that many in Washington, D.C., refused to believe their results were legitimate. When they were asked to retake their exams, they scored even higher.

Their success didn't stem from individual brilliance alone, but from their collective ability to embrace vulnerability and allow it to show them their need for mutual support. As one of the group's members, George Cooper, put it, "We decided early in the game that we are all going to either sink or swim together. We were serious about this. I can remember sitting in the head at night after lights out, just drilling each other back and forth until it literally hurt, because we were convinced that if one of us made it, we were all going to make it."[11] The story of the Golden 13 demonstrates the profound power of friendship.

These men shared a common question: How do we succeed in the face of insurmountable odds? They embraced their vulnerability, offered mutual support, and remained accountable to one another through their grueling twenty-hour days.

Their journey shows that our traveling companions are not just an important part of a meaningful life; they can be the very essence of it. The relationships we nurture with friends and guides remind us that we are deeply loved and capable of receiving the support we need as we press forward in the life we've been given. Meaning is not always found in the destinations we reach, but in the stories we write and later retell with those who've walked beside us.

## *Personal Agency: Aligning Desire with Meaningful Contribution*

The final dimension of a meaningful life involves a desire for the flourishing of others. This is the true litmus test for a healthy relationship to desire: Do I want the wholeness, growth, intimacy, pleasure, and meaning for my neighbor, or just for myself? If our desires fail to eventually serve the well-being of others, we risk turning them into tools for selfish ambition, thus contributing to the suffering of those around us.

Consider the father who chases after his "desire" for meaningful work but abandons his children in the process. Or the infamous Tuskegee syphilis study, where doctors, driven by a desire for scientific advancement, lied to six hundred Black men by telling them they were being tested and treated for "bad blood," a local term for several ailments. In reality, they were withholding a diagnosis and proper treatment for syphilis that roughly two-thirds of the men had.[12] Selfish desire, in any form, is a threat to human flourishing.

When we discover how to align our personal agency with making a meaningful contribution to others, we begin to hear the voice of our true calling. This calling is not a fixed destination but an ongoing dialogue between our innermost desires and the world around us—where it both inspires us and breaks our heart.

To cultivate our calling requires a twofold attunement. First, we need to be keenly in tune with our own desires, becoming intimately familiar with the themes in our life that matter most to us—our "yes." But we also need to take time to attune to the world around us, paying attention to what is broken or beautiful, and noticing what calls out to us. Our calling exists at the intersection of these two forces, where we are most alive and where the world, whether in its beauty or its pain, bids us to engage more fully.[13]

A compelling example of calling is seen in the life of Bryan Stevenson, the civil rights lawyer and author of *Just Mercy*. Stevenson felt burdened not only to tell the truth about our country's prison system but also to inspire others to collectively shape the future. He understood that confronting America's painful past would meet significant resistance, but he also believed that through the courage to face the truth, doors to healing and justice could be opened.

In 2018, Stevenson's passion led him to create the National Memorial for Peace and Justice and the Legacy Museum in Montgomery, Alabama. Visitors can walk among 800 steel monuments bearing the names of more than 4,400 Black people killed in lynchings between 1877 and 1950. The museum invites visitors to travel through 400 years of American history—showing the devastating legacy of enslavement, racial terrorism, segregation, and mass incarceration. Stevenson channeled his raw desire for justice and his awareness of historical racial atrocities to create a haunting and breathtaking memorial.[14] It's an inspiring example of how personal purpose, when directed toward the common good, creates a remarkable contribution to society.

## *What Story Does Your Life Tell?*

This raises an important question: What story does your life tell? At the beginning of our journey into desire, our pursuit of meaning may have been focused on making a name for ourselves, accumulating possessions, and measuring our worth against others. Or perhaps we were so consumed by anxiety or the need to please others that we couldn't fathom our lives holding any real significance.

Yet, as we mature, we begin to resonate with Rainer Maria Rilke's insight that we grow by being defeated by ever greater things.[15] Over time, we become less driven by lesser desires, like people-pleasing or performance metrics, and more drawn toward living out our calling—one that brings personal joy and promotes the welfare of others. In this pursuit, we find ourselves longing to be defeated not by fleeting ambitions, but by the enduring values that have inspired so many remarkable individuals before us: history, compassion, courage, justice, and love.

There are two types of light that can sharpen our clarity about purpose: stadium lights and starlight. In his book *Stolen Focus,* Johann Hari uses the metaphor of stadium lights to represent collective causes and efforts that unite us, such as cancer awareness, civil rights, environmental stewardship, or community service. Stadium lights shine brightly when we join together to support a shared goal, broadening our perspective and reminding us that we are part of something larger than ourselves.

In contrast, starlight is best seen in the darkest, most remote places—symbolizing the introspection, personal discovery, and spiritual insight that come when we leave the familiar world. These lights appear when we intentionally seek time alone or with a trusted guide, to experience solitude, a rite of passage, spiritual practices, or simply a retreat into nature. Sometimes, though, we find ourselves under starlight not by choice, but because something in our life has fallen apart, forcing us into the wilderness. In these moments, starlight guides us to deeper questions that are often obscured by the constant distractions of daily life. While we may reach for our phones thousands of times a day, starlight compels us to reach within, searching for answers in the vastness of the world both within and around us.[16]

Reflect on what might be inhibiting you from cultivating your calling. Do you find yourself dominated by personal ambition or endless striving, exhausted by hustle or self-sabotage? Or do you feel overwhelmed by the constant demands of others, to the point that you have no idea about your own needs or direction? In either case, your sense of agency—your capacity to effect meaningful change—will be underdeveloped. The more we attune to our inner world, the more we recognize which type of light we need in any given season.

If you're struggling with existential dread or find yourself stuck in a cycle of prioritizing ambition over connection to others, it may be time to step toward the stadium lights, where you can see a story at play that is larger than your individual concerns. However, if you've never taken time to reflect on your own desires and have habitually neglected your own soul in the service of others, it might be wise to prioritize starlight for the time being. Doing so will ensure that your contributions come from a place of authenticity and reduce your susceptibility to burnout.

While it's never an either-or situation, there are seasons in life when recalibration is necessary. This is why attuning to our own hearts is so critical. Sometimes it's the pain of the world that calls us into action, while other times, the beauty of the world beckons us to engage more passionately. Both are essential, but what does your heart most need right now? If you're uncertain, experiment by seeking out both types of light in the next month and noticing where the deepest joy lies.

## *The Surprising Benefit of Supporting Others*

While we've discussed the benefits of self-care, research has shown that caring for others has even more powerful effects on our well-being. In one study, participants were divided into three groups, each tasked with focusing on a different action each day. One group was asked to perform an act of kindness for someone else, another group told to hold someone in their thoughts with affection or prayer, and the third group to focus on an act of self-care. At the end of the study, those who performed acts of kindness for others had healthier immune responses and less inflammation than the other two groups. Interestingly, the self-care group finished third.[17]

As Sahil Bloom and Arthur Brooks put it, "Happy people love people, use things, and worship the divine; unhappy people use people, love things, and worship themselves."[18] The desire to make a positive difference in the lives of others is not only a sign of personal maturity; it also leads to greater personal happiness and health. Let's turn to a few ways you can start.

### PRACTICAL WAYS TO SEEK THE FLOURISHING OF OTHERS

- START LOCALLY. You don't need to travel far to find a cause or a person in need of love. Look within your neighborhood or town. Where is it hurting? What issues exist? Where is it already beautiful? Listen and learn as much as you can before taking action; you might find an organization already doing remarkable work that you can join with to foster greater healing or flourishing.
- ASSESS YOUR RESOURCES. Consider what you have to offer— time, talents, finances, or practical experience. Who in your community could benefit from what you have?
- IDENTIFY YOUR PASSIONS. What themes resonate with you? Do you enjoy youth sports, mental health, beautification of a neighborhood, food, etc.? Frederick Buechner says it well: "The place God calls you to is the place where your deep gladness and the world's deep hunger meet."[19]
- EMBRACE MUTUALITY. Many people enter communities to give something back and say something along the lines of "I received so much more than I gave." While partially true, this can hinder the development of genuine relationships. Center mutuality in your relationships, not just service.

### *The Capstone of a Meaningful Life: Becoming a Transitional Character*

When we faithfully live out our calling, work toward the flourishing of others, and allow our hearts to be shaped in the wilderness, we position ourselves to become what Dr. Carlfred Broderick calls a transitional character:

A person, who, in a single generation, changes the entire course of a lineage. Who somehow finds a way to metabolize the poison and refuse to pass it on to their children. They break the mold. Their contribution to humanity is to filter the destructiveness out of their own lineage so that the generations downstream will have a supportive foundation upon which to build protective lives.[20]

There are few greater legacies than becoming a transitional character. This transformation is the result of iterative movements we make toward living with greater meaning and purpose. We see this in the stories of Lauren, Kenji, the Golden 13, and Bryan Stevenson. Each of their journeys is significant because they became transitional characters, impacting not only their families but, in some cases, society as a whole. Their path didn't start with grand ambitions to revolutionize society or disrupt the status quo. It began with honoring the spark of life within themselves and developing the inner defiance to refuse the life and society they were pressured to accept. The capstone of a meaningful life is not what we achieve, but who we become—transitional characters who break destructive cycles for future generations.

## Conclusion

A meaningful life is formed through the practices of solitude, intentional relationships, and the pursuit of agency. Solitude provides the intentional space and time for reflection and personal growth; relationships help us stay connected and accountable to our best desires; and personal agency guards against our natural drift into self-absorption, filling us with the longing to contribute fully to others and future generations. When we cultivate these practices, we find our hearts alive with purpose and satisfied with meaning.

As you've gotten in touch with your desires, I hope you've gained a greater sense of their beauty and power. While many use desire to escape life or build temples for themselves, we are learning to let desire push us toward a more embodied, loving, and purposeful existence than we could have ever imagined. Before we conclude our time together, I want to offer a few final thoughts on how to live well into desire. It's time to reflect on your journey, learn how to protect your five core longings from imbalance and stagnation, and create the environment that will allow your desires to evolve and flourish in the years ahead.

# Conclusion:
# The Ongoing Journey
# of Desire

AT THE END OF ANY GREAT JOURNEY, IT'S IMPORTANT TO PAUSE, take out a map, and reflect on how far we've come. This moment is no exception. As you look back, I hope you're inspired by how vast and intricate the desires are within you. They are the foundation of everything that matters in your life.

We began this book with an invitation to excavate your childhood story instead of dismissing it or overlooking the significance of it. From there, we explored how to live through the crucibles in our life, ensuring that our desires for growth are rooted in authenticity. We then ventured into the heart of intimacy, learning how to navigate its obstacles and develop the skills needed to build a lifetime of love. We explored sex, discovering the profound revelations and healing it can provoke. Finally, we explored how habits of solitude, relationships, and personal agency help us satisfy our longing for meaning and purpose.

Throughout this book, you have encountered stories of individuals reaching critical inflection points in their relationship with desire: people like Lauren, who reclaimed her life from a mother who governed her desires; Leslie and Ryan, who had avoided sexual desire but eventually allowed it to heal them; and Kenji, whose life was unexpectedly transformed thanks to a cinnamon roll. Each of them felt stuck in an unwanted dimension of their life, but eventually allowed their desire for more to lead them onto the unpredictable, sometimes anxiety-inducing path toward a fuller, more authentic life.

Truth be told, I don't know what shape or direction your desires should take from here. However, I do know it's all too easy to revert to our default modes of operating, even after we've recognized the importance of cultivating a better relationship with desire. Many will read this book and gain insights about intimacy but continue to neglect those they purport to love. Others may reconnect with their faith, only to use it to spiritually bypass the heartaches and relational tension that lie ahead. Some may become Joan of Arcs in their fields of work, making an indelible contribution to the world, while their intimate relationships or mental health implode. These regression patterns are common, but they are also clarion calls, signaling the need to return to a holistic and robust relationship to desire.

## *Three Final Desire Recommendations*

To sustain your growth in the years ahead, I want to leave you with three final recommendations: Find your village, recognize that life comes through death, and remind yourself, as often as you need, of the immense beauty inside you.

### FIND YOUR VILLAGE

In *The Wild Edge of Sorrow,* author Francis Weller speaks to our collective longing for life in a "village."[1] Villages are communities that embody several characteristics: They care deeply about our growth, maturity, and healing; they include elders who possess the strength and wisdom to guide us; and they are available when we need them. A village could be found through friends in your neighborhood, your local church, or a place like a café. While proximity is important, the most essential feature is a consistent place where you are deeply known and can offer that gift to others as well. While this vision for community is powerful, a village like this can be hard to come by in our increasingly fragmented and individualistic society.

Sometimes, the best we can do is to seek out communities that offer a partial fulfillment of the village. We join a local fitness community to support our physical health. We join a faith community that invites us into a story larger than ourselves and, hopefully, allows elders and younger generations to connect with one another. We seek out a mental health professional to guide us through challenges we haven't known how to navigate. When we find these pieces of a village, we experience something powerful: solidarity, guidance, and support when we're on the brink of giving up.

The sad reality is that we would all be healthier if there were strong villages around us. Consider two of the leading mental health struggles of our day—anxiety and depression. Would we be as anxious if we knew that an entire village had us covered? If the elders of a community initiated younger generations into a meaningful way of life and supported them through setbacks, would 44 percent of college students be experiencing depression?[2] Think about the conflicts in our romantic relationships—would we rely so heavily on our partners for emotional support, validation, and fulfillment if we were connected to an entire community? We are made for interdependence, but we live in a world that places a greater value on independence. Our mental and relational health struggles reveal how essential it is that we find or create our village.

To build a village, start by identifying a few areas where you feel a deep longing for support. Invite a few friends or acquaintances to reflect on their own, and begin a conversation about how to co-create a village that fosters connection and growth. Whenever possible, seek out elders who have navigated the terrain you're traveling through. For example, several of my clients who are entrepreneurs say the best thing they've done for their careers and sanity was to intentionally gather with colleagues at different stages of their business journeys. Elder entrepreneurs often provide invaluable perspectives on navigating growth and overcoming obstacles, while younger entrepreneurs bring solidarity and fresh insights into technology and innovation within evolving industries.

No matter your field or stage of life, the key is to meet consistently, share vulnerably, and collectively define and commit to the purpose of your time together. A timeline of three to nine months is a good starting point. We often overestimate what a community can offer in the first month or two, but underestimate the far-reaching changes that years of intentional connection across multiple communities can bring.

We often get stuck in our search for a village for two main reasons. First, we may already belong to a community, but the gatherings feel shallow, failing to address our deeper challenges and longings. Second, many of us feel isolated, longing for allies or guides yet unsure where or how to begin. In either case, a sense of paralysis and futility can set in, leaving us to wonder: *Is there a place where I can be deeply known and truly developed?* The good news is that both of these challenges have solutions.

If you're interested in learning more about resources and communities my team and I have created, see page 323. These resources are designed for groups to go deeper and for individuals to get more connected to others on a shared journey. Remember, there will always be crucibles that leave us confused and lonely, but you don't need to go through your entire life confused or alone. Seek communities that foster curiosity and growth, and if you don't find one that checks all the boxes, keep assembling the pieces—or create one with a few other friends.

### LIFE COMES THROUGH DEATH

Desire teaches us to hold the mysterious tension between death and resurrection. This pattern is present everywhere. The food we eat must die for us to live. A salmon swims back to its birth waters to spawn new life within days of its death. Our ego must die for new life to come to our identity and relationships. For anything to live, something must die.

The same is true for our desires. Every day, we wake up one day closer to our death. The reality of our mortality is meant to provoke us to ask: How do we want to live? But if we avoid thinking about death, or if we believe deep down that desire should be a progressive journey toward fulfillment, we will be dismayed when pain arrives.

The odds are, at some point in the next few years, your vision of the good life will break down and you will experience barrenness in a significant area of your life. This may occur when the parent you once admired turns out to be considerably dysfunctional; when the career aspiration you built your life upon crumbles; or when the partner you picked to improve your life, or the child you thought would complete you, has chosen instead to bless you with a reality check.

The hardest, most important years of our life are lived, as the poet says, between two worlds: one world dead, the other that feels powerless to be born.[3] This is the terrain of barrenness, an essential metaphor for the heartache and powerlessness that life can bring. Some desires die because they have served their purpose or can no longer sustain us, but others die for no reason at all, and everything within us knows it's not the way it's supposed to be. Even when the breakdown is necessary, it still hurts like hell. David Foster Wallace put it best: "Everything I've ever let go of has claw marks on it."[4]

These experiences show us that desire is not a security system to protect us from pain, nor is it a tool for an emotional pick-me-up. Desire is a heart-expansion project. When we lose someone or something we love, our hearts are meant to crack open. And when we experience the sweetness of life or goodness beyond what we thought possible, our hearts are meant to grow with awe and gratitude. Through the loss and satisfaction that desire brings, we learn that grief and joy are not enemies, but siblings.

## REMEMBER YOUR BEAUTY

Your desires are one of the most beautiful things about you. You may still struggle to fully believe this. Even after recognizing the systems and stories that have conditioned us to distrust our desires, the programing and lingering civil wars can obscure our ability to see how stunning we really are. Beauty and judgment both vie for the right to narrate our lives, but our task is to choose which one will author our future.

According to Dan Siegel, the brain is an anticipation machine, constantly shaping our expectations of life based on past experiences and the meaning we've assigned to them.[5] An unexamined life convinces us that life is happening to us and against us—we expect rejection before it comes, brace for disappointment in our longings, and remain stuck in cycles of limiting beliefs. But the same mechanism that keeps us trapped in the anticipation of dread has the power to set us free. The more we embrace our beauty and genuinely believe we are worthy of love, the more our brain begins to anticipate goodness. With every step we take to heal and integrate our story, we're not just reshaping our thoughts; we're actively rewiring our future.

The ultimate goal of this journey into desire has been to deepen our capacity to love—ourselves, others, and the world around us. Love transforms and expands our capacity to desire. It turns the civil wars of our lives into playgrounds of discovery. The childhood stories we were once too ashamed to tell become sacred when we learn to love the child within. The truths we once feared would break us become the crucibles that remake us into people of great strength and kindness. The barriers to intimacy crumble and form into bridges of connection. Pleasure is no longer something we avoid or chase to escape our lives, but a way to fully awaken our bodies to delight. And years that once felt listless and futile begin to fall away, revealing stars of meaning and purpose to guide us forward. Desire, rooted in love, is one of the most incredible forces in the world.

If you ever lose your way on this journey, return to your heart. There, you'll find the stories that have formed you—the innocence of the desires that first captured you, the experiences of pain and joy that have etched the contours of your face, and the passions that have always burned within you. Your heart is the wellspring of your core longings, a place you can always revisit to be reminded of all that is good, true, and beautiful within you. May your awareness deepen and your gratitude grow for the stunning heart you've been given.

# Acknowledgments

To the leaders in the fields of psychology, neuroscience, philosophy, and theology—thank you for the integrity and passion in your labor. My desire to integrate these fields was possible only because of the women and men who came before me and honored their longing to ask better questions and press into new frontiers.

To my clients—you've taught me how to write words that matter. Your deepest pain and most searching questions fuel my research and writing. Your stories have led me into the depths of hell and into glory—all of which I needed to witness to write this book.

To my agent, Mark Tauber—I'm the beneficiary of your decades of work in this field, and because of your support, this book found its way into a more expansive world. Thank you for understanding my longings—and my angst—about this project from the beginning.

To my editor, Derek Reed—you have an uncanny ability to honor what's on the page while calling it toward something more. Thank you for trusting your hunches and being bold enough to name the places where my ideas needed development. Your work made this book sharper, stronger, and more authentic.

To Jessalyn Foggy, Ashley Shoemaker, Theresa Zoro, Alisse Goldsmith-Wissman, and so many others at Random House—thank you for going above and beyond at every stage of this process.

To Gary and Nan Smith—what incredible support, playful presence, and faithfulness you've offered to us at every stage of this project, all amid living with "golden guts."

To Paul Squires—your expertise, diligence, and extraordinary research abilities were foundational to this project. The path analyses and data work you carried out were remarkable. You brought decades of wisdom and gave countless hours to bringing order to massive datasets. I'm endlessly grateful.

To Dan Allender—you are the person on this earth who has taught me the most about the beauty and madness of desire. This book wouldn't have been conceived—let alone written—without your kind and surprising presence in my life. I'm continually taken aback by the ways you see and engage the human heart, and I long to become more like you.

To Ron Carucci—one of the most gracious friends and brilliant minds I've ever known. Thank you for the countless hours you gave to this work—from whiteboarding structure to refining what meandered to anchoring me in the boldness this vision required. Readers may never fully grasp what you've contributed to both *Unwanted* and *Desire*, but I do.

To Graham and April Smith—you two remain a mystery to me. How a couple can be so generous, available, and committed to the belief that anything is possible both unnerves and inspires me. Graham—you are a rare man. You continually challenge me to see possibilities I am often too reluctant to consider.

To my children—your desires are beautiful, holy, and breathtaking. They've disrupted me in ways that have, indeed, made me quite cranky. But they are re-forming me in ways you'll never fully know. What an honor to be your dad. I like you both so freaking much.

Heather—my love. You have witnessed my desires in all their varied forms. Some have brought heartache into our marriage and family. Others—through miles and miles of conversation and love—have grown into longings that now carry us into the mystery of what lies ahead. Thank you for showing me a heart, a body, and a love that is fully alive.

# Desire Research Statement

**T**HROUGHOUT THIS BOOK, WE'VE EXPLORED THE INTRICATE terrain of desire—how it shapes our relationships, our growth, and our purpose. Many of the observations and insights shared here are informed by my clinical work and research. In this appendix, I invite you to take a deeper look at the study findings and data that have shaped these discussions. This is where theory meets practice, providing a glimpse into the evidence behind the concepts you've read. To all of you who love data: You're welcome.

## *Purpose of the Research*

The primary aim of this research was to investigate the topic of desire across the lifespan. Specifically, the study examined how adverse childhood experiences, family systems, behavioral patterns, and core beliefs contribute to personal, relational, sexual, and professional flourishing—or challenges—in adulthood. Too often, individuals are taught to resolve their symptoms rather than engage the deeper drivers of their problems. While existing research supports connections between the past and present, this study sought to refine and deepen these insights.

Central to this inquiry was the development of the Holistic Desire Assessment (HDA), a comprehensive survey designed to evaluate variables influencing desire. The HDA includes 7 scales and 26 subscales:

- Family (7 subscales)
- Childhood (2 subscales)
- Partner (4 subscales)

- Knowledge (2 subscales)
- Well-Being (4 subscales)
- Sex & Stress (6 subscales)
- Adult Desire (1 subscale)

Analyses were conducted at the subscale level to provide detailed insights into the relationships among variables, while scale-level data offered a broader perspective on factors influencing adult desire.

A secondary goal was to report reliability and validity evidence for the HDA, its scales, and its subscales as tools for exploring the multifaceted nature of desire.

## Study Design and Sample

The study utilized a convenience sampling method in which more than 8,000 persons were invited to participate via mailing lists and social media from psychoeducation and mental health organizations. This resulted in 4,081 adult participants (a 51 percent response rate), all over eighteen years old, who completed the HDA anonymously.

Participants accessed the survey via an online link, confirming their eligibility before proceeding. Demographic data collected included gender, sexual orientation, age, ethnicity, marital status, education level, birth order, family size, household income, religious affiliation, and relationship status. No personally identifiable information was collected. For the couples version of the survey, a random number was assigned to each participant, which uniquely categorized the participant in the dataset and ensured their anonymity to the researchers.

## Demographic Overview

- GENDER: 39 percent female, 60.5 percent male, .5 percent other
- SEXUAL ORIENTATION: 89.8 percent heterosexual

- AGE RANGE: 18 to 86 (25 percent aged 18–31; half were between 18 and 41)
- ETHNICITY: 80.6 percent white
- RELATIONSHIP STATUS: 61.9 percent in committed relationships, 9.6 percent single

## HDA Reliability and Validity

The HDA's 26 subscales, comprising 221 self-report items rated on a 1–5 scale, demonstrated strong reliability, with 21 subscales achieving a Cronbach's alpha above 0.70, indicating internal consistency. Scale-level averages and model fit statistics further validated the tool's utility (e.g., CFI = 0.962, RMSEA = 0.067).

## Data Analysis and Key Findings

Various statistical methods were employed, including path analysis, stepwise regression, and logistic regression. These techniques illuminated the complex interplay of variables impacting adult desire.

## Path Analysis Insights

Path analysis enabled the researchers to explore various theories or models of how the variables combine and interact to impact an outcome of interest. For example, the set of family subscales were combined with the well-being subscales to understand how they impact adult desire. The path analysis made it possible to identify core drivers of adult desire. To facilitate interpretation and reporting of the path analysis results, variables identified by a path analysis were further analyzed using logistic and stepwise regression. Logistic regression enabled the researcher to report impacts of core variables on outcomes using odds ratio.

A core finding in this research is that parent-child relationships and family dynamics interact complexly and impact the nature of adult desire. These relations were explored and clarified using path analysis. The path model in Diagram 1 expresses how parent relationships (positive and negative relationships with one's mother or father and a needy mother or father) and childhood stress impact childhood desire and adult anxiety. In turn, these connections impact adult desire directly and through enmeshment—a very strong focus on the family. Each of the variables in the path model are statistically significantly related to other variables, as indicated by the arrows. The quality of a path model is evaluated using a set of statistics. This set of statistics provided strong evidence for the validity of the path model in Diagram 1 (CFI = .962, TLI = .924, RMSEA = .067, SRMR = .032).

The Comparative Fit Index (CFI) compares the model's fit to a baseline (independence) model where all variables are assumed to be uncorrelated. Higher values indicate a better fit. The CFI ranges from 0 to 1; .962 indicates an excellent. The Tucker-Lewis Index (TLI) is similar to the CFI, but it adjusts the index for model complexity by penalizing (lowering the index) for including variables in the path model without substantial improvement in the path model fit. Like CFI, TLI ranges from 0 to 1. It is also known as the Non-Normed Fit Index (NNFI). A TLI of .924 represents an excellent fit with a minimal (if any) penalty.

The Root Mean Square Error Approximation (RMSEA) is an absolute fit index measuring how well the path model approximates the population covariance matrix, adjusted for model complexity. It estimates the lack of fit per degree of freedom. Smaller values indicate a better fit. An RMSEA value of .067 indicates a very good fit. The path model's Standardized Root Mean Square Residual (SRMR) is 0.032. The SRMR is also an absolute fit index that measures the standardized difference between observed and predicted correlations. Lower values mean better fit. The value of .032 is an excellent fit. Given the high reliabilities of the variables measured by HDA, the high degree of goodness of fit for the path model in Diagram 1 to the data provides evidence for the validity of the HDA and provides the researchers with confidence in the conclusions made from these findings.

## DIAGRAM 1

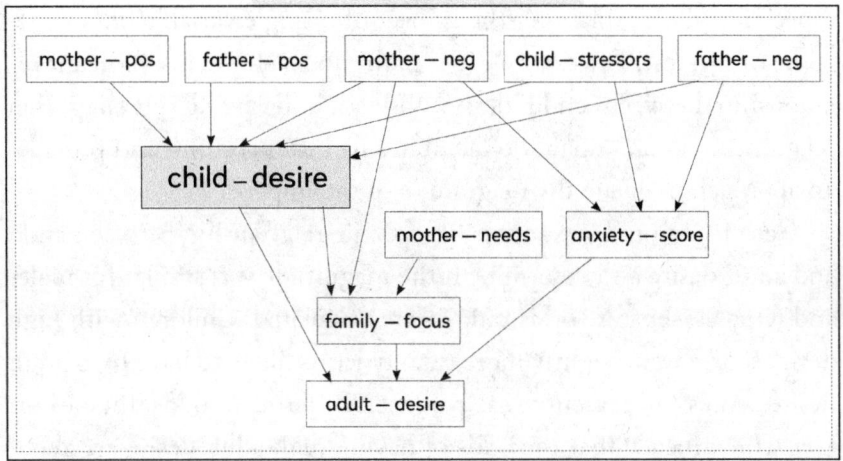

## *Stepwise Binary Logistic Regression*

A complementary approach to identifying the variables that have the greatest impact on adult desire is to examine the direct effects of the variables using a model simpler than a path analysis. To that end, the researchers examined the path model variables using stepwise binary logistic regression. Binary logistic regression was selected because the assumption of the normality of the dependent variable *adult desire* can be relaxed and simply modeled as a binary variable. The results were consistent with the findings from the path model. Child desire, family focus, and anxiety score all had statistically significant direct effects on adult desire. The stepwise binary logistic regression further indicated that child stressors and a negative mother relationship also had direct effects on adult desire. The stepwise binary logistic regression model achieved 75 percent accuracy in predicting a high versus a low adult desire score.

## *Logits & Odds Ratios*

One benefit of logistic regression is that the impact of variables on adult desire is expressed as logits, which are logarithms of odds ratios.

Therefore the results can be readily interpreted as odds ratios. As discussed above, odds ratios are a convenient method to interpret results, especially when explaining the impact of a single variable on an outcome of interest. For example, the path model shows a significant relationship between child desire and adult desire. Expressing that relationship as an odds ratio facilitates its interpretation and provides an approach to gauge the magnitude of the impact.

Case in point: To examine the specific relationship between child and adult desire and determine if the magnitude was similar for males and females, separate odds ratios were calculated. Children with high desire scores were slightly more than twice as likely to have high adult desire scores (65 percent vs. 32 percent). In terms of odds, the ratio is 4.17, which means that the odds of having high adult desire are about 4.17 times higher for those with high child desire compared to those with low child desire. This relationship was examined for males and females separately, and the results were consistent (not statistically different, $p > .05$).

Similarly, when examining another relationship observed in the path model, high levels of child stressors lead to greater adult anxiety. The odds ratio is 2.6 for this relationship, meaning that children with high levels of stressors are 2.6 times more likely to have high adult anxiety scores compared to children with low child stressor scores. Again, no significant differences were found between males and females. These nonsignificant results for males and females support the generalization of the results. These odds ratio examples were not derived from the logits obtained from the stepwise binary logistic regression but are simple, two-variable relationships.

## Sources of Funding

This research was made possible through the generous contributions of individual donors, who funded the survey design and analysis. Additional financial support was provided by Stringer Counseling LLC, reflecting our commitment to advancing understanding of desire and its impact on personal and relational growth.

## *Implications and Applications*

So, what can we conclude about all of this data? This research under-scores desire as a multifaceted and dynamic force shaped by history, relationships, and psychological well-being. By isolating variables such as parent-child dynamics, childhood stressors, and family enmesh-ment, the findings highlight how unresolved past experiences shape adult desire.

The study's insights advocate for interventions prioritizing holistic healing. The results of the Holistic Desire Assessment enable clini-cians to trace desire-related difficulties to their origins, offering a road map for targeted therapeutic strategies. This paradigm shift—from symptom-focused to systemic approaches—has profound implica-tions for therapy, psychoeducation, and resource development.

Perhaps most significantly, the research suggests that the very chal-lenges hindering adult desire can become pathways for healing and transformation. By addressing these connections, individuals and cli-nicians can foster integrated expressions of desire, aligning history, identity, and potential for meaningful growth.

# *Online Resources*

IT IS MY HOPE THAT THIS BOOK WILL OPEN A CONVERSATION about desire, one that continues long after these pages end. For those who want to explore further, I've created a set of online resources designed to help you reflect on your story and engage the five core desires in practical ways.

### Jay's Website

Your central hub for books, events, intensives, and additional resources.

https://www.jay-stringer.com

### The Desire Self-Assessment

Discover where you are strong, underdeveloped, or over-indexed in the five desires, and receive compass headings to guide your growth.

https://www.thedesireassessment.com

### The Journey into Desire

An online course designed to help you understand your desires, what has shaped them, and how they can guide the life you long to live.

https://www.thejourneycourse.com

### Podcast

Exploring the five core desires with leading thinkers, clinicians, and storytellers.

https://url.us.m.mimecastprotect.com/s/C83ECOYZkJcA6yXAo UrsMsGtTzB?domain=jay-stringer.com

### Instagram

For ongoing reflections, research, and conversation:
https://www.instagram.com/jay_stringer_

### Email

Have a question or want to share something you're learning? I'd love
to hear from you.
jay@jay-stringer.com

# Notes

**INTRODUCTION**

1. Amanda Reill, "A Simple Way to Make Better Decisions," *Harvard Business Review*, December 5, 2023, https://hbr.org/2023/12/a-simple-way-to-make-better-decisions.
2. James Cornwell et al., "Motivation and Well-Being Across the Lifespan: A Cross-Sectional Examination," *The Journal of Positive Psychology* 18, no. 1 (2022): 1–7, https://www.researchgate.net/publication/361633197_Motivation_and_well-being_across_the_lifespan_A_cross-sectional_examination.
3. Victoria Waldersee, "How Your Motivations Change as You Get Older," YouGov, July 5, 2018, https://yougov.co.uk/topics/society/articles-reports/2018/07/05/how-your-motivations-change-you-get-older.
4. From Yuval Noah Harari, *Homo Deus: A Brief History of Tomorrow* (Harper, 2017).
5. Ana Bridges et al., "Sexual Scripts and the Sexual Behavior of Men and Women Who Use Pornography," *Sexualization, Media and Society* 2, no. 4 (2016), https://www.researchgate.net/publication/309441770_Sexual_Scripts_and_the_Sexual_Behavior_of_Men_and_Women_Who_Use_Pornography.
6. BBC 5Live Women's Poll, Savanta ComRes, November 21, 2019, https://comresglobal.com/wp-content/uploads/2019/11/Final-BBC-5-Live-Tables_211119cdh.pdf.
7. Leah Sharman et al., "Prevalence of Sexual Strangulation/Choking Among Australian 18–35 Year-Olds," *Archives of Sexual Behavior* 54, no. 2 (2024): 465–80, https://pubmed.ncbi.nlm.nih.gov/38961025/.

**CHAPTER ONE**

1. See Matthew Arnold, "Grand Chartreuse," where he writes: "Wandering between two worlds one dead / The other powerless to be born / With nowhere yet to rest my head, / Like these, on earth I wait forlorn," Poetry Foundation, https://www.poetryfoundation.org/poems/43605/stanzas-from-the-grande-chartreuse.
2. R. Nardou et al., "Psychedelics Reopen the Social Reward Learning Critical Period," *Nature* 618 (2023): 790–98, https://doi.org/10.1038/s41586-023-06204-3.

**CHAPTER TWO**

1. Ronald Rolheiser, *The Fire Within: Desire, Sexuality, Longing, and God* (Paraclete Press, 2021), 8.
2. James Hollis, *The Middle Passage: From Misery to Meaning in Midlife* (Inner City Books, 1993).
3. David Schnarch, *Brain Talk: How Mind Mapping Brain Science Can Change Your Life & Everyone in It* (Sterling Publishers, 2018).

**CHAPTER THREE**

1. A Duke University Medical School study found that babies whose mothers were affectionate and attentive tended to grow up as happier, more resilient, and less anxious adults. The psychologists rated the mother's affection on a scale from "negative" to "extravagant." Eighty-five percent of mothers showed normal affection, nearly 10 percent were less affectionate, and about 6 percent showed high levels of affection. Thirty years later, the study participants were interviewed about their emotional well-being. Those who had received high levels of affection from their mothers were far less likely to feel stressed or anxious as adults. They also reported few conflicts with peers and had fewer distressing social interactions. See J Maselko et al., "Mother's Affection at 8 Months Predicts Emotional Distress in Adulthood," *Journal of Epidemiology & Community Health* 65, no. 7 (2011): 621–25, https://jech.bmj.com/content/65/7/621.

2. Bessel van der Kolk, *The Body Keeps the Score: Brain, Mind, and Body in the Healing of Trauma* (Penguin Books, 2015), 116.

3. The English psychoanalyst Donald Winnicott coined the notion of a "good enough mother," recognizing that children do not need (nor could they ever have) perfect parents. See D. W. Winnicott, *Playing and Reality*, 2nd ed. (1953; Routledge Classics, 2005).

4. Susan S. Woodhouse et al., "Secure Base Provision: A New Approach to Examining Links Between Maternal Caregiving and Infant Attachment," *Child Development* 91, no. 1 (2019): e249–65, https://doi.org/10.1111/cdev.13224.

5. Jay Stringer, Holistic Desire Survey.

6. Sam V. Wass et al., "Infants' Visual Sustained Attention Is Higher During Joint Play Than Solo Play: Is This Due to Increased Endogenous Attention Control or Exogenous Stimulus Capture?," *Developmental Science* 21, no. 6 (2018): e12667, https://doi.org/10.1111/desc.12667.

7. Victoria Leong et al., "Speaker Gaze Increases Information Coupling Between Infant and Adult Brains," *Proceedings of the National Academy of Sciences of the USA* 114, no. 50 (2017): 13290–95, https://doi.org/10.1073/pnas.1702493114.

8. E. Kross et al., "Social Rejection Shares Somatosensory Representations with Physical Pain," *Proceedings of the National Academy of Sciences of the USA* 108, no. 15 (2011): 6270–75, https://www.pnas.org/doi/10.1073/pnas.1102693108.

9. Shanta R. Dube et al., "Childhood Abuse, Neglect, and Household Dysfunction and the Risk of Illicit Drug Use: The Adverse Childhood Experiences Study," *Pediatrics* 111, no. 3 (2003): 564–72, https://doi.org/10.1542/peds.111.3.564.

10. Jay Stringer, *Unwanted: How Sexual Brokenness Reveals Our Way to Healing* (NavPress, 2018), 30.

11. Daniel J. Siegel coined the simple and powerful concept of "rupture and repair." See https://drdansiegel.com/.

12. Sheila Gregoire, *She Deserves Better: Raising Girls to Resist Toxic Teachings on Sex, Self, and Speaking Up* (Baker, 2023), 146.

**CHAPTER FOUR**

1. Candace B. Pert, *Everything You Need to Know to Feel Go(o)d.* (ReadHowYouWant .com, 2010), 13.

2. A. Roberts et al., "PTSD Is Associated with Increased Risk of Ovarian Cancer: A Prospective and Retrospective Longitudinal Cohort Study," *Cancer Research* 79, no. 19 (2019): 5113–20, https:doi.org/10.1158/0008-5742.CAN-19-1222.

3. Esme Fuller-Thomson et al., "The Link Between Childhood Sexual Abuse and Myocardial Infarction in a Population-Based Study," *Child Abuse and Neglect* 36, no. 9 (2012): 656–65, https://doi.org/10.1016/j.chiabu.2012.06.001. The researchers assumed that abused men would be more prone to high-risk behavior, such as smoking or drinking,

which would account for the higher rate of heart attacks. To the team's surprise, the impacts of abuse were more direct, quite independent of behavior factors.

4. Arline T. Geronimus et al., "Do Black Women Experience Stress-Related Accelerated Biological Aging?," *Human Nature* 21, no. 1 (2010): 19–38, https://link.springer.com/article/10.1007/s12110-010-9078-0. This was consistent with higher rates of poverty, stress, hypertension, obesity, and related health conditions.

5. J. Li et al., "The Risk of Multiple Sclerosis in Bereaved Parents: A Nationwide Cohort Study in Denmark," *Neurology* 62, no. 5 (2004): 726–29, https://doi.org/10.1212/01.WNL.0000113766.21896.B1.

6. Quoted in Bono, "A Clenched Fist and an Open Hand: Lessons Learned from Desmond Tutu," *Time,* December 31, 2021, https://time.com/6132224/desmond-tutu-bono.

7. Jay Stringer, Holistic Desire Survey.

8. Penguin Random House, "Avery Celebrates 5 Years of *Atomic Habits* and an Astounding 260 Weeks on the NYT Bestseller List," November 21, 2024, https://global.penguinrandomhouse.com/announcements/avery-celebrates-5-years-of-atomic-habits-an-astounding-260-weeks-on-the-nyt-bestseller-list/.

9. Stringer, Holistic Desire Survey.

10. Ibid.

11. Bessel van der Kolk, *The Body Keeps the Score: Brain, Mind, and Body in the Healing of Trauma* (Viking, 2014), 43.

12. William Faulkner, *Requiem for a Nun* (Doubleday, 2012), 73.

**CHAPTER FIVE**

1. Carl Jung, *Jung's Seminar on Nietzsche's Zarathustra* (Taylor & Francis, 1997), 1473–74.

2. Julian of Norwich, *Revelations of Divine Love,* Long Text, Chapter 18. Modern translations vary, but one common phrasing is: "First the fall, and then the recovery from the fall, and both are the mercy of God." Also phrased as, "And commonly, first we fall and later we see it: and both of the Mercy of God." Also quoted here: Richard Rohr, *Falling Upward: A Spirituality for the Two Halves of Life,* rev. ed. (Josey Bass, 2023), vi.

**CHAPTER SIX**

1. John O'Donohue, *To Bless the Space Between Us: A Book of Blessings* (Doubleday, 2008), 61.

2. Will Guidara, "The Secret Ingredients of Great Hospitality," TED Talk, September 2022, https://www.ted.com/talks/will_guidara_the_secret_ingredients_of_great_hospitality.

3. John O'Donohue sent a letter that included the words: "May you find in yourself a courageous hospitality toward what is difficult, painful, and unknown." O'Donohue, *To Bless the Space,* 60; "A Blessing for a Friend on the Arrival of Illness," https://www.jhrehab.org/2016/11/30/for-a-friend-on-the-arrival-of-illness/.

4. Carol Dweck, *Mindset: The New Psychology of Success* (Ballantine, 2016), 6.

5. Dweck, *Mindset,* 7.

6. Daniel J. Siegel, *Mindsight: The New Science of Personal Transformation* (Bantam Books, 2010), 116.

7. R. E. Pyke, "Sexual Performance Anxiety," *Sexual Medicine Reviews* 8, no. 2 (2020): 183–90, https://doi.org/10.1016/j.sxmr.2019.07.001.

8. J. K. McNulty et al., "Longitudinal Associations Among Relationship Satisfaction, Sexual Satisfaction, and Frequency of Sex in Early Marriage," *Archives of Sexual Behavior* 45 (December 2016): 85–97, https://link.springer.com/article/10.1007/s10508-014-0444-6.

9. C. E. Leavitt et al., "The Role of Sexual Mindfulness in Sexual Wellbeing, Rela-

tional Wellbeing, and Self-esteem," *Journal of Sex & Marital Therapy* 45, no. 6 (2019): 497–509, https://www.tandfonline.com/doi/full/10.1080/0092623X.2019.1572680.

**CHAPTER SEVEN**

1. Brené Brown, *Atlas of the Heart,* Season 1, Episode 1, "The Language of Emotion and Human Experience," aired March 31, 2022, Max.

2. David Schnarch, *Passionate Marriage: Keeping Love and Intimacy Alive in Committed Relationships* (W. W. Norton & Co., 2009), 59.

3. Brené Brown, "How to 'Brave the Wilderness' & Find True Belonging," *The Marie Forleo Podcast,* YouTube, September 12, 2017, https://www.youtube.com/watch?v=A9Fopg KyAfI.

4. Michael E. Kerr and Murray Bowen, *Family Evaluation: An Approach Based on Bowen Theory* (W. W. Norton & Co., 1988).

5. E. S. Allen et al., "Premarital Precursors of Marital Infidelity," *Family Process* 47, no. 2 (2008): 243–59, https://doi.org/10.1111/j.1545-5300.2008.00251.x.

6. Sue Johnson, *Hold Me Tight: Seven Conversations for a Lifetime of Love* (Hachette: Little Brown Spark, 2008), 47.

7. British psychoanalyst and author Neville Symington contends that one of the ways narcissism manifests is through an individual's shortcuts. According to Symington, shortcuts are indicators that we are relying on outside sources for validation rather than developing deep and authentic connections with ourselves and others, particularly in moments of pain. When there is no face to bear witness to grief and no elders to guide us through the complexities of life, we are most susceptible to the shortcuts and shiny things of our culture. See Neville Symington, *Narcissism: A New Theory* (Routledge, 1993).

8. Mary Kowalchyk et al. "Narcissism Through the Lens of Performative Self-Elevation," *Personality and Individual Differences* 177 (July 2021), https://doi.org/10.1016/j .paid.2021.110780.

9. Annie Dillard, *Pilgrim at Tinker Creek* (1974; Harper Perennial, 1979), 36.

10. Matthew 5, *The Message: The Bible in Contemporary Language,* copyright © 1993, 2002, 2018 by Eugene H. Peterson. All rights reserved.

11. Hope Reese, "How a Bit of Awe Can Improve Your Health," *The New York Times,* January 3, 2023, https://www.nytimes.com/2023/01/03/well/live/awe-wonder-dacher -keltner.html.

12. A. Chirico et al., "Effectiveness of Immersive Videos in Inducing Awe: An Experimental Study," *Scientific Reports* 7 (April 2017), https://doi.org/10.1038/s41598-017 -01242-0.

13. Chirico et al., "Effectiveness of Immersive Videos in Inducing Awe."

14. Dacher Keltner, *Awe: The New Science of Everyday Wonder and How It Can Transform Your Life* (Penguin Press, 2023), 74.

**CHAPTER EIGHT**

1. John Gottman and Nan Silver, *The Seven Principles for Making Marriage Work: A Practical Guide from the Country's Foremost Relationship Expert* (Three Rivers Press, 1999).

2. David Morris Schnarch, *Passionate Marriage: Love, Sex, and Intimacy in Emotionally Committed Relationships* (W. W. Norton & Co., 1997), 49.

3. *The Simpsons Movie,* directed by David Silverman, Mike B. Anderson, and Gregg Vanzo, 20th Century Fox, 2007.

4. Gottman and Silver, *The Seven Principles for Making Marriage Work,* 116.

5. Sheila Wray Gregoire and Dr. Keith Gregoire, *The Marriage You Want: Moving Beyond Stereotypes for a Relationship Built on Scripture, New Data, and Emotional Health* (Baker Books, 2025), 113.

**CHAPTER NINE**

1.   Men reported higher levels of infidelity—nearly twice the rate of women: 28 percent for men and 15 percent for women. When men had a higher ratio of positive experiences with their partner, the odds of infidelity were 3:10. But when their relationship was bent toward negativity, the odds of infidelity were 5:10, an increase of 65 percent. When women reported a higher ratio of positive experiences with their partner, the odds were 1.3:10. But when their relationship was marked by negativity, it was 2.4:10, an increase of 88.1 percent.

2.   National Domestic Violence Hotline, https://www.thehotline.org/; Office on Violence Against Women, U.S. Department of Justice, https://www.justice.gov/ovw/resources-for-survivors.

3.   Daniel B. Wile, *After the Honeymoon: How Conflict Can Improve Your Relationship* (self-published, 1988), 12–13.

4.   Julia Schwartz Gottman and John Gottman, *Fight Right: How Successful Couples Turn Conflict into Connection* (Harmony, 2024), introduction.

5.   J. M. Gottman and R. W. Levenson, "A Two-Factor Model for Predicting When a Couple Will Divorce: Exploratory Analyses Using 14-Year Longitudinal Data," *Family Process* 41, no. 1 (2002): 83–96, https://doi.org/10.1111/j.1545-5300.2002.40102000083.x.

6.   Dan Allender and Steve Call, *The Deep-Rooted Marriage: Cultivating Intimacy, Healing, and Delight* (Thomas Nelson, 2025), 6, 30, 80.

7.   Ami Rokach and Sybil H. Chan, "Love and Infidelity: Causes and Consequences," *International Journal of Environmental Research and Public Health* 20, no. 5: doi:10.3390/ijerph20053904. See also M. Tafoya and B. H. Spitzberg, "The Dark Side of Infidelity: Its Nature, Prevalence, and Communicative Functions," in *The Dark Side of Interpersonal Communication*, 2nd ed., Brian H. Spitzberg, William R. Cupach, eds. (Routledge, 2007).

8.   Ingrid Solano et al., "Pornography Consumption, Modality and Function in a Large Internet Sample," *The Journal of Sex Research* 57, no. 1 (2020): 92–103, https://doi.org/10.1080/00224499.2018.1532488. This study found that 91.5 percent of men and 60.2 percent of women reported having consumed porn in the past month. The three modalities of porn consumed were written pornography, pictures, and videos.

9.   J. H. Kim et al., "Sociodemographic Correlates of Sexlessness Among American Adults and Associations with Self-Reported Happiness Levels: Evidence from the U.S. General Social Survey," *Archives of Sexual Behavior* 46 (March 2017): 2403–15, https://link.springer.com/article/10.1007/s10508-017-0968-7. These figures tend to rise as people age. Another study surveyed 1,900 married adults aged 57–85 and found that 40 percent had not had sex the previous year. See Y. Zhang et al., "Study of Partnered Sex, Relationship Quality, and Mental Health Among Older Adults," *The Journal of Gerontology: Series B* 75, no. 8 (2020): 1772–82, https://doi.org/10.1093/geronb/gbz074.

10.   For men, the quality of their sexual relationship made no statistical difference as to whether they might pursue extramarital affairs.

11.   Jamie Ballard, "A Quarter of Americans Are Interested in Having an Open Relationship," YouGov, April 26, 2021, https://today.yougov.com/society/articles/35503-open-relationships-gender-sexuality-poll.

12.   Kim Parker and Rachel Minkin, "Views of Divorce and Open Marriages," Pew Research Center, September 14, 2023, https://www.pewresearch.org/social-trends/2023/09/14/views-of-divorce-and-open-marriages/. Half say they are somewhat or completely unacceptable, and 16 percent say they are neither acceptable nor unacceptable.

13.   Jessica Wood et al., "Motivations for Engaging in Consensually Non-Monogamous Relationships," *Archives of Sexual Behavior* 50 (May 2021): 1253–72, https://doi.org/10.1007/s10508-020-01873-x.

14.   Rebecca Moody, "Screen Time Statistics: Average Screen Time by Country," Com-

paritech, March 26, 2025, https://www.comparitech.com/tv-streaming/screen-time-statistics.

15. "Screen Time vs. Lean Time Infographic," CDC (Archive), last reviewed January 29, 2018, https://www.cdc.gov/nccdphp/dnpao/multimedia/infographics/getmoving.html.

16. Daniel de Visé, "Americans Are Drinking as Much Alcohol Now as in the Civil War Days," *The Hill*, June 12, 2023, https://thehill.com/policy/healthcare/4043030-hard-liquor-consumption-is-up-60-percent-since-the-1990s/.

17. Overweight & Obesity Statistics, "Prevalence of Overweight and Obesity: Adults," National Institutes of Health: National Institute of Diabetes and Digestive and Kidney Diseases, last reviewed September 2021, https://www.niddk.nih.gov/health-information/health-statistics/overweight-obesity#:~:text=More%20than%201%20in%203,who%20are%20overweight%20(27.5%25).

18. Catalina Woldarsky Meneses and Leslie S. Greenberg, "The Construction of a Model of the Process of Couples' Forgiveness in Emotion-Focused Therapy for Couples," *Journal of Marital and Family Therapy* 37, no. 4 (2011), 491–502, https://doi.org/10.1111/j.1752-0606.2011.00234.x.

## CHAPTER TEN

1. David Schnarch, "Normal Marital Sadism," blog, Crucible Institute, May 2012, https://crucible4points.com/normal-marital-sadism/.

2. James Clear, *Atomic Habits: An Easy & Proven Way to Build Good Habits & Break Bad Ones* (Avery, 2018), 27.

3. The rabbi Jesus hints at this in John 14:2: "My Father's house has many rooms; if that were not so, would I have told you that I am going there to prepare a place for you?" Leaving had little to do with geography, but it did entail a radical transfer of loyalties.

4. Daniel A. Cox, "The State of American Friendship: Change, Challenges, and Loss Findings," from the May 2021 American Perspectives Survey, June 8, 2021, https://www.americansurveycenter.org/research/the-state-of-american-friendship-change-challenges-and-loss/.

5. Sara Berg, "What Doctors Wish Patients Knew About Loneliness and Health," AMA, July 14, 2023, https://www.ama-assn.org/delivering-care/public-health/what-doctors-wish-patients-knew-about-loneliness-and-health.

6. "Aging and Health Matters: Loneliness Puts Older Adults at Risk for Serious Medical Problems," podcast presented by the Centers for Disease Control and Prevention, May 2020, https://tools.cdc.gov/podcasts/media/pdf/316995_Loneliness_Risks_for_Older_Adults.pdf; "Health Effects of Social Isolation and Loneliness," Centers for Disease Control and Prevention, May 15, 2024, https://www.cdc.gov/social-connectedness/risk-factors/index.html.

7. Andrew Huberman, "Science of Social Bonding in Family, Friendship & Romantic Love," Huberman Lab, December 20, 2021, https://www.hubermanlab.com/episode/science-of-social-bonding-in-family-friendship-and-romantic-love.

8. The foundation of our social homeostasis is the bond we had with our primary caregiver, but it can be redirected to friendships and romantic partners later in life.

9. The dorsal raphe nucleus is responsible for mediating social homeostasis and is rich with dopamine. It will influence you to crave social interaction if you are not at your right level.

## CHAPTER ELEVEN

1. Peggy J. Kleinplatz, "The Erotic Encounter," *Journal of Humanistic Psychology* 36, no. 3 (1996): 105–23, https://doi.org/10.1177/00221678960363008.

2. Derby Herbenick et al., "Changes in Penile-Vaginal Intercourse Frequency and Sexual Repertoire from 2009 to 2018: Findings from the National Survey of Sexual Health

and Behavior," *Archives of Sexual Behavior* 51 (November 2022), 1419–33, https://doi.org /10.1007/s10508-021-02125-2.

3. Peggy Orenstein, *Girls & Sex: Navigating the Complicated New Landscape* (Harper, 2016), 47.

4. Sexual difficulties are generally classified in four categories. 1. Desire disorders (lacking sexual desire or interest in sex). 2. Arousal disorders (unable to become physically aroused or excited). 3. Orgasm disorders (delay or absence of orgasm). 4. Pain disorders (pain during intercourse). It's important to note that sexual problems may be due to an underlying physical condition like diabetes, heart disease, alcoholism, neurological disorders, or a negative side effect from medications (antidepressants, high-blood-pressure meds, and hormones [e.g., Lupron and Zoladex]). General medical conditions should always be explored before the deep psychological work that this book is focused on can begin.

5. Including: 19 percent of women reported lubrication issues; 11 percent had frequent pain during sex.

6. The combined prevalence of minimal, moderate, and complete impotence was 52 percent. The prevalence of complete impotence tripled from 5 to 15 percent between subject ages 40 and 70 years. H. A. Feldman et al., "Impotence and Its Medical and Psychosocial Correlates: Results of the Massachusetts Male Aging Study," *Journal of Urology* 151, no. 1:54–61, doi:10.1016/s0022-5347(17)34871-1. PMID: 8254833.

7. Raymond R. Rosen, "Prevalence and Risk Factors of Sexual Dysfunction in Men and Women," *Current Psychiatry Reports* 2 (June 2000): 189–95, https://link.springer.com /article/10.1007/s11920-996-0006-2; E. O. Laumann et al., "Sexual Dysfunction in the United States: Prevalence and Predictors," *Journal of the American Medical Association* 281, no. 6 (1999): 537–44, https://jamanetwork.com/journals/jama/fullarticle/188762.

8. Samuel L. Perry and Cyrus Schleifer, "Till Porn Do Us Part? A Longitudinal Examination of Pornography Use and Divorce," *Journal of Sex Research* 55, no. 3 (2017): 284–96, https://www.tandfonline.com/doi/full/10.1080/00224499.2017.1317709.

9. J. H. Kim, W. S. Tam, and P. Meunnig, "Sociodemographic Correlates of Sexlessness Among American Adults and Associations with Self-Reported Happiness Levels: Evidence from the U.S. General Social Survey," *Archives of Sexual Behavoir* 46, no. 8:2403–15, doi: 10.1007/s10508-017-0968-7.

### CHAPTER TWELVE

1. Suzanne Iasenza, *Transforming Sexual Narratives: A Relational Approach to Sex Therapy* (Routledge Press, 2020), 9.

2. "State Policies on Sex Education in Schools," National Conference of State Legislatures, updated October 1, 2020, https://www.ncsl.org/health/state-policies-on-sex -education-in-schools.

3. Kelli Stidman Hall et al., "The State of Sex Education in the United States," *Journal of Adolescent Health* 58, no. 6 (2016): 595–97, https://www.jahonline.org/article/S1054 -139X(16)30004-0/fulltext; Laura Duberstein Lindberg et al., "Changes in Adolescents' Receipt of Sex Education, 2006–2013," *Journal of Adolescent Health* 58, no. 6 (2016): 621–27, https://www.jahonline.org/article/S1054-139X(16)00051-3/fulltext.

4. Richard Weissbourd et al., "The Talk: How Adults Can Promote Young People's Healthy Relationships and Prevent Misogyny and Sexual Harassment," Making Caring Common Project, Harvard Graduate School of Education, https://static1.squarespace .com/static/5b7c56e255b02c683659fe43/t/5bd51a0324a69425bd079b59/1723734772299/mcc _the_talk_final.pdf.

5. "Young People, Pornography & Age Verification," British Board of Film Classification (2020), https://www.yourbrainonporn.com/relevant-research-and-articles-about -the-studies/pornography-and-adolescents-studies/young-people-pornography-age -verification-british-board-of-film-classification-january-2020/.

6. E. F. Rothman et al., "The Prevalence of Using Pornography for Information About How to Have Sex: Findings from a Nationally Representative Survey of U.S. Adolescents and Young Adults," *Archives of Sexual Behavior* 50, no. 2 (2021): 629–46, https://doi.org /10.1007/s10508-020-01877-7.

7. Being female increases the odds of having sex education by 80 percent; childhood trauma increases the odds of having sex education by 516 percent; having a positive father increases the odds of having sex education by 75 percent; and the age you first see porn increases the odds of having sex education by 16 percent.

8. Carol Rinkleib Ellison, "A Research into Some American Women's Sexual Concerns and Problems," *Women & Therapy* 24, no. 1–2 (2002): 147–59, https://doi.org/10.1300 /J015v24n01_17.

9. David M Schnarch, *Intimacy and Desire: Awaken the Passion in Your Relationship* (Beaufort Books, 2009).

10. Jay Stringer, *Unwanted: How Sexual Brokenness Reveals Our Way to Healing* (NavPress, 2018), 98.

11. Ana J. Bridges et al., "Aggression and Sexual Behavior in Best-Selling Pornography Videos: A Content Analysis Update," *Violence Against Women* 16, vol. 10 (2010), https:// journals.sagepub.com/doi/10.1177/1077801210382866; Gail Dines, *Pornland: How Porn Has Hijacked Our Sexuality* (Beacon Press, 2010).

12. Emily F. Rothman and Avanti Adhia, "Adolescent Pornography Use and Dating Violence Among a Sample of Primarily Black and Hispanic, Urban-Residing, Underage Youth," *Behavioral Sciences* 6, no. 1 (2016), https://doi.org/10.3390/bs6010001.

13. Perry et al., "Till Porn Do Us Part?", 1–3.

14. Researchers from Brigham Young University completed a study of 813 university students and found that 87 percent of men and 31 percent of women use porn, and that 67 percent of men and 49 percent of women find pornography use to be acceptable.

15. Stringer, *Unwanted,* 179.

16. A. Cano and K. D. O'Leary, "Infidelity and Separations Precipitate Major Depressive Episodes and Symptoms of Nonspecific Depression and Anxiety," *Journal of Consulting and Clinical Psychology* 68, no. 5 (2000): 774–81, https://doi.org/10.1037/0022-006X.68.5.774.

17. Sheila Wray Gregoire et al., *The Great Sex Rescue: The Lies You've Been Taught and How to Recover What God Intended* (Baker Books, 2021), 187. For discussions of the prevalence in the general population, see P. T. Pacik and S. Geletta, "Vaginismus Treatment: Clinical Trials Follow Up 241 Patients," *Journal of Sexual Medicine* 5, no. 2:e114–e123, doi: 10.1016/j.esxm.2017.02.002; I. P. Spector and M. P. Carey, "Incidence and Prevalence of the Sexual Dysfunctions: A Critical Review of the Empirical Literature," *Archives of Sexual Behavior* 19:389–408, doi: 10.1007/BF01541933.

18. Elizabeth E. Stanley et al., "Gap in Sexual Dysfunction Management Between Male and Female Patients Seen in Primary Care: An Observational Study," *Journal of General Internal Medicine* 40, no. 4:847–53, doi:10.1007/s11606-024-09004-1.

19. D. A. Kalmbach et al., "The Impact of Sleep on Female Sexual Response and Behavior: A Pilot Study," *Journal of Sexual Medicine* 12, no. 5 (2015): 1221–32, https://doi .org/10.1111/jsm.12858.

20. Ronette L. Kolotkin et al., "Obesity and Sexual Quality of Life," *Obesity* (September 6, 2012): 472–79, https://doi.org/10.1038/oby.2006.62.

21. Ibid.

22. L. C. Ferreira et al., "Predicting Couple Satisfaction: The Role of Differentiation of Self, Sexual Desire, and Intimacy in Heterosexual Individuals," *Sexual and Relationship Therapy* 29, no. 4 (2014): 390–404, https://doi.org/10.1080/14681994.2014.957498.

23. Emily Nagoski, *Come as You Are: The Surprising New Science That Will Transform Your Sex Life* (Simon & Schuster, 2015), 149.

24. Fatigue tends to exacerbate stress as well. In addition, overall poor health that impacted stress levels was found to be a particularly problematic component for men's ability

to maintain sexual desire over time. See S. Murray and R. Milhausen, "Factors Impacting Women's Sexual Desire: Examining Long-Term Relationships in Emerging Adulthood," *Canadian Journal of Human Sexuality* 21, no. 2 (2012): 101–15, https://www.researchgate.net /publication/287600143_Factors_impacting_women's_sexual_desire_Examining_long -term_relationships_in_emerging_adulthood.

25.   Juliana M. Kling et al., "Menopause Management Knowledge in Postgraduate Family Medicine, Internal Medicine, and Obstetrics and Gynecology Residents: A Cross-Sectional Survey," *Mayo Clinic Proceedings* 94, no. 2 (2019): 242–53, https://pubmed.ncbi.nlm.nih.gov/30711122/.

26.   M. S. Christianson et al., "Menopause Education: Needs Assessment of American Obstetrics and Gynecology Residents," *Menopause* 20, no. 11 (2013): 1120–25, doi: 10.1097 /GME.ob013e31828ced7f. PMID: 23632655; https://pubmed.ncbi.nlm.nih.gov/23632655/.

27.   Miriam K. Forbes et al., "Sexual Quality of Life and Aging: A Prospective Study of a Nationally Representative Sample," *Journal of Sex Research* 54, no. 2 (2017): 137–48, https:// doi.org/10.1080/00224499.2016.1233315.

28.   David Schnarch, *Passionate Marriage: Keeping Love and Intimacy Alive in Committed Relationships* (W. W. Norton & Co., 2009), 76.

29.   Markus H. Schafer and Laura Upenieks, "Do Sexual Expectations Matter for Older Men and Women? Anticipated Sexual Futures and Late-Life Sexuality Over Two Decades," *The Gerontologist* 63, no. 2 (2023): 240–50, https://doi.org/10.1093/geront /gnac071.

30.   David Lee and Josie Tetley, "'How Long Will I Love You?'—Sex and Intimacy in Later Life," International Longevity Centre UK, February 2017, https://ilcuk.org.uk/wp -content/uploads/2018/10/ILC-UK-How-long-will-I-love-you-1.pdf.

31.   J. M. Twenge et al., "Declines in Sexual Frequency Among American Adults, 1989–2014," *Archives of Sexual Behavior* 46 (March 2017): 2389–2401, https://doi.org/10.1007 /s10508-017-0953-1.

32.   Stacy Lindau et al., "A Study of Sexuality and Health Among Older Adults in the United States," *New England Journal of Medicine* 357, no. 8 (2007): 762–74, https://www .nejm.org/doi/full/10.1056/NEJMoa067423.

33.   "When estrogen plummets following menopause, the vaginal lining thins, vaginal walls become less elastic, and lubrication diminishes. These changes can result in vaginal dryness, burning, or itching that is exacerbated during entry. Topical estrogen—as a cream, a suppository, or a ring that releases the hormone over three months—can help plump up vaginal tissues and aid lubrication. A vaginal insert containing dehydroepiandrosterone (Intrarosa), which was approved by the FDA in 2016, is an alternative for breast cancer survivors who don't want to risk absorbing estrogen. Water-based lubricants and longer-lasting silicone-based lubricants can also make penetration less painful."—"Yes, You Can Have Better Sex in Midlife and in the Years Beyond," Women's Health, Harvard Medical School, September 30, 2021, https://www.health.harvard.edu/womens-health/yes-you -can-have-better-sex-in-midlife-and-in-the-years-beyond.

34.   Andrea Muraskin, "Does Sex Get Better with Age? This Senior Sex Therapist Thinks So," NPR, May 6, 2023, https://www.npr.org/sections/health-shots/2023/05/06 /1174167603/does-sex-get-better-with-age-this-senior-sex-therapist-thinks-so.

35.   Gustaf Bruze et al., "Associations of Bariatric Surgery with Changes in Interpersonal Relationship Status: Results from 2 Swedish Cohort Studies," *JAMA Surgery* 153, no. 7 (2018): 654–61, https://jamanetwork.com/journals/jamasurgery/fullarticle/2676728.

### CHAPTER THIRTEEN

1.   While these three dynamics cast the widest net, there will inevitably be several topics missed. In some cases, the logic and wisdom of these chapters can be contextualized to other sexual difficulties you face, but in other cases, more personal research will be needed to find relevant resources.

2. John Bancroft et al., "The Dual Control Model: Current Status and Future Directions," *The Journal of Sex Research* 46, no. 2–3 (2009): 121–42, https://doi.org/10.1080/00224490902747222.

3. Emily Nagoski, *Come as You Are: The Surprising New Science That Will Transform Your Sex Life* (Simon & Schuster, 2015), 51.

4. Sheila Wray Gregoire et al., *The Great Sex Rescue: The Lies You've Been Taught and How to Recover What God Intended* (Baker Books, 2021).

5. Peggy Orenstein, *Boys & Sex: Young Men on Hookups, Love, Porn, Consent, and Navigating the New Masculinity* (HarperCollins, 2020), 80.

6. Wednesday Martin, "The Bored Sex," *The Atlantic*, February 14, 2019, https://www.theatlantic.com/ideas/archive/2019/02/women-get-bored-sex-long-term-relationships/582736/.

7. Martin, "The Bored Sex."

8. David A. Frederick et al., "What Keeps Passion Alive? Sexual Satisfaction Is Associated with Sexual Communication, Mood Setting, Sexual Variety, Oral Sex, Orgasm, and Sex Frequency in a National U.S. Study," *The Journal of Sex Research* 54, no. 2 (2017): 186–201, https://doi.org/10.1080/00224499.2015.1137854.

9. See Sheila Wray Gregoire et al., *The Great Sex Rescue: The Lies You've Been Taught and How to Recover What God Intended* (Baker Books, 2021), 41–44; and Lisa Wade, *American Hookup: The New Culture of Sex on Campus* (W. W. Norton & Co., 2017), 117.

10. Wade, *American Hookup*, 159.

11. David A. Frederick et al., "Differences in Orgasm Frequency Among Gay, Lesbian, Bisexual, and Heterosexual Men and Women in a U.S. National Sample," *Archives of Sexual Behavior* 47, no. 1 (2018): 273–88, https://link.springer.com/article/10.1007/s10508-017-0939-z.

12. James Hollis, *Under Saturn's Shadow: The Wounding and Healing of Men* (Inner City Books, 1994), 104.

13. Esther Perel, *Mating in Captivity: Unlocking Erotic Intelligence* (Harper, 2006).

14. John Gottman, "Couples That Have a Good Sex Life Do Two Things," in YouTube video series *Making Relationships Work*, Gottman Institute, September 9, 2015, https://www.youtube.com/watch?v=0TLrK52-thY.

15. Nagowski, *Come As You Are*, 241.

16. Jean H. Kim et al., "Sociodemographic Correlates of Sexlessness Among American Adults and Associations with Self-Reported Happiness Levels: Evidence from the U.S. General Social Survey," *Archives of Sexual Behavior* 46, no. 8 (2017): 2403–15, https://link.springer.com/article/10.1007/s10508-017-0968-7. The term "sexless marriage" can sometimes refer to couples who have not had sex in the last six months, the last year, or the last five years. This survey defined it as not having sex in the last year.

17. "Ejaculation Frequency and Prostate Cancer," Harvard Health Publishing, January 19, 2022, https://www.health.harvard.edu/mens-health/ejaculation_frequency_and_prostate_cancer. Compared to men who reported 4–7 ejaculations per month across their lifetimes, men who ejaculated 21 or more times per month had a 31 percent lower risk of prostate cancer (other lifestyle factors were taken into account).

### CHAPTER FOURTEEN

1. Arthur C. Brooks, "How to Want Less," *The Atlantic*, February 8, 2022, https://www.theatlantic.com/magazine/archive/2022/03/why-we-are-never-satisfied-happiness/621304/.

2. This question is inspired by the poet Mary Oliver's famous line "Tell me, what is it you plan to do with your one wild and precious life?" in "Poem 133: The Summer Day," *New and Selected Poems* (Beacon Press, 1992).

3. Naman Gopal Srivastava, "'My Goggles Filled Up with Water': Michael Phelps Swam Blind for Over 175m to Achieve One of His Biggest Career Achievements,"

*Essentially Sports*, June 6, 2022, https://www.essentiallysports.com/us-sports-news
-swimming-news-my-goggles-filled-up-with-water-michael-phelps-swam-blind-for
-over-175m-to-achieve-one-of-his-biggest-career-achievement/.

4.   Carl Jung, *Archetypes of the Collective Unconscious* (1934).

5.   Bill Plotkin, *Soulcraft: Crossing into the Mysteries of Nature and Psyche* (New World
Library, 2003), 91–95.

6.   Cara Feinberg, "The Mindfulness Chronicles," *Harvard Magazine*, August 19,
2010, https://www.harvardmagazine.com/2010/08/the-mindfulness-chronicles.

7.   Diane Ackerman, *Deep Play* (Knopf Doubleday: Vintage, 2000), 8.

8.   This insight is from Rollo May, *The Courage to Create* (W. W. Norton & Co.,
1975), 34.

9.   Eugene Peterson, *Working the Angles: The Shape of Pastoral Integrity* (Eerdmans,
1987), 71.

10.   "PISA 2018 Results (Volume III): What School Life Means for Students' Lives,"
Organisation for Economic Co-operation and Development, December 3, 2019, 177,
https://www.oecd.org/en/publications/pisa-2018-results-volume-iii_acd78851-en
.html.

11.   The participants in the study could sit still or walk, but they were banned from talking, reading, or using screens. Before and after each outing, samples of saliva, which contains the stress hormone cortisol, were collected from each volunteer. Analysis revealed
that the biggest drops in cortisol occurred in the first twenty to thirty minutes.

12.   Andrew Huberman, "How to Increase Your Willpower and Tenacity," Huberman
Lab, October 9, 2023, https://www.hubermanlab.com/episode/how-to-increase-your-will
power-and-tenacity.

13.   Bruce Grierson, "What If Age Is Nothing but a Mind-Set?," *New York Times*,
October 22, 2014, https://www.nytimes.com/2014/10/26/magazine/what-if-age-is-nothing
-but-a-mind-set.html.

14.   Shannon Karl, "The Intersection of Childhood Trauma and Addiction," *Counseling
Today*, April 2021, https://www.counseling.org/publications/counseling-today-magazine
/article-archive/article/legacy/the-intersection-of-childhood-trauma-and-addiction.

15.   E. Crouch et al., "Adverse Childhood Experiences (ACEs) and Alcohol Abuse
Among South Carolina Adults," *Substance Use & Misuse* 53, no. 7 (2018): 1212–20.

16.   Anna Lembke, *Dopamine Nation: Finding Balance in the Age of Indulgence* (Dutton,
2023), 99.

17.   Dan Allender, CSL 518, *Sexual Disorders*, November 7, 2007, The Seattle School of
Psychology and Theology (formerly Mars Hill Graduate School), lecture.

18.   Yuval Noah Harari, *Homo Deus: A Brief History of Tomorrow* (Harper, 2017), 15.

19.   Lembke, *Dopamine Nation*, 103–4.

20.   Nancy M. Petry et al., "Shortened Time Horizons and Insensitivity to Future Consequences in Heroin Addicts," *Addiction* 93, no. 5 (1998): 729–38, https://onlinelibrary
.wiley.com/doi/10.1046/j.1360-0443.1998.9357298.x.

21.   Johann Hari, *Stolen Focus: Why You Can't Pay Attention—and How to Think Deeply
Again* (Crown, 2023).

22.   Gloria Mark et al., "No Task Left Behind? Examining the Nature of Fragmented
Work," *CHI 2005*, University of California, Irvine, Donald Bren School of Information
and Computer Science, https://ics.uci.edu/~gmark/CHI2005.pdf. The "switch cost effect"
also reduces the quality of our work (resulting in more mistakes), lowers the amount of
information we can retain, lessens our ability to get into a flow state of creativity, and
blunts our decision-making abilities.

23.   Johann Hari, "Your Attention Didn't Collapse. It Was Stolen," *The Guardian*,
January 2, 2022, https://www.theguardian.com/science/2022/jan/02/attention-span-focus
-screens-apps-smartphones-social-media; Hari, *Stolen Focus*.

24.   John Steinbeck, *Cannery Row* (Viking Press, 1945).

25. James Hollis, *Swamplands of the Soul (Studies in Jungian Psychology by Jungian Analysis)* (Inner City Books, 1996), 72.

26. Søren Kierkegaard, *The Concept of Anxiety: A Simple Psychologically Oriented Deliberation in View of the Dogmatic Problem of Hereditary Sin,* trans. Alastair Hannay (Liveright Publishing, 2015; originally published 1844), 187.

27. "Massimo Bottura," *Chef's Table,* created by David Gelb, season 1, episode 1, Boardwalk Pictures and Netflix, April 26, 2015.

28. Ron Carucci, *To Be Honest: Lead with the Power of Truth, Justice and Purpose* (Kogan Page, 2021), 78.

29. Amanda Hughes et al., "Elevated Inflammatory Biomarkers During Unemployment: Modification by Age and Country in the UK," *Epidemiology and Community Health* 69, no. 7 (2015): 673–79, https://jech.bmj.com/content/69/7/673.

30. P. Butterworth et al., "The Psychosocial Quality of Work Determines Whether Employment Has Benefits for Mental Health: Results from a Longitudinal National Household Panel Survey," *Occupational and Environmental Medicine* 68, no. 11 (2011): 806–12, https://doi.org/10.1136/oem.2010.059030.

31. H. Bosma et al., "Low Job Control and Risk of Coronary Heart Disease in Whitehall II (Prospective Cohort) Study," *BMJ* (February, 1997): 558–65, https://doi.org/10.1136/bmj.314.7080.558.

32. "Our Research on the Connection Between Strategic Purpose and Motivation," PwC, Strategy&, 2019, https://www.strategyand.pwc.com/gx/en/unique-solutions/capabilities-driven-strategy/approach/research-motivation.html.

33. Joseph Campbell, "An Experience of Being Alive," Joseph Campbell Foundation, YouTube, December 14, 2022, https://www.youtube.com/watch?v=qJm5-5JI4dU.

## CHAPTER FIFTEEN

1. Rollo May, *The Courage to Create* (W. W. Norton & Co., 1975), 12, 13.

2. Ashlee Vance, *Elon Musk: Tesla, SpaceX, and the Quest for a Fantastic Future* (Harper Collins, 2015).

3. Ron Carucci, "Why Success Doesn't Lead to Satisfaction," *Harvard Business Review,* January 25, 2023, https://hbr.org/2023/01/why-success-doesnt-lead-to-satisfaction.

4. Carucci, "Why Success Doesn't Lead to Satisfaction."

5. James Hollis, *Swamplands of the Soul (Studies in Jungian Psychology by Jungian Analysis)* (Inner City Books, 1996), 65.

6. C. S. Lewis, *The Four Loves* (1960; Harcourt, 1988), 65.

7. Julianne Holt-Lunstad et al., "Social Relationships and Mortality Risk: A Meta-analytic Review," *PLoS Medicine* 7, no. 7 (2010): e1000316, https://doi.org/10.1371/journal.pmed.1000316.

8. Daniel A. Cox, "The State of American Friendship: Change, Challenges, and Loss," Survey Center on American Life, a project of the American Enterprise Institute, June 8, 2021, https://www.americansurveycenter.org/research/the-state-of-american-friendship-change-challenges-and-loss/.

9. Daniel J. Siegel, *The Mindful Brain: Reflection and Attunement in the Cultivation of Well-Being* (W. W. Norton & Co., 2007), xiv, 28.

10. *Amadeus,* directed by Milos Forman, Orion Pictures, 1984.

11. P. Stillwell, "Oral History: The Golden Thirteen," *Proceedings* 113, no. 5 (1987): 1011, https://www.usni.org/magazines/proceedings/1987/may/oral-history-golden-thirteen (accessed March 2025).

12. "About the Untreated Syphilis Study at Tuskegee," Centers for Disease Control and Prevention, September 4, 2024, https://www.cdc.gov/tuskegee/about/index.html.

13. Frederick Buechner, *Wishful Thinking: A Seeker's ABC* (HarperOne, 1973), https://www.frederickbuechner.com/quote-of-the-day/2022/11/14/vocation.

14.   Bryan Stevenson, National Memorial for Peace and Justice and The Legacy Museum, https://legacysites.eji.org/about/.

15.   Rainer Maria Rilke, *The Book of Images: Poems / Revised Bilingual Edition*, English trans. Edward Snow (North Point Press, 1994), 213.

16.   Johann Hari, *Stolen Focus: Why You Can't Pay Attention—and How to Think Deeply Again* (Crown, 2023).

17.   Arthur C. Brooks and Oprah Winfrey, *Build the Life You Want: The Art and Science of Getting Happier* (Portfolio/Penguin Publishing Group, 2023), 74.

18.   Sahil Bloom, *The 5 Types of Wealth: A Transformative Guide to Design Your Dream Life.* (Ballantine Books, 2025), 161.

19.   Frederick Buechner, *Wishful Thinking: A Seeker's ABC* (HarperOne, 1972), 118–19.

20.   C. B. Broderick, *Marriage and the Family* (Prentice Hall, 1992), 14.

## CONCLUSION

1.   Francis Weller, *The Wild Edge of Sorrow: Rituals of Renewal and the Sacred Work of Grief* (North Atlantic Books, 2015).

2.   "College Students' Anxiety, Depression Higher Than Ever, but So Are Efforts to Receive Care," University of Michigan School of Public Health, March 9, 2023, https://sph.umich.edu/news/2023posts/college-students-anxiety-depression-higher-than-ever-but-so-are-efforts-to-receive-care.html. The Healthy Minds Study was based on web surveys taken from 96,000 U.S. students across 133 campuses.

3.   Matthew Arnold, "Grand Chartreuse," Poetry Foundation, https://www.poetryfoundation.org/poems/43605/stanzas-from-the-grande-chartreuse.

4.   David Foster Wallace, *Infinite Jest* (Little, Brown, 1996), 607.

5.   Daniel J. Siegel, *Mindsight: The New Science of Personal Transformation* (Bantam Books, 2010), 148.

# Index

ABOUT THE AUTHOR

JAY STRINGER is a licensed therapist, researcher, and speaker who helps people uncover and reshape the story beneath self-sabotage, disconnection, and shame. He is the award-winning author of *Unwanted: How Sexual Brokenness Reveals Our Way to Healing.* He lives in New York City with his wife, Heather, and their two children.

**ABOUT THE TYPE**

This book was set in Caslon, a typeface first designed in 1722 by William Caslon (1692–1766). Its widespread use by most English printers in the early eighteenth century soon supplanted the Dutch typefaces that had formerly prevailed. The roman is considered a "workhorse" typeface due to its pleasant, open appearance, while the italic is exceedingly decorative.

Also available from bestselling author

# JAY STRINGER

# Desire
## THE WORKBOOK

A Guided Journey into the Longings
That Shape Our Lives

### JAY STRINGER
Bestselling author of UNWANTED

CONVERGENT